# THE NEW SECURITY AGEN
# REGION

CU01433512

# The New Security Agenda in the Asia-Pacific Region

Edited by

**Denny Roy**
*Strategic and Defence Studies Centre*
*The Australian National University*
*Canberra*

First published in Great Britain 1997 by
**MACMILLAN PRESS LTD**
Houndmills, Basingstoke, Hampshire RG21 6XS and London
Companies and representatives throughout the world

A catalogue record for this book is available from the British Library.

ISBN 978-1-349-25703-4     ISBN 978-1-349-25701-0 (eBook)
DOI 10.1007/978-1-349-25701-0

First published in the United States of America 1997 by
**ST. MARTIN'S PRESS, INC.,**
Scholarly and Reference Division,
175 Fifth Avenue, New York, N.Y. 10010

ISBN 978-0-312-17371-5

Library of Congress Cataloging-in-Publication Data
The New security agenda in the Asia-Pacific region / edited by Denny
Roy.
p.   cm.
Includes bibliographical references and index.
ISBN 978-0-312-17371-5 (cloth)
1. National security—Asia.   2. National security—Pacific Area.
I. Roy, Denny, 1960–  .
UA830.N485  1997
355'.03305—dc21                                          97–11429
                                                            CIP

10   9   8   7   6   5   4   3   2   1
06  05  04  03  02  01  00  99  98  97

# Contents

# Notes on the Contributors

**John Chipman** is Director of the International Institute for Strategic Studies, London.

**Paul Dibb** is Professor and Head of the Strategic and Defence Studies Centre, Australian National University.

**J. Soedjati Djiwandono** is Head of the Department of International Relations, Centre for Strategic and International Studies, Jakarta.

**Alan Dupont** is a Research Fellow in the Strategic and Defence Studies Centre, Australian National University.

**Aurelia George Mulgan** lectures in the School of Politics, University of New South Wales, Australian Defence Force Academy.

**Stuart Harris** is Professor and Convenor of the Northeast Asia Program, Research School of Pacific and Asian Studies, Australian National University.

**Philip Howard** is a researcher with the Project on Environment, Population and Security in the Peace and Conflict Studies Program, University of Toronto.

**Robert O'Neill** is Chichele Professor of the History of War at All Souls College, Oxford.

**Denny Roy** is a Research Fellow in the Strategic and Defence Studies Centre, Australian National University.

**Gerald Segal** is a Senior Fellow at the International Institute for Strategic Studies, London; Director of the United Kingdom Economic and Social Research Council's Pacific Asia Programme; and Co-Chair of the European Council for Security Cooperation in the Asia-Pacific region.

**Stewart Woodman** is Director of Graduate Studies at the Strategic and Defence Studies Centre, Australian National University.

# List of Acronyms

| | |
|---|---|
| ACSA | Acquisition and Cross-Servicing Agreement |
| ADB | Asian Development Bank |
| AEW&C | Airborne Early Warning and Control |
| AFTA | ASEAN Free Trade Agreement |
| APEC | Asia Pacific Economic Cooperation |
| ARF | ASEAN Regional Forum |
| ASEAN | Association of Southeast Asian Nations |
| $C^3$ | Command, Control and Communications |
| $C^3I$ | Command, Control, Communications and Intelligence |
| CBM | confidence building measure |
| CIS | Commonwealth of Independent States |
| CLO | Cabinet Legislative Office (Japan) |
| COCOM | Coordinating Committee on Multilateral Export Controls |
| CSCE | Conference on Security and Cooperation in Europe |
| CTBT | Comprehensive Test Ban Talks |
| DMZ | demilitarised zone |
| EASR | East Asia Strategy Report |
| ECOWAS | Economic Organisation of West African States |
| EFTA | European Free Trade Area |
| EU | European Union |
| FM | Foreign Ministry (Japan) |
| FPDA | Five-Power Defence Arrangements |
| GATT | General Agreement on Tariffs and Trade |
| GCC | Gulf Cooperation Council |
| GDP | gross domestic product |
| GNP | gross national product |
| IMF | International Monetary Fund |
| IPR | intellectual property rights |
| JDA | Japan Defence Agency |
| JSTARS | Joint Strategic Airborne Reconnaissance System |
| LDP | Liberal Democratic Party (Japan) |
| MFN | most favoured nation |
| NAFTA | North American Free Trade Agreement |
| NATO | North Atlantic Treaty Organisation |
| NDPO | National Defence Programme Outline |
| NPT | Non-Proliferation Treaty |
| OAU | Organisation for African Unity |

| OECD | Organisation for Economic Cooperation and Development |
| OSCE | Organisation on Security and Cooperation in Europe |
| PECC | Pacific Economic Cooperation Council |
| PMC | Post-Ministerial Conference |
| PNG | Papua New Guinea |
| ROC | Republic of China |
| SAARC | South Asian Association for Regional Cooperation |
| SAR | search and rescue |
| SDF | Self-Defence Forces |
| SDP | Social Democratic Party (Japan) |
| SEATO | Southeast Asia Treaty Organisation |
| SLOCs | sea lines of communication |
| UAV | unmanned aerial vehicle |
| UN | United Nations |
| UNCAR | United Nations Conventional Arms Register |
| UNCLOS | United Nations Convention on the Law of the Sea |
| UNHCR | United Nations High Commissioner for Refugees |
| US | United States |
| WEU | West European Union |
| WTO | World Trade Organisation |
| ZOPFAN | Zone of Peace, Freedom and Neutrality |

# 1 Introduction: Old and New Agendas
Denny Roy

Traditionally, the field of strategic studies has been dominated by influential Western military thinkers who focused on the causes of war and the uses of military power. The Cold War, which made the US–Soviet confrontation the central feature of strategic studies, reinforced these tendencies within the field. A few years on, we can now characterise the 'old' security agenda of the Cold War era. The primary foci of study were Europe, the great powers, and major war. In most analyses, the term 'security' was narrowly understood as protection of territory and population from military attack by foreign governments. Most discussion of conflict in the mainstream security literature assumed the prevention of war lay in some form of military deterrence.

But with the end of the Cold War, this well-worn approach appears inadequate, perhaps even obsolete, as a framework for analysing the security challenges of the present and future Asia-Pacific region. The inability of the Cold War approach to deal with the security challenges of the post-Cold War era is clear if we consider some of the most prominent events of the last few years, including the conflict in the former Yugoslavia, the war between the rebels in Chechnya and the Russian central government, the tensions in the Spratly Islands and across the Taiwan Strait, and the tribal violence in Rwanda.

Previously fundamental (and, for many people, comfortable) conceptual premises are now being rethought. In the new security agenda, attention has shifted to regional conflicts, especially in the Asia-Pacific region and the Middle East, and to the dangers of medium-sized regional wars. The concept of security is open to broader interpretation, and a variety of unconventional threats to security is recognised. Even mainstream strategic fora are examining the possibility of a 'zone of peace', 'security communities', or other alternatives to what Thomas Hobbes described as the 'war of all against all'. Instruments of state power other than military force demand consideration as means of obtaining the state's goals. The value of traditional military alliances and of the United Nations as vehicles for preventing conflict are being reassessed. States are hard-pressed to design a long-term national strategy with no identifiable 'enemy' even in the short term, especially when the increasing costs of first-rate weapons systems combined with competing demands for public funds severely limit defence budgets for most countries.

Policies grow out of basic assumptions, and flawed assumptions have all too often spawned poor policies. Clearly, the tools and models of the past must give way to more innovative and creative expertise in the field of security studies. The changing strategic landscape of the post-Cold War era demands that the Asia-Pacific region's important bilateral and multilateral relationships be re-evaluated, important new non-military threats be identified, and the new demands on strategists be understood. Otherwise, policy-makers and analysts may find themselves caught in the old trap of preparing to fight the previous war. Accordingly, this book is designed to provide an overview of likely security challenges in the Asia-Pacific region during the near to medium term and to suggest effective strategies for meeting these challenges.

This book has two central themes. The first is the important question of which parts of the 'old' agenda should be retained, and what new elements should be added. These few years of post-Cold War readjustment present a valuable opportunity to strategic reassessment and conceptual retooling. The immediate prospect for major war is minimal and the foreign policies of all the major powers suggest a desire for reconciliation and a recognition of the benefits of peaceful cooperation. Yet the squalls that may develop into tomorrow's conflicts are already visible on the horizon. To make best use of this transitional period, strategic thinkers must determine which principles and lessons from the past have enduring validity, and to understand the significance of new security developments. While many aspects of the new security envionment in the Asia-Pacific region have changed, some fundamental tenets of international politics persist. It is crucial that the next generation of security analysts and planners is wise enough to discern what to keep, what to throw away, and what to add.

Several of the chapters emphasise the necessity of conceptual change, introducing along the way some of the most important aspects of the New Security Agenda. Both Paul Dibb and Robert O'Neill assert that the prospect of global nuclear war has become unlikely, but that the future holds potential new security threats (albeit on a smaller scale) that may prove as vexing as the Cold War nuclear threat and require the same amount of attention from strategists. These new threats include what O'Neill terms the problems of 'unintended chaos': conflicts that are not the direct result of conscious policies by national governments. Alan Dupont surveys some of these 'unconventional' security threats, which include environmental degradation, transnational organised crime, uncontrolled migration, infectious disease, and the potential damage of international market forces upon domestic economies. Philip Howard highlights the issue of 'ecological security', increasing conflict resulting from competition over increasingly scarce natural resources such as water, timber and arable land. Howard notes that the potential for violence is greater within politically unstable states – including newly democratising countries. Stuart Harris discusses the close connection between international security and economic issues, which has never been greater than in the post-

Cold War era, and cautions against assessing political events and strategies without accounting for economic motives and consequences. Dupont provocatively asserts that traditional notions of security that focus on threats to territory and state sovereignty are too narrow to comprehend the more subtle and multifaceted threats governments and peoples face today, and that the defence structures of most countries are poorly suited to the challenges of the future. Stewart Woodman envisages warfare of the future and finds that despite the popular acclaim for technological advances that promise to make combat precise and relatively 'bloodless', information-intensive warfare may have disturbing implications, including pushing warfare into areas that make human control more difficult, thus increasing the potential for crisis escalation, and creating an additional incentive for states without first-rate technological capabilities to acquire long-range delivery systems, possibly with nuclear warheads, as a relatively cheap equaliser.

Other passages add balance to the discussion by demonstrating the continuing validity of some aspects of the 'old' security agenda. O'Neill concludes that while the names have changed, the primary dangers of the new era largely fit into the framework of traditional security studies. While recognising many security 'discontinuities' in the post-Cold War age, Paul Dibb's 'The Emerging Strategic Architecture in the Asia-Pacific Region' concludes that an old-fashioned balance of power, in which medium-sized powers can play a key role, is the most promising approach for maintaining order and deterring the unilateral use of force. Dibb also questions the notions that economic power has made military power irrelevant and that Asia has achieved permanent peace and stability. Economic prosperity alone does not guarantee peace, he writes, while the region still faces challenges such as nationalism, territorial disputes, several unstable domestic political regimes, nuclear proliferation, and the construction of a new post-Cold War order in the absence of mature multilateral security organisations. John Chipman warns that the new emphasis on 'regionalism', the belief that smaller countries should themselves solve the political problems in their own neighbourhoods with minimal involvement by larger outsiders and by means suited to local cultures and circumstances, understates the enduring realities of international politics. It is 'hubris', Chipman says, to believe this approach will be successful without recognising the persistence of power politics and great-power influence.

The second central theme is the changing nature of security in the Asia-Pacific region itself. The general assertions of the New Security Agenda – the inseparability of economics from security issues, the emergence of unconventional or 'unintended' security threats, the revolution in military affairs created by new technologies, and the new emphasis on regional security approaches – apply as much to the Asia-Pacific region as any other region of the globe; indeed, the Asia-Pacific region has provided inspiration and empirical support to many of the concepts and theories of the New Security Agenda.

The region's two most important long-term security issues are both affected by the end of the Cold War and will strongly condition the post-Cold War security environment: the rise of Chinese power and the US–Japan alliance. This book addresses both of these issues. Gerald Segal contends that peace in the Asia-Pacific would be best served if a growing China accepts the liberal norms and institutions that prevail among the established democracies, and offers a 'road map' leading to this outcome.

Aurelia George Mulgan notes that the end of the Cold War finds among the Japanese declining public support for continued hosting of US bases, reluctance to provide logistical and perhaps combat support in the event American forces engage in hostilities in the region, and discomfort over the prospect of converting the alliance from an anti-Soviet to an anti-Chinese pact, given Japan's sense that it enjoys a 'special relationship' with China. Reflecting the strategic ambiguity of the post-Cold War world, the revised security agreement avoids identifying any particular enemy to allow maximum flexibility to meet future contingencies that are today unknown.

Southeast Asia's security approach is a mix of old and new, writes J. Soedjati Djiwandono. Local conflicts persist despite the end of the Cold War since, as he points out, many are essentially indigenous and cannot be completely blamed on superpower instigation. Southeast Asian states also recognise that competition among the great powers will continue to play itself out within the region, although it is likely to take less militarised forms. Nevertheless, he takes a strongly regionalist position: Southeast Asia ultimately must bear responsibility for its own security and stability, and should develop its own framework, eschewing irrelevant European models and institutions.

The New Security Agenda is, of course, a contested concept. Taken as a whole, the chapters in this volume provide a thorough discussion of what this new agenda might consist of, although it is clear that some items are more controversial than others. Equally importantly, the authors provide abundant ideas on how these new strategic possibilities will affect the Asia-Pacific region. Thinking through these possibilities is befitting in an area of the world that appears destined to become the globe's economic and political centre by the early twenty-first century.

# 2 World Order: New Challenges at the Global Level

Robert O'Neill

Global security challenges tend not to be at the forefront of our minds in the mid-1990s. The ending of the Cold War may not have brought peace to the world, but it has led to a profound sigh of relief now that the huge, tightly organised armed forces of East and West are no longer poised to strike each other and the home territories on which their command systems are based on the instant. I am sorry that it is my task to disrupt that sense of security by examining several dangers which remain potent, and which will require political attention at the highest levels if they are not to become as worrisome as the Cold War used to be.

## THE PROBLEM OF UNINTENDED CHAOS

Before moving to discuss the problems of conflict arising from deliberate action, let us first recognise the dangers of unintended chaos – of conflict which occurs not because anybody has clearly willed it but because disaster has overwhelmed a substantial sector of the world and threatens to spill over onto the remainder. The causes of such problems, amply identified in the literature on conflict in the post-Cold War era, include environmental disasters, resource depletion and uncontrolled population movement.

The probability of such events occurring is not recognisably high at present, but my optimism may rest partly on ignorance of underlying developments. Depletion of the ozone layer, for example, could result in decreased habitability of those parts of the earth's surface beneath the holes, or changes in the movement of oceanic currents might lead to climatic disasters such as storms or the lowering of temperatures. Environmental security is now a very important aspect of international security, and the findings of the Rio conference, for example, deserve close study. But until we understand more fully the environmental consequences of our actions and lifestyles, and the ways in which those consequences can further affect our well-being, these issues have all too little leverage on governments and public opinion.

Resource depletion is a less complex issue, in that we have some idea, however approximate, of the extent of mineral deposits and agricultural production, and of the time it will take to deplete non-renewable resources.

5

At present most time-lines are comfortably distant and we give little thought to pushing them yet further away, because that is considered to be the task of future generations. We have coped with whatever legacies we were left by our forebears so we can feel justified with getting by as well as we can and leaving tomorrow's problems to tomorrow's people. We may not, however, have the luxury of following that precept once we have a fuller understanding of what we are now doing to influence the prospects of human civilisation's continuance into the distant future.

Uncontrolled population movements, such as millions fleeing from famine in Africa, boat people by the thousands off the coasts of Southeast Asia, Russian refugees streaming into Germany or Algerians pouring into the south of France have been somewhat overplayed in the literature and on our television screens. Such dangers exist but not on the scale that the Jeremiahs have forecast. Generally, these problems may be coped with by a combination of normal state border controls and the supply of humanitarian relief at the points of origin and first refuge. But at the same time let us not put out of our minds entirely the possibility that collapse of governmental services or inadequacies in basic essentials for human life are potential problems whose causes need to be thought about now, and to which pre-emptive measures might usefully be applied.

The import of these preliminary remarks is that global organisation and vision, if not global government, is increasingly necessary. If we remain overwhelmingly national in our organisations, our debates and our outlooks, we run higher risks of unintended disasters being visited on the international system as a whole than if we think of ourselves as a single group of beings on one crowded planet. The old analogy of our being aboard Spaceship Earth still has relevance.

## THE INTENTIONAL USE OF FORCE

A major concern of this book, however, is the intentional application of force: how people might seek to use it; what their motives might be; what levels of threat they can pose; and what measures we can take to protect ourselves from the consequences of such action. What are the contingencies that we have to think about at the global level, looking into the next decade?

## THE PROSPECT OF GLOBAL WAR

Global war cannot be taken off our list for study. Several major powers have weaponry with a global reach. There are several religions and value systems which range over enough of the globe to have potential for bringing many nations into conflict. Economic linkages may promote stability through interdependence but they can also promote jealousy, rivalry and a desire to eliminate the competition and take their resources over. Economic growth does not always strengthen peace: it can tempt a state with a grievance to be truculent or downright aggressive. It may be true that modern democracies do not go to war with each other, but we have not had all that long to put that theory to the test. It may be that when every state is a liberal democracy, national hatreds will still be intense because that is the way some people are. Think of the charming attitudes of British football hooligans towards their fellow democrats in Belgium or Spain. Will people of such blind prejudice never form part of a national government? And let us not forget that not every powerful state is yet a practising liberal democracy, and that in some, nationalistic military spokesmen continue to command attention and political support.

The most potent sources of widespread warfare in the coming decade are three-fold: frustrated aspirations in Russia, an isolated and resentful China, and a militant form of Islam which resorts to violence on a spasmodic basis.

## Russia

The type of development in Russia that is most alarming to contemplate is a collapse into a kind of civil war, out of which a hard-line faction either seizes control or threatens to use force against its internal opponents, or against external powers thought to be friendly towards them. This is a far cry from the old Cold War scenarios, which would require a reincarnation of the Warsaw Pact if they were to have relevance to our future. Now that the states of Central and Eastern Europe have experienced freedom, and are making reasonable economic progress, they will not endure Russian domination with the relative docility of the 1950s and 1960s. It took, after all, six years of Nazi occupation and isolation from the West to reduce them to a condition of near helplessness. They will not be easy pickings again for a long time. Hence the Russian Army will not regain its crucially important jumping-off point in central Germany, and Western Europe will not be under the kind of acute threat which would inhibit the development of more positive and stabilising relations with Russia.

The situation for Russia's neighbours is somewhat different, as many of them are still very dependent on Russia for markets, supply of essential items including energy, expertise of many kinds, and even protection. Belarus has recently chosen to re-enter the fold with Russian management of its foreign and defence policies and perhaps the unification of their currencies. Others such as Kazakhstan and Kyrgyzstan have made special arrangements with Russia, and it is possible that yet more will succumb to a combination of threats and enticements to place Moscow in effect in charge of territory of much the same extent as that of the old Soviet Union. Ukraine is likely to be an exception, feeling sufficiently powerful to be able to stand up to Moscow and with enough direct contact with the West to take heart in maintaining its policy of independence. Kiev could manage affairs badly, of course, and end up falling back into Moscow's clutches through ineptitude, but again this is a very different situation to that of an integrated Soviet Union, run by a system based on coercion and centralised authority.

The worst contingency the West will have to face out of events in Russia therefore is a consolidated Commonwealth of Independent States, in which Russia runs the foreign and defence policies and commands the military and the internal security surveillance, and military expenditures edge back upwards. It still will not be a very powerful state in economic terms; it will lag behind the West increasingly in all kinds of technological development; and but for the power of its strategic missile force, it will lack the means of threatening the West directly until such time as Poland and the Baltic states should be incorporated into the Western alliance system. This means that the question of technological inferiority will matter even more than it did during the Cold War. The terrain on which the opposing forces were arrayed lent credibility to the massed armoured forces which the Soviets could launch against NATO. Much of Germany was within a day's reach of a fast tank, of which the Soviets had plenty. When the vital ground of Western Europe is several hundred miles away, either the Russians would have to reconquer their old domain – no easy task in itself – or rely on sophisticated long-range strike forces which they lack, and against which the West can develop highly effective defences. The nuclear problem remains, and I shall return to it later in this discussion, but the old bogey of a Russian conventional assault against which the West would have no other recourse than to threaten the strategic use of nuclear weapons is a thing of the past. And it will not reappear unless reform in Russia proves to be vastly more successful than it has been to date.

This is not to dismiss Russia as a cause of serious conflict on and outwards from its own periphery. States such as China, Poland, the Baltics, Finland, Ukraine, Georgia, Turkey, Iran and Afghanistan will not be able to remain relaxed about the security of their border regions. This is especially true of the smaller countries. A clash with Poland would cause great alarm in the West and lead to all kinds of tensions in its relations with Russia, particularly if Poland were to become a full member of the North Atlantic alliance. But that will depend ultimately on the US Senate's approval. Much has to happen before there is even a treaty extension to ratify. And the net effect for the West is that while a strong expansion base is necessary, the prospect of a major armed clash with a resurgent, remilitarised Russia is remote.

## China

A second major power which poses problems in its relations with the external world is China. It is currently a much more successful state than Russia, but it has yet to go through the political turmoil which will follow the departure of Deng Xiaoping. It could suffer from a series of internal upheavals as the Communist Party is taken over by political reformers, or it could fall into a state of internal division, even civil war, should the leaders of the People's Liberation Army decide to become involved. While my inclination is to think that the Chinese will find a way through the rapids ahead without a collapse in the authority of central government, and without embracing liberal democracy, the events of 1989–91 serve to remind us that surprising events can happen. Such events in the future would have wider repercussions, immediately affecting decisions taken in Pyongyang, Taipei and Hanoi, and flowing on through the Asia-Pacific region to Washington. And we should not forget that the Chinese retain a nuclear arsenal of whose sure control we could not be certain in the event of a collapse of central authority, or the military getting out of hand.

But even assuming the Chinese will maintain stability through their coming transition, there will still be severe problems in regional relations. We have seen recently how emotively driven the Beijing government is on the question of Taiwan. All Beijing achieved was to make the Taiwanese value their independence all the more and rally behind Lee Tenghui. Beijing's sabre-rattling also served to bring the United States down off the fence in defence of Taiwan: a major international humiliation for the Chinese leadership, which they will probably feel more keenly than most might imagine. Now that Taiwan has officially embraced the forms of democracy, their cause has acquired a new moral dimension for liberal Americans, reinforcing the special affection underpinned by guilt that American conservatives have always shown towards the old Republic of China. Given the tensions raised in the US–China relationship by human rights, intellectual property and trade issues generally, it is not easy to see how these two great powers of the Pacific can coexist harmoniously in the foreseeable future.

This is not necessarily a state of affairs which will lead to military clashes, but the events of March 1996 showed clearly that it takes but a small miscalculation and Chinese missiles will slam into Taiwanese territory or shipping. The temptation to seize Quemoy and Matsu may prove too great for some ambitious regional Chinese military commander, even if the project were not appealing to the government. Any of these events would force the United States to side more fully with Taiwan. Washington now has to see that the Taiwanese are well supplied with modern defensive weaponry, and kept up to date technologically. It has deployed special naval forces to the Taiwan Strait. Any further Chinese provocation of Taiwan will push the United States into more direct support for its former ally. The Taiwanese leadership has been given a special scarcity value by the clumsy efforts of Beijing to dictate to the United States to whom it can and cannot give a visa. The United States will probably refrain from throwing sand in Chinese eyes by giving President Lee another visa in the immediate future, but suddenly contact with Taiwanese leaders has a special attractiveness in United States political circles. This whole episode has served to show how strongly passions can be aroused and we cannot exclude the possibility that relations between China and Taiwan will lead to hostilities, further humiliation for China and deeper involvement of the United States in Taiwan's defence.

The wider issue of China's relations with the whole region is a further cause for concern. First and foremost, from a global perspective, is the nature of links with Japan. History does not encourage us to think that the conduct of this relationship will be either smooth or free from contradictions. There is a natural complementarity between the two great states which will sustain cooperation, particularly in the field of trade. But it would be naïve in the extreme to imagine that the trade relationship will be free of acute tensions as China becomes more directly a competitor with Japan and, with a lower cost structure, a highly successful one. Japan, with its continuing close relationship with the United States, is likely to be supportive of Taiwan in the event of a crisis. Japan will also want to have influence in the Korean peninsula (which it is building through investment, trade and the provision of energy to the North), Eastern Siberia and the Sea of Okhotsk. Chinese interests may differ, particularly over North Korea, but in a more general sense neither power will want to feel that the other is successfully establishing a sphere of influence in Northeast Asia which consigns the other to a minor role.

China's role in Southeast Asia also gives cause for concern. The area to which Beijing has laid claim in the South China Sea cannot prove other than embarrassing for itself, even if the peace is preserved there. Should conflict return to the Paracels and Spratlys, it is probable that the United States will again take the side of the underdogs, for a variety of reasons from balance of power considerations to a feeling of closer rapport with the ASEAN states. Sino-Vietnamese relations retain their natural tensions, only now Vietnam is bolstered by a sense of belonging to a close-knit regional organisation and will stand up strongly for what it believes to be its rights and interests. Settlement of the issue of the conflicting territorial claims in the South China Sea will be a formidably difficult matter.

Paul Dibb has given us a very valuable analysis of the problems of maintaining a stable balance of power in the Asia-Pacific region in his recent Adelphi Paper.[1] It will not be easy for the region as a whole to establish a framework for managing the conflicting interests and ambitions of the many states which make it up. There will be ways in which they can collide. The interests of the middle and smaller powers may not receive the respect that they would hope for from the great powers. A stronger, but somewhat isolated China can only increase these difficulties. The United States will be a welcome source of stabilising influence for many years to come in the Asia-Pacific region, but why should the US continue to bear that responsibility?

**Radical Islam**

In mentioning radical Islam I am not wishing to do more than acknowledge the tensions already existing between the West and the more radical religious-political factions of the group of Islamic states. At present radical Islamic forces are very limited in their power to cause harm. Terrorism, money, training and inspiration are the main ways in which the more extreme elements can exert influence. But should even one of these groups acquire a nuclear warhead, we would be in a vastly different situation, to which I shall return shortly.

But finding a modus vivendi with these groups will not be a matter of a few years and a few small compromises. Some of the problems are virtually permanent ones: the existence of Israel; the slow but relentless erosion of ancient values and cultures by Western liberal democracy, materialism and individualism; the political fragility of many of the friendlier Islamic states towards the West; the dependence of the West on oil from the Islamic states; and the importance of the markets which these countries offer to the West. They have the potential to motivate significant numbers of young people to hostility against the apparent source of all their problems. For as long as the available means of destruction are limited to weapons which kill people by dozens rather than hundreds of thousands, we may feel that we have time on our side. Should this situation change, the world can become a very different place in which to live and conduct business. But even the present level of violence is unacceptable and deserves our active concern. Saddam Hussein may have been foolish when he invaded Kuwait, but look at the costs he inflicted on the world, his own people and the environment in the process.

He was defeated in a military sense but remains a potent political force. He is unlikely to have an opportunity to break out again, but he is not the first and will not be the last Islamic leader to want to play the role of Saladin and defeat the invading arms of Western influence.

## Regional War

All three of the above sets of problems have obvious regional dimensions. They will present themselves almost certainly as regional issues before becoming global concerns. There are many other individual cases to be watched which lack the potential to escalate to the level of a global crisis, particularly now that the Cold War is over. They include the Baltic states, the Caucasus, Central Asia, the southern Gulf states, Afghanistan, South Asia, a purely local confrontation between North and South Korea, parts of Africa such as the Maghreb, and Israel.

It is worth noting that there are other regions which have been severely troubled in the past, such as Southeast Asia, and Central and South America, which have built stability out of crisis through effective regional cooperation. From a global perspective the lesson is clear: the development of good regional organisations should be encouraged and supported by everyone with either expertise or resources to offer. If this movement towards regional solutions for regional problems can be stimulated, the potential of local issues to escalate to become regional or even global concerns can be reduced greatly. There is therefore a global interest in assisting troubled regions to develop their own linkages, organisations and treaties, each in its own way, thereby taking some of the burden off the overtaxed United Nations, not to mention the United States and NATO.

## National and Subnational Conflicts

Intra-state conflicts are the most common form of war in the world today. If any generalisation as to their causes is valid it is that they come from bad government, failed economic systems and unrelieved social tensions. The best remedy – and the only effective one in the long term – is self-help. But how is its potential to be developed in states whose various factions are polarised and locked in mortal combat? One of the best answers given in the past was that of the Marshall Plan. There have been many other examples on a less spectacular scale. But the key element is the provision of intelligently targeted financial assistance and technical advice on development – political, social and economic. The scale required in the world today makes this a global challenge, both to the United Nations and to all those powers which have something to offer, not just the United States.

## THE LIMITATION OF THE USE OF FORCE

While all the above points of analysis make clear that there are exploiters of violence in the world who respect neither international conventions nor the rule of international law in a more general sense, there are many other more responsible governments and leaders who will be guided by agreed international restrictions on the use of force. These agreements range from 'no first use' declarations, to the banning of certain types of weapons, the prohibition of the transfer of militarily related technology to certain states, the placing of particular types of targets off limits in war, the holding of commanders responsible as individuals for any war crimes committed by personnel under their authority, the institution of demilitarised zones, the establishment of observer groups in troubled areas, agreed limitation on production levels and stocks of particular weapons, and the institution of a series of confidence-building measures between potential opponents.

The conflict in Bosnia has emphasised the growing role that international law is playing as a means of reducing the harm suffered in conflicts of all types. The building of greater respect for international law is another global challenge of formidable dimensions. The forces of example and participation are particularly potent in the building of such respect. Just as the Soviets and the Americans both recognised during the Cold War that their own individual security could be enhanced by the placing of agreed limitations on weapon systems, force deployments and operational methods, so should other states which can cause severe trouble in the post-Cold War era be brought to see the wisdom of this approach. Once the point is established more clearly in regions such as the Balkans, the periphery of Russia, South Asia, East Asia and the Pacific, and the Middle East, we need to consider its practical implications: what new measures are necessary in each region for the successful voluntary limitation of the use of force? The banning of land mines, difficult though it would be to carry through into effect, is a good case in point. The recent 31-nation talks held in Vienna to establish a regime to limit the transfer of arms and military technology to pariah states is another worthwhile endeavour. In effect this body would replace COCOM, but its sponsors would include several of those states at which COCOM's efforts were directed, particularly Russia. It must be noted, however, that these negotiations broke down on the issue of whether or not the United States was seeking to gain commercial advantage out of the limitations proposed.

## Peace-keeping and Peace-enforcement

Both peace-keeping and peace-enforcement are in high demand, and there is no indication that the need for them will slacken. More struggling states seem likely to succumb to internal conflicts. There are many bilateral conflicts which have to be regulated before they can be resolved, and the continued emergence of determined aggressors such as Saddam Hussein and those of the states of the former Yugoslavia demonstrate that enforcement often has to precede peace-keeping.

Although the United Nations can authorise, legitimise and control the operations of peace-keeping forces, it has no forces of its own to deploy. In the field of peace-enforcement the UN's roles are much more restricted – essentially to those of authorisation and legitimisation. Operational control is delegated to a leading power, and the viability of each undertaking rests entirely on the dedication of the political leadership and legislatures of the major power providing the forces. The UN *by itself* can do nothing in the fields of peace-keeping and peace-enforcement. The UN was established by Britain, the Soviet Union and the United States to extend the life of their Second World War alliance and make it serve as the basis of world order for the indefinite future. They constituted the UN so that all major decisions would have to come back to them as individual governments for approval. They agreed to add France and China to the circle of veto powers, but since 1945 the constitution of the Security Council has not changed in this key aspect. How appropriate reform is to be achieved is a problem beyond the scope of this discussion, but what to expect in the absence of such reform is very clearly within the scope of this analysis.

Peace-enforcement essentially depends on the United States, both in terms of having its approval for any major UN commitment and for the actual command, control, movement and supply of the necessary forces. Britain and France have important supporting roles to play but each has run its armed forces down to the point at which neither could command a major force, nor supply one much over a division in size – as the Gulf War and recent operations in Bosnia have made clear. Britain and France are dependent on the United States for command and control, intelligence, and some transport and other logistical support. Russia can play only a nominal role and China is neither interested in nor capable of taking a significant part of this burden. The best contribution Russia and China have made in recent years was to refrain from using their vetoes against policies on which the other three permanent members of the Security Council were agreed.

Essentially this means that the future of peace-enforcement is in the hands of the US Senate. I will not say that this in itself is a new challenge to world order, but it is a major limitation on the ability of the United Nations to act as an impartial arbiter with some real strength. Increasingly as the finances of the UN become more and more straitened, so the degree of American participation in and support for peace-keeping operations will determine their scope and effectiveness. The political wind in the US is blowing in the face of the UN. This does not augur well for the prospects of the United Nations as a practical resolver of disputes and a potent bringer of peace to troubled states and peoples. The possible paralysis facing the UN underlines the desirability of exploiting more fully the potential of regional cooperation for the building of security. At least in that context it is informed regional voices which most affect the outcome, not people in New York and Washington driven by very different agendas and handicapped by slender knowledge of the issues at stake in a conflict. Sadly, few regional organisations to date have shown themselves capable of taking effective action. The final and most obvious remedy is self-help at the national level. If electors want effective decision-making power to remain in the hands of their own governments, their states need to be strong and self-reliant. Otherwise their fates will be settled in part by the use or non-use of the military power of others. This challenge sometimes needs to be recognised more explicitly by the governments of states bordering on troubled areas when they are tempted to rely on the provision of external support.

## THE EXISTENTIAL THREAT OF WEAPONS OF MASS DESTRUCTION

The Cold War has left many legacies: some, such as the agreed framework of arms control and confidence-building measures, are helpful; others, such as the development of weapons of mass destruction, are decidedly unhelpful. The previous Australian government played an important role in the establishment of a more effective system of control of chemical weapons. In its last year in office it set its sights on a much more ambitious project: the elimination of nuclear weapons. As a member of the Canberra Commission on that subject, let me speak to its objectives and its work.

During the Cold War itself I thought that nuclear weapons on balance served a useful purpose: that of deterrence. As a military historian I could see that nuclear weapons had no fruitful role in the fighting of wars, but if they helped to prevent a huge one from being fought, that was all to the good. More importantly if their protection established a framework of confidence in the West in its own security, on the basis that a much smaller proportion of its resources were devoted to military purposes than in the East, and fewer of its young men had to bear the burden of two years' conscription, it was as well that nuclear weapons were in the Western arsenal. The inability of the West to meet the Lisbon force goals of 1952 underlines the predicament we would have been in during the 1950s and 1960s without nuclear weapons. There was also the fact that the Russians had nuclear weapons after 1949. Handing them two sets of strategic advantages with Stalin at the helm would have been lunacy.

But now we are in a different situation. Should Russia become a rogue state, the world can deal with it by political, economic and conventional military means, unless of course such a Russian leadership should choose to use their massive nuclear arsenal. With the collapse of the Warsaw Pact the balance of nuclear advantage has swung in the opposite direction. Whereas during the Cold War the most probable object of a nuclear threat was Moscow, and the most probable originator of that threat was NATO, today the most probable target of a nuclear threat is the United States, and the most probable issuer of the threat is a bunch of desperadoes, so hate-filled that they do not care that their actions virtually are an act of suicide (if they are caught). These desperadoes do not have to be restricted to the ranks of Russian extreme nationalists. They can be extremists of many kinds. Think of the Islamic radicals who tried to blow up the World Trade Center in New York, or of a Saddam Hussein, or the North Koreans or, coming closer to home, of the Unabomber or the right-wing militias of the United States itself. If any of these had access to a single nuclear warhead, how safe would the citizens of New York or the legislators of Washington feel? Had the people who bombed the World Trade Center had a suitcase with 100 pounds of highly enriched uranium – about the size of a grapefruit – they could have destroyed the southern third of Manhattan, including the whole of the financial district and most buildings up to 20th Street.

The only solution to this problem lies in stricter proliferation control, and that requires the existing nuclear weapons powers to take the disarmament measures that they promised to take when they signed the Treaty. The rest of the world will not tolerate a much tighter system of surveillance and policing which leaves the five nuclear armed powers free to do what they like, thereby maintaining a unique class structure in the international order. For as long as this class exists there will be a natural inclination for some ambitious leaders to want to join it.

The problem of lack of control over the contents of the vast Russian nuclear arsenal has been splendidly analysed in the recent Harvard report, *Avoiding Nuclear Anarchy*.[2] The dangers are clear and action is needed. This is a time of opportunity and Australia can play an important role as a catalyst of international debate, just as it did in the field of chemical weapons. In the meantime the United States government has to consider how to maintain deterrence against all those who might seek to use nuclear weapons against it – to the extent that they can be deterred. The Russians have to ponder the problems of sustaining and modernising their own nuclear forces, and convince the world that they have the whole arsenal under firm control. The Chinese, who are on record as saying that they really do not want nuclear weapons at all and will disarm when the others do, risk further isolation and suspicion for their efforts to modernise. The British and French wonder how they will pay for the next round of modernisation which will be necessary if their tickets for the nuclear club are to remain current. The near-nuclears and the undeclared owners of nuclear weapons have to be watched carefully. They, and any who join them, will have to be brought into the nuclear disarmament dialogue – no easy matter in the case of a state which has nuclear weapons but refuses to admit it. These are challenges to world order which are new and extremely serious. If they defeat us the penalties will be unthinkable.

## THE PROBLEM OF HEGEMONY

The final problem I shall mention is a structural one: the consolidation of both official governmental power and non-governmental influence in the hands of a very small group of nations, of which the United States will be the most prominent. Others sharing in this concentration of power will include Japan, the major states of Western Europe and probably China, but each of these will be dependent on the United States in several key ways, not the least of which will be the provision of security.

The world has been through a wave of integration in the past generation, especially with the formation of the European Communities then the European Union, with its outer bailey the European Free Trade Area; ASEAN and its enlargement to include Vietnam; the North American Free Trade Area; Mercosur in South America; and the nascent APEC. There are others to mention in Africa, the Caribbean, the Gulf, the Arab states and the Commonwealth, although the first group are much the more cohesive. But this wave may be about to lose its strength. Dangerous signs of nationalist reassertion are evident in Europe and the United States, in response, it must be admitted, to excessive regulation and standardisation.

Perhaps in the Asia-Pacific region the drive for integration may generate less of a backlash, but this remains to be seen. The region is far bigger than Europe or North America, and the variety of states and interests to be accommodated is much more complex. It will be interesting to see the outcome, but it would be prudent to expect a slowing of integration here as elsewhere. One consequence of failure to integrate much further than at present will be to leave the political power of the leading states relatively untrammelled, and the gap in influence between them and the remainder of the community of nation-states will only widen. It is unclear as to whether this degree of political prominence can be turned into economic leadership, but the way in which the United States has regained economic strength in recent years suggests that the two are not incompatible.

There are natural limits to the development of a hierarchy of nations because the burdens of leadership are substantial, and the greater competitive powers of the states lower in the rank order will enable some of them to move upwards. But we may all come increasingly to feel that we should have votes for the US President and Senate because they will have so much direct influence on what happens in the world outside the United States.

What about the United Nations? Its charter is widely accepted as the basis of international order. Unfortunately the UN can do nothing significant without the active approval of most of the Permanent Five on the Security Council, and any one of them can block effective action. The most powerful and active of these five is the United States, so the authority and capacity of the UN rest substantially and increasingly on the political debate within the United States. Finding a way to move forward to a wider sharing of power and responsibility among the members of the Security Council, which will be acceptable to all of the Permanent Five, is another new challenge for world order.


CONCLUSIONS

We are moving out of the era of global wars. Regional wars abound, but even they can be reduced in frequency and scope as energetic human beings take charge of their own lives and the quality of government of the systems they live under. Potential for unintended conflict remains substantial and can grow if the causes are neglected, but here again the challenges are obvious and the penalties of failure to heed warnings will be painful. The world will not do enough, but it will not be wholly blind to problems such as environmental degradation, resource depletion and uncontrolled movement of populations. The control of weapons of mass destruction is an urgent matter. It is a complex problem but it can only become worse if we do not tackle it quickly. At least the problem will have a high political profile in future years. There are grounds for hope.

A modicum of team spirit for tackling the challenges of peace-keeping and peace-enforcement exists, but it will not be enough to cover all the deserving cases which will arise. Regional associations would be wise to take on more responsibility for their own areas. For those states which lack such a body to assist them, their best recourse is self-help, boosted by whatever assistance the more secure and richer members of the international community will give them.

All of us would be wise to be less dependent on the United States. The US will not oppose such efforts. The principal opposition will come from those within our own electorates who want an easy ride. They should be told that dependence does not offer an easy ride in the long term.

Educated people everywhere are becoming more aware of their opportunities. New information technology is opening up avenues to knowledge, understanding and influence. As this democratic power asserts itself – and it can do so only slowly and in a disjointed way – it will create a field of force in which legislators will work. It can counter the centralising of power which events of the twentieth century have fostered. The exercising of democratic power can be for good or for evil, it can be wise or foolish and short-sighted. The choices are ours. They may seem small and inconsequential but their overall effect is crucial. The combined efforts of millions of people took us through the era of the two world wars. The real challenge to all of us now in the new international setting is to carry this process another step or two forward. Reducing the incidence of regional wars and eliminating nuclear weapons would not be a bad beginning.

## NOTES

1. Paul Dibb, *Towards a New Balance of Power in Asia, Adelphi Paper 295,* IISS/OUP, Oxford and New York, 1995.
2. Graham T. Allison, Owen R. Cote Jr, Richard A. Falkenrath and Steven E. Miller, *Avoiding Nuclear Anarchy: Containing the Threat of Loose Russian Nuclear Weapons and Fissile Material,* MIT Press, Cambridge, Massachusetts, 1995.

# 3 The New Regionalism: Avoiding Strategic Hubris
John Chipman

The message that virtually all areas of the world wished to promote in the aftermath of the Cold War was that the time had now come for regional solutions to regional problems. Effective regionalism could dampen local disputes and enfranchise the people of the region to find solutions that were compatible with their regional preferences. Some, in the face of malevolent power, have turned away from this perhaps misguided notion. This is the case for the states of the Gulf Cooperation Council (GCC). Saddam Hussein saw regionalism as an opportunity but was blinded to the important residual interest that the US held in preserving influence in the Gulf. He could not imagine the scale of the resources that the US was willing to deploy to uphold a certain regional balance of power and the importance to the US of the security of access to oil the US saw came with that balance. The failures of Arab intramural diplomacy to contain Saddam Hussein and to find a solution to his invasion of Kuwait has thus had the dual effect of diluting if not sinking the political interest in pan-Arabism, and of encouraging the Gulf states in particular to import American power as the best and only means of defending themselves. Regionalism in the Gulf is maintained only in a cosmetic form.

Some, who were unprepared for regionalism, regretted the obligations that regionalism imposed. African states feared their marginalisation from the mainstream of international security. While in the 1970s and 1980s they lamented the exploitation of their weakness by the superpowers in their competition with each other, as the 1990s opened they saw that as West–East relations began to take on the substance and form of previous North–South relations, the rich countries in the West would see their security interests more engaged in providing assistance to Eastern Europe and the former Soviet Union than to themselves. Leaders who had mastered the technique of playing East against West, now found their countries descending into geopolitical insignificance. And indeed, witnessing the reactions of the international community to Somalia and Rwanda, it is difficult not to conclude that Africa has become a strategic ghetto: a no-go area in which the international community has no interests, and in any case fears to tread. Regionalism, for Africans, is depressing.

The Europeans and the Asians find themselves in a different position again, struggling to find the right balance between regional self-sufficiency and the

20

retention of the American link. One of the many lessons, for Europeans, but perhaps too for others, of the crisis in the former Yugoslavia is this: if states begin to address an issue exclusively on regional terms, and express a desire for outsiders to stay out, their later ability to collaborate effectively, on the basis of a common analysis of the problem and towards a commonly aimed for solution with that outside power, is severely hampered. When the United States began to engage itself in the Yugoslav problem it did so on the basis of a different analysis of the problem. The principal transregional organisation, NATO, had not been used as a forum for consultation to harmonise views.

One of the lessons for Asians, and perhaps too, for others, of the March 1996 crisis in the Taiwan Strait, is that dialogue and mutual understanding of different national perspectives is a necessary but insufficient condition for conflict prevention: it depends for its credibility on the capacity physically to deter the resort to force in dispute settlement. The development of cooperative security mechanisms must not obscure the need to assure that an overall balance of power remains.

Some of these lessons had to be learned again, because they were first forgotten. An intellectually depressing feature of the end of the Cold War has been the tendency of some strategists to write of international affairs as if one needed entirely to start with a new set of strategic principles. This is especially true of those who had an understandable distaste for power politics, and who looked forward to the day when different sets of axioms could govern international affairs than those which prevailed during the Cold War. All ends of all types of wars usher in a romantic period, when even the most practically minded are inspired to presume that international behaviour can be reconstructed on a fresh set of norms. The early panegyric of the so-called 'New World Order' owed something to this impulse. But it is striking how long a certain idealism about the possibilities of escaping from strategic truths that had no special origin in the Cold War and therefore did not die with it, has lasted in the minds of academic writers on international affairs and some government officials. And it is even more disconcerting to see those who would wish to usher in a new style of international behaviour ignore some of the profound changes in global and regional politics which make one-dimensional solutions to the challenges of the contemporary era inapplicable.

The idea of regionalism, which remains a dominant feature of contemporary strategic discourse, especially suffers from this twin tendency to dismiss certain everlasting truths about the nature of international politics, and equally to ignore some of the genuine changes in international politics that limit the effectiveness of the regionalist's art form as normally defined. Regionalism and regional security organisations are important contributions to the management of international security, but they are invariably only partial answers to the security challenges that arise in most places. The virtue of regionalism and of the institutions that give regionalism an operational capability is that they can help develop locally derived and therefore locally supported norms to guide regional security behaviour. On this basis, they provide an initial context in which interested states can judge and act on challenges to the peace that affect the members. The hubris of regionalism is to suppose that regionalism is ex hypothesi the best approach to the resolution of regional issues, and that outside influence can only have a neo-imperial motivation, or must be paid for in the currency of political dependency. The hope for regionalism is that it can cultivate norms of behaviour and ingrain habits of cooperation that eradicate the resort to force as a method of settling disputes. The danger of regionalism is that it can seduce those who invest heavily in it to act as if the preservation of a regional institution and its norms can be more important than the pursuit of the best solution to a problem.

The lesson of half a decade of regionalism since the end of the Cold War is two-fold. First, states in various parts of the world owe an obligation to themselves and to international society as a whole to cooperate in order independently to be able to pre-empt and deter the local use of force to settle disputes. But regionalism cannot just become a wider form of nationalism, where the accent on a local style of politics and diplomacy is so strong that it makes constructive dialogue and cooperation with outside friends and allies ineffective. Second, the powers of the West, and especially the United States, need themselves to be good regionalists and develop foreign policies towards regions which incorporate an appreciation of the workings of regional dynamics. But their interests in regional security cannot be assured by an intellectual, or worse, physical isolationism which impedes them from influencing regional trends to make them compatible with wider global realities.

WHAT IS REGIONALISM?

Regionalism, in general, is the tendency towards and preference for regional systems or methods. It seeks to defend a certain cultural disposition, and aims towards a degree of autonomy in the management of regional affairs. In the sphere of international security, regionalism is the attempt by a group of states to order their relations amongst each other in such a way as to advance commonly agreed aims, to avoid local conflict and to manage it, if it does break out, as much as possible, on a regional basis. The presumption of the Cold War was that this aspiration could not be met because the interests of the superpowers in regional affairs was such that local solutions to local conflicts was not on the cards. It is certainly true that virtually none of the regional conflicts of the 1970s and 1980s was solved primarily, or even partly, by such regional organisations as existed. It is equally true that outside powers today are not prone to invent fanciful reasons as to why their strategic interests may be at stake in some far-away place just to preserve their prestige. And it is undeniable that political, social, economic and military challenges are now considered first at the regional level, with leaders placing the compass close to home and drawing a tighter circle for their immediate interests.

But it does not follow from these assertions that the current international environment is especially propitious for the politics of regionalism and for regional organisations. One cannot consider regionalism as an easy alternative to the globalism that many thought characterised the Cold War, nor can regionalism be a form of escapism, or its mere existence a palliative to the challenges of nationalism.

True regional security in almost all places of the world requires a happy marriage between local cooperation and constructive engagement from the outside. This is the only way to avoid the creation of strategic ghettos on the one hand, and the reappearance of sphere of influence politics on the other.

## WHAT IS THE INTERNATIONAL FRAMEWORK IN WHICH REGIONALISM OPERATES?

Against this background, how does the structure of the present international system affect the saliency of regionalism, in its usual forms, for the effective management of regional affairs?

The overarching feature is the shifting nature of the regions themselves. Regions are not mere geographical facts, they are political constructs that carry a geographical name. And like French wine, regional appellations have to be carefully controlled if they are not to be dismissed as unmarketable. The existence of a regional solidarity cannot be merely asserted, it has to be proven over time and be seen to reflect political and economic realities which ordinary citizens recognise.

With the collapse of the Berlin Wall and the release of the forces of nationalism which this both permitted and inspired, the world has witnessed a remarkable change in its political geography. Some regions have lost their previous geopolitical salience: few now talk of the politics of Southwest Asia in the same way that they did in 1979 at the time of the Afghan war. Old regions have been reborn, so that now, talking of the geopolitics of Central Asia makes sense. And indeed one cannot now understand the potential outcomes of the Afghan civil war without appreciating the Central Asian elements to it. Countries that were previously seen as front-line states do not have the same geopolitical relevance: Turkey's status has thus been reduced from a country which was the anchor of NATO in the southern flank, to one simply surrounded by unstable actors on all sides, and with less assurance than it might have had in the past for automatic support of its policies. Changes in political geography inspire new initiatives in national strategy which find their expression in institutional preferences. Thus, Germany, seeing the countries of the Warsaw Pact regain their real independence, wants to ensure that it has, in the official phrase, 'Western countries to its East'. Hence the German interest in NATO and EU expansion. Russia's own loss of empire has encouraged it to find an institutional way of preserving some influence over its former political wards through the CIS. It has also been inspired to seek for the OSCE a central place in European security politics, if only partially to displace NATO's primacy.

The end of the Cold War was felt globally, but the changes in political geography this brought forth were naturally greatest in Eurasia. Other regions have political earthquakes awaiting which might have equally dramatic regional consequences. If and when the present uncertain peace process in the Middle East is concluded, the end of the formal Arab–Israeli conflict will bring forth an equally tectonic shift in the regional rules of international politics. The domestic politics and the international affairs of the Middle East have been for the last half century determined by the conflict between Arab and Israeli. When this, at least officially, is brought to an end with the conclusion of treaties with Lebanon, Syria and Israel, at least three things will happen. First, many of the regimes which depended on the conflict with Israel to maintain autocratic forms of power may find themselves less able to extract support from their populations and could fall. Second, a period of musical chairs diplomacy will ensue with different states seeking different forms of regional agreements to secure their interests in the new era: we see hints of this already with Turkish–Israeli security pacts and Qatari–Israeli business deals. Third, the opponents of the peace process will organise themselves more effectively transnationally, thus creating new challenges to the existing conservative structures. These changes will immediately have their impact on regional political organisations. The Arab League's relevance was already challenged by the Gulf War and the coalition that was formed against Iraq. Once the Arab boycott against Israel is lifted, what Arab leader will think – genuinely – that the Arab League is the first point of contact for the solution of a regional problem? The Gulf Cooperation Council is bound to be further weakened by the individualist foreign policies of its members, which would become all the greater if any of the regimes actually fall.

In Asia, certain modest adjustments have taken place in regional relationships owing to new political developments. Thus ASEAN, following the official end of the Cambodian conflict, has sought to expand to bring in others who logically have a place in regional politics. A question others will ask here is whether its special strategic culture will be able to cope both with an expanded membership and with a potentially different agenda. Equally important will be to know whether its model can be readily translated into a wider security context. But there are changes which are taking place now, and which may suddenly emerge that may affect more dramatically regional relationships, and thus require enormous flexibility by regional institutions. Any unification of Korea, even if the product would still be the smallest state in Northeast Asia, would change some of the strategic calculations of both China and Japan. The economic strength of many of China's regions and the different external suitors each entertains introduces a form of regional relationships which does not perfectly correspond to formal international boundaries. China's regions have forms of external relations with other states which give them particular interests in interstate politics. And the politics of Chinese unification, if this is what one can call China's collection of policies towards the Spratlys, Hong Kong and Taiwan, will affect political calculations of how the region is to be defined and therefore of regional dynamics.

All this is to suggest that good regionalism needs to derive from good geopolitics, and like all geopolitics, regionalism needs to be flexible in the face of political change, something which is not often facilitated by the fact much regional politics takes place in an institutional form. If regions change, so must the politics of regionalism, both for outside actors and for regional ones.

## THE CHALLENGES TO REGIONALISM

There are four principal challenges to regionalism today. These have varying influence in different regions but no region is entirely immune from their actual or potential impact. The first comes from below: the forces of parochialism and nationalism which challenge both regional constructs and the states that comprise them. With ethnic reassertion and new claims for self-determination, has come a privatisation of violence. In many places the state's monopoly control over the use of force is challenged, and the tribute which citizens wish to pay to regional entities is limited by their primordial loyalties: nationalists to the state; ethnic warriors often to the one they would wish to establish for themselves.

A second challenge comes from without, and it is the, often unevenly felt, fear of a local great power and its presumed attachment to the virtues of coercive force to settle problems. In Europe, the Eastern Europeans and the Baltic states remain distrustful of Russia, and wish to animate the US and Western European states to guarantee their security against a threat that is not perceived the same way by existing NATO states. In the Gulf, the states of the GCC have different types of fears about Iran and Iraq, and while they are sceptical of the wisdom of the US policy of dual containment, they are largely unwilling to engage either of these states in constructive dialogue. In Asia, there are privately expressed fears about China's growing power, but few if any overt champions of a US-led policy of containment. The dilemmas of how to couple policies of dialogue with those of deterrence plague most regional security structures in the world's most important areas.

The third challenge to regionalism which flows from this last is the perceived itinerant nature of US engagement in regional security and the schizophrenic regional attitude towards it. This is strongest in Europe where for many years Europeans have regretted the weight of the US in regional affairs but equally lamented the absence of its leadership when moods of isolationism set in. Claims of security autonomy in any region can inspire the US to withdraw, while insufficient burden-sharing can cause tensions in a relationship which risks the same result. At the same time, a proven capacity to engage the US can stultify regional growth. This is evidently the case in the Gulf where the GCC has been able to postpone indefinitely any politically sensitive decision on military integration since it sees its military salvation so completely in American support. The relationship between regional organisations and the US in areas of its strategic interest are bound continuously both to challenge and constrain the nature of regionalist ambitions as well as the local analysis of regional dilemmas. This will be all the more the case when subjects that pertain to a globalist agenda, like non-proliferation, have to be handled in a regional context, and sometimes in ways that challenge regional analyses of the problem.

The fourth challenge to regionalism is the general challenge of all strategy, which is how to harness, in appropriate manners, the economic, political, diplomatic and military elements of external policy to an agreed end. In Europe the economic and security policies towards Eastern Europe and Russia are bifurcated by the institutional division of labour between the European Union and NATO. An important debate in Asia is whether economic inter-dependence is a sufficient counter to the forces of nationalism. In both regions, as in others, crises are rarely effectively handled by the ostensibly relevant regional organisation, but by a collection of individual powers from the region and beyond, which have the right mixture of political, economic and military attributes to weigh in heavily and force a congenial outcome.

## WHAT ARE THE LIMITATIONS AND POSSIBILITIES OF REGIONALISM?

Given these challenges to the regionalist ethos it is worth pointing out the limitations, but also the possibilities of regionalism. In the security realm, regionalism really has four tasks, all of which are challenging enough, but none of them, even if brought together successfully, can provide adequate answers to the security questions that are likely to be posed.

The first is the primary obligation of any collective security structure, and this is the elaboration of norms and agreed patterns of behaviour that are deemed acceptable by the regional society. The Organisation of African Unity (OAU) in the early 1960s established its most important norm, that the borders inherited from colonial times should not be challenged. This norm is fraying at its edges, but its invocation set important and by-and-large useful parameters for considering regional disputes within Africa. The OSCE in Europe is elaborating a complex security model for the twenty-first century which aspires to find ways to ensure that existing norms and confidence-building measures can properly be applied. Most small regional organisations, including ASEAN, see as one of their principal roles the creation of a security community in which a regional culture of appropriate behaviour is devised and recognised. Yet often, regional organisations exclude from their agendas discussion of real or potential security issues, thus the South Asian Association for Regional Cooperation (SAARC) excludes the discussion of bilateral disputes, while ASEAN's highly lauded renunciation of interference in the internal affairs of states may be found wanting if an important regional state has a succession crisis, and the domestic effects of this cannot be domestically contained. A maxim for consideration: regionalism, quite understandably, reflects the interests in the status quo; the test of its utility lies in its effectiveness when a regional status quo is challenged.

The second is the creation, for want of a better term, of a common foreign and security policy, on which a regional identity can be asserted more widely. It is axiomatic that a national position shared by others is a national position strengthened, and so states that are members of regional organisations have an interest in forging a regional consensus when they can. But the availability of a common forum can rarely force states to abide by an institutionalised consensus. The dilemma of regionalism is that without common policies, regionalism has no purpose, but a regionalist consensus is often fragile and one is struck by how often regional groupings are frustrated by various types of 'go-it-alone' politics. Germany within the EU went solo on the recognition of Croatia and Slovenia and managed to drag others, against their better instincts, with it. Qatar and Oman, within the GCC, have often pursued independent foreign policies, in pursuit of their own interests, and sometimes in pursuit simply of their wish to frustrate Saudi Arabia, the intramural hegemon. The Czech Republic, thinking itself the most Western of the Eastern European states, has broken the Visegrad consensus, and sought to deal with the West without consulting Poland, Hungary and Slovakia as much as was originally presumed by these states when the Visegrad group was established. And one is entitled to view the recent arrangements between Australia and Indonesia as evidence by the latter that the multilateral arrangements of which it is formally a part, should not be the only focus of foreign policy. Common policies therefore are important but they will rarely supplant important national perceptions. Another maxim: regionalism has its limits as an organiser of external policy.

Two tasks that go beyond the creation of norms and the development of common foreign and security policies are tasks which transform collective security organisations into their elder and more cold-blooded brothers: collective defence organisations. One is the capacity for regional peace-keeping. Few regional organisations do this at all, and this is a constant lament of the UN Secretary General, who has called for regional organisations to take up more of the burden for regional peace-keeping. One organisation that has done regional peace-keeping, the ECOWAS in Liberia, has not fared well. Not only was the Nigerian-led force treated with suspicion regionally, but it inspired the deployment of a UN force whose avowed purpose was to supervise the activities and the neutrality of the locally sanctioned and deployed force. If there were ever more eloquent testimony to the cynicism with which regional organisations are held within regions themselves it is the evident preference for external peace-keepers. A second task which regional organisations can give themselves is for actual collective defence, and here too there is no real example, outside NATO (and in theory the WEU), of states which give themselves a real security guarantee. And therefore so long as groups of states within a region may risk a concerted threat to their security, they have to find ways to import countervailing power, and the very need to do this is bound to compromise the purity of the regionalist impulse.

CONCLUSION

What, in this context that I have sketched out, are the key axioms that should govern our contemporary understanding of regionalism?
The first is that regional isolationism is as bad as national isolationism. Regions cannot immunise themselves either from the effects of global trends, or from the unsavoury effects of neighbourhood strife. On the contrary, good regionalism requires the development of policies towards the neighbourhood and the world beyond. In doing this, however, it is important to avoid the tendency to grant institutions a more sacrosanct importance than the strategic interests that their members genuinely hold. The EU sometimes conducted policy in Yugoslavia in a way more relevant to managing intramural concerns than to managing the conflict of Yugoslavia. And some in Europe were surprised to read in Asian newspapers that some Asian leaders regretted the introduction of American power to deter more robust use of Chinese force against the island of Taiwan since it would make the next meeting of the ASEAN Regional Forum more awkward.

Second, in most places of the world, especially in Europe, the Middle East and Africa, but no doubt eventually in Asia too, effective regionalism will require a willingness to consider the external impact of internal politics. We live in an age where the domestic politics of one country, can quickly become the domestic politics of its neighbour: internal conflict is commutable. In these circumstances an understandable reluctance to comment, and even act on the internal problems of neighbours could later be interpreted as an act of strategic negligence. This at least, is what many accused the Europeans of in Yugoslavia.

The third is that cooperative security – which is a principal feature of the new regionalism – and balance of power must coexist. Indeed, more often than not, it is the existence of some kind of balance of power, often externally assured, that enables regional states to engage in the politics and practice of cooperative security. Forgetting this is a form of strategic hubris which can have tragic ramifications.

Regionalism is often a necessary strategy for assuring healthy diplomatic relations within a particular region, it is rarely a sufficient condition or strategy for the assurance of peace in the vicinity of the region. Regional emperors who shed their links with external powers which play a balancing role will find in their regional relations that they have no clothes. Cooperative security tempers the coldness of pure balance of power politics, in that it offers opportunities for small states to address their concerns with each other without reference to a great power, and equally allows them the opportunity to deal with a local large power in terms that do not immediately imply a threat to that power. But cooperative security is dangerous when pursued alone, for it encourages the malevolent to grab their security interests without sufficient regard for the declared interest of others.

Finally, the solution of crisis will often come about through the ad hoc formation of powers from within and without a region who are best equipped, historically, diplomatically, economically and militarily, to deal with a special issue. Contact Group politics are bound to proliferate. We saw the relevance of the Contact Group and ultimately of the US in dealing with the Bosnia crisis in 1995. In April 1996 the US called on a group of four states – itself, China, and the two Koreas – to re-ignite efforts to finalise a peace treaty on the Korean peninsula. Contact Group politics are useful, because they bring relevant powers together in an ad hoc fashion without institutionalising the directoire politics which smaller powers in regions fear. But it is worth pointing out that the Contact Group ethos on which states are bound to rely when regional structures become too unweildy, owes more to nineteenth-century concepts of the balance of power than to twenty-first-century notions of cooperative security. The techniques of cooperative security that are useful to create an atmosphere of peaceful interaction lose their relevance once conflict breaks out, or needs quickly to be contained. I suspect that the new regionalism will not permanently be able to escape the old power politics.

# 4   New Dimensions of Security

Alan Dupont

## WHAT DOES SECURITY MEAN?

It is probably true to say that 'security' is one of the most commonly used words in the English language today. Certainly in the realm of international relations, debates about the meaning and scope of security feature prominently in the academic literature of the 1990s in much the same way as deterrence dominated the agenda of the 1950s and 1960s, interdependence that of the 1970s, and peace, or peace studies, that of the 1980s. Given the widespread penetration and usage of the concept, one would imagine that there would be a correspondingly widespread understanding and consensus about what security means. In fact, the opposite is the case. Security, or national security as it is most commonly known, is arguably one of the least understood and most contested concepts to enter the lexicon and discourse of international relations. This ambiguity, it should be noted, is not confined to the modern era. In the early 1960s, the British historian, Michael Howard, bemoaned 'the appallingly crude conceptual standards'[1] which applied to national security, while a decade earlier, the American academic, Arnold Wolfers, thought that the concept might 'not have any precise meaning at all'.[2] Others have compared the difficulty of defining national security with attempting to encapsulate a human emotion like anger – it is an 'uncertain quality: it is relative not absolute: it is largely subjective and takes countless forms'.[3] It is instructive to analyse why security has proved to be such an elusive concept, because the answer to this question sheds light on the contentious and important issue of how security should be perceived in the world of the 1990s and beyond.

The etymological roots of security are clear enough. Security originates from the Latin *securus*, meaning free from danger, safe. These two elements, the notion of danger or threat, and the desire for protection against danger, are central to virtually all definitions of security. But there consensus ends. The first major point of contention is between those who believe that the primary object or referent point of security should be the state, and those who believe that it should be the individual or humanity at large. This I will refer to as the 'who' of security. The second area of disagreement concerns the nature and hierarchy of threats, or the 'what' of security.

As the term national security implies, much of the traditional thinking and theorising about security has been cast in terms of the nation-state. At the

31

systemic or structural level, the debate has tended to concentrate on the most effective means of preserving the integrity and balance of the system of states itself.[4] At the unit level, these concerns are typically expressed in terms of defending the sovereignty and territoriality of individual states from the hostile or predatory intentions of others. Survival of the state as a political, cultural and social entity, and freedom from war or external aggression, are usually considered to be the key measures of security. Some definitions differentiate between internal and external threats to security, while others include the freedom to pursue the national interest, usually without elaborating what the national interest might be. The other element most commonly mentioned is the protection of core values, and the assurance of future well-being.[5] These are recurring themes and indicate the focus and preoccupation of mainstream thinking on security.

Outside the mainstream, although growing in influence, are those who regard security more prosaically, and are inclined to define it in terms of protecting the individual from hunger, disease, repression and the more serious vicissitudes of daily life.[6] Adherents of this approach argue that the object of security should be the individual, or humanity in general, rather than the state, which has no meaning if dissociated from its human context and identity.[7] There are several permutations of this school of thought, but they are most commonly associated with notions of human or global security.[8] A representative definition can be found in the 1994 United Nations Human Development Report, which contends that 'the concept of security has for too long been interpreted narrowly .... It has been more related to nation states than people .... Forgotten were the legitimate concerns of ordinary people who sought security in their daily lives.'[9] In between these two diametrically opposed positions are those who assert that the needs and concerns of the state and the individual must be balanced with those of subnational and non-state actors. Richard Ullman, for example, defines threats to national security as 'an action or a sequence of events that (1) threatens drastically and over a relatively brief period of time to degrade the quality of life for the inhabitants of a state, or (2) threatens significantly to narrow the range of policy choices available to a state or to private, non-governmental entities (persons, groups, corporations within the state)'.[10]

The second major area of disagreement concerns the hierarchy and nature of threats, or the 'what' of security. The majority of definitions, implicitly or explicitly, regard military threats as the primary cause of insecurity, usually expressed in terms of the potential for major, conventional armed attack against the territory or resources of the state, or more limited forms of military contingencies, such as low-level incursions, or strikes against vulnerable, high-value targets. Threats of a political nature aimed at undermining internal stability or political independence form a second widely accepted component. These may be presented either in unit or structural terms; for example, challenges to existing borders or the balance of power. Or they may be domestically focused, such as threats to the leadership or authority of a particular ruling elite, or from other ethnic, religious or social groups within the state. Threats are also sometimes couched in terms of their impact on values, mores and social cohesion.

## THE SECURITY ORTHODOXY

Before proceeding to analyse how these issues are changing the way in which we think about security, one first needs to understand why the security orthodoxy of the Cold War years privileged its military dimension and enshrined the state as the primary object of security. The principle answer to this important question lies in the way the tenets of classical realism have shaped and influenced thinking about international society and security since the basic structure of the contemporary state system was first laid down at the Treaty of Westphalia in 1648.[11] Realists trace their philosophical roots back to the writings of the European political theorists, Machiavelli and Thomas Hobbes, and before them to the Greek sage and historian Thucydides. They hold a fundamentally pessimistic view of human nature and conceive of international politics as an arena of conflict, where anarchy is the ordering principle and sovereign states the central actors, engaged in an unending and brutal struggle for supremacy.[12] The basic driving force of this anarchical society of states is the 'concept of interest defined as power'. Power is also sometimes considered to be an end in itself.[13] The objective is survival, or national security, but this is often implied rather than specifically articulated.[14] The principal systemic concern of realists is how to maintain a stable balance of power among the competing states.[15]

The origins of modern realism can be traced to the breakdown in the post-First World War order in the 1930s, but the longevity of its ideational reign cannot be explained by the consequences of this breakdown alone.[16] Perhaps the most important reason for the strength of realist thinking in the following decades was the advent of the Cold War, which heralded an era of unprecedented global competition between the two dominant states of the period, the former Soviet Union and the United States. Although the contest between Moscow and Washington was played out on a multidimensional stage, including in the economic and ideological domains, the enduring images of that contest were essentially military and political. In an era symbolised by the familiar, if disturbing, mushroom cloud signature of thermo-nuclear detonations, and the physical realities of the Berlin Wall, the realist logic of security through military strength seemed apt and unassailable.

The strategic preoccupations of the Cold War were institutionalised by the growth of a United States national security establishment, largely policy orientated and concerned with the notion of war prevention and, later, war management. Since the United States had assumed the role of standard bearer and protector of the West's political and spiritual heritage, it was hardly surprising that American academic thinking on security became the accepted Western orthodoxy. And it was the orthodoxy of realism which prevailed. The Cold War also encouraged the development of a sub-discipline of international relations which we know today as Strategic Studies. Strategic Studies reinforced the realist bias towards the military aspects of national security, producing as Buzan has noted, a 'large volume of empirical literature on the problems of military policy', but giving little attention to alternative approaches or interpretations of security.[17] The conceptual 'underdevelopment' of security contrasted quite sharply with the other key concepts of international relations, and it was not until the late 1970s that academics and practitioners began to explore alternative ways of thinking about security which challenged the statist, militarised, balance-of-power prescriptions of realism.

This change in thinking coincided with the passing of the shrill confrontational early phase of the Cold War and the establishment of an uneasy detente between the two rival superpowers and their coalitions of lesser powers. The first real challenge to the realist paradigm of security came from a reinvigorated liberalism where a new generation of scholars began to write about the emerging phenomenon of globalisation, later to be given the label of interdependence.[18] Although the notion of interdependence was not conceived as a security construct, it nevertheless struck at the core of the realist understanding of security in three critical areas. First, interdependence challenged the pre-eminence of the state because it postulated that there were multiple channels connecting societies, many of which were outside the prerogative of national governments. Second, it argued that military aspects of security should not dominate the agenda of interstate relations because states have to deal with multiple issues which are not arranged in a clear hierarchy. Third, it questioned the utility of military force as an effective instrument for achieving security in a world increasingly characterised by widening circles of interlocking economic interests and political integration.[19]

## NEW THINKING

Reflecting these attitudinal changes, in the late 1970s an international commission headed by the former West German Chancellor, Willy Brandt, called for a new, more inclusive approach to security, which would incorporate the non-military agenda of complex interdependence.[20] This was followed by the Palme Commission in 1982, which developed some of the themes of the earlier Brandt Commission and formulated the notion of Common Security.[21] Common Security represented a significant departure from the realist security paradigm because it eschewed competitive, zero-sum notions of deterrence and power, and emphasised instead cooperation, dialogue and confidence building, averring that genuine security could never be achieved unless all states recognised and accepted the legitimate security concerns of others. In essence, 'achieving security with others, not against them'.[22] While Common Security recognised the need for a more multidimensional definition of security, its primary concern was still the military realm.

At the same time that the concept of common security was being articulated in Europe and further afield, Asian countries had also begun to re-examine their security policies and concepts in the light of changes in the global and regional security environments. Japan's confidence in the efficacy of its omni-directional foreign policy had been severely shaken by the United States' defeat in Vietnam, and the oil shock of 1973. Painfully aware of its dependence on overseas raw materials and energy resources, the Japanese developed a new concept of Comprehensive Security, designed to pre-empt economic as well as strategic threats to national security.[23] The ASEAN states, most notably Malaysia and Indonesia, also began to advance security concepts which had a distinctly regional flavour in both form and substance. Like Japan they subscribe to a comprehensive view of security. Unlike Japan, however, the ASEAN nations give primacy in their security to the requirements of internal stability, national development and social harmony, reflecting their concern with regime maintenance, their relative weakness as nation-states and their sense of vulnerability to internal threats and external intervention.[24]

While both Common and Comprehensive Security mark a significant departure in thinking about security from that of the realist orthodoxy, neither fully recognises the import of an emerging range of new security issues which fundamentally challenge the norms and utility of both the realist and liberal concepts of security, in their classical as well as contemporary formulations. These issues tend to be complex, multidimensional and transnational in form and impact. For the most part, they stretch the boundaries of traditional thinking about security. Some are economic; others relate to the earth's physical environment; many are new manifestations of age-old phenomena.[25] They range from concerns about international financial flows and market access, to food scarcity, resource depletion, global warming, transnational crime, illegal migration, virulent new strains of diseases, and a host of other issues not previously associated with security and foreign policy. Together they form the core of a new security agenda.[26]

## ECONOMIC SECURITY

Ironically, given its current military connotations, the modern concept of national security actually evolved from an economic and welfare interpretation of the national interest by the American historian Charles Beard in the 1930s. Beard's study was framed in the context of the Great Depression and the era of the New Deal, and was principally concerned with the economic and welfare interests of the United States.[27] Within a few years, this economic orientation was quickly displaced by the more pressing and immediate politico-military concerns associated with the rise of fascism, Nazism and militarism in Europe and Japan. Throughout this period, and even at the height of the Cold War, protection of national economic assets and well-being was widely accepted as a core security interest. However, economics was generally seen as being relevant to security only as a component of military power, as Paul Kennedy has so brilliantly chronicled in his book *The Rise And Fall Of The Great Powers*.[28]

The problem with this rather narrow conceptualisation of economic security is that it tends to underplay the role of trade and resource issues as causes of conflict. It also gives insufficient recognition to the reality that national governments, particularly in developing states, are today far more vulnerable to the vagaries and volatility of a rapidly globalising world economy than at any time in human history.[29] This has direct implications for both the 'who' and 'what' of security. The fundamental point is that economic threats to security in the form of disruptions to global commerce and financial transactions, economic coercion, trade sanctions, protectionism, resource disputes and arguments over market share and market access constitute a whole range of relatively new threats to security which may be just as serious and pervasive as traditional politico-military threats. Some liberals have drawn attention to these dimensions of economic security by producing studies on the linkages between trade, security and conflict. Richard Rosencrance, for example, argues that higher levels of international commerce are associated with a lower incidence of war; others argue that international trade can mitigate the anarchy of the international system by giving participating states a greater stake in economic cooperation, thereby increasing the absolute gains of all units in the system.[30] For the most part, however, economics and security have generally been regarded as discrete, and sometimes even hermetically sealed domains, particularly in the policy arena.[31]

ENVIRONMENTAL SECURITY

Perhaps the issue most associated with the new security agenda of the post-Cold War era is what has come to be known as environmental or ecological security. The argument here is that the earth's physical environment is under increasing stress from the combined effects of uncontrolled population growth, diminishing natural resources, climatic change and pollution, which over time have the capacity to erode the very foundations of global order, and threaten the security of humankind. At one end of the 'who' of the environmental security spectrum is the image of a malnourished, destitute and itinerant victim of a local tribal conflict in the developing world, caused by a dispute over water or grazing rights, or the destruction of habitat. At the other end of the spectrum is the possibility that island micro-states may disappear altogether because of rising sea-levels induced by global warming, or the Armageddon-like prospect of the earth being destroyed by a meteor strike. If the latter example seems more appropriate to a convention of *Star Trek* 'groupies' rather than the more sober deliberations of a conference on international security, consider that the Pentagon has been exploring, for some years now, how to apply some of the technology developed for anti-ballistic missile defence to the problem of destroying earth-bound meteors.

The environment as a security issue was first raised some 15 years ago, but the subject has really only gained currency in academic and policy circles since the late 1980s.[32] One of the more prescient and influential writings in recent years on the subject of environmental security and other non-state, non-military security challenges is an article authored by the American journalist, Robert Kaplan, in early 1994.[33] Entitled 'The Coming Anarchy', Kaplan asserts that the environment will become 'the national security issue of the early twenty-first century' and the 'core foreign policy challenge from which most others will ultimately emanate ...'.[34] As an example, Kaplan cites the case of China, which he portrays not as an emerging world power, but as a fractured, disaggregating collection of disparate regions where economic development is uneven, and economic prospects threatened by still uncontrolled population growth, soil degradation, deforestation and a host of other environmentally related security and developmental problems.[35] However, perhaps the most scholarly and persuasive statement of the case for treating the environment as a security problem has been made by the Canadian academic Thomas Homer-Dixon, the Head of the Project on Environment, Population and Security at the University of Toronto.[36]

I will leave others to articulate in more detail the arguments of Homer-Dixon. Let me, however, make two points about environmental security. It seems to me that there is a compelling case to be made that the environment interacts with security at a number of different levels, either as a direct cause of serious conflict, or as a contributing element. If one were to measure a global hierarchy of threats, those resulting from environmental degradation would rank, in many cases, more highly than traditional military security concerns. Second, environmental security issues transcend the logic and conceptual framework of realism because they are frequently beyond the jurisdiction and control of any one state, and are not amenable to resolution by military force or coercion. While liberalism would appear to offer a more promising and empathetic framework for analysing and responding to the environmental dimension of security, here too there are problems. Although some of the tenets of complex interdependence can be applied to environmental concerns, liberalism is still too inclined to view international security through the lens of the state, and to focus on the security implications of trade densities and economic transactions.

## UNREGULATED POPULATION FLOWS

The case for moving beyond traditional conceptions of security is strengthened further if one looks at two other aspects of the new agenda – unregulated population flows and transnational crime. Unregulated population flows, or illegal migration as it is more commonly known, I define as the forced or unsanctioned movement of people across borders and within states for economic reasons, or as a consequence of war, persecution or environmental factors. This definition includes not only those people classified as refugees by the United Nations, but also internally displaced persons as well as undocumented or illegal migrant workers. Large-scale migration of people is, of course, not a new phenomenon. Indeed, history is replete with examples of polities and civilisations being destroyed, supplanted or enriched by inflows of people from alien cultures and ethnically distinctive groups.

Until recently, however, the unregulated movement of people was not an issue which engaged or concerned defence or foreign policy establishments, nor was it considered to be a matter of national or international security. What is changing this perception is the dramatic increase in the number of illegal population movements, globally and regionally, and the realisation that these movements are inextricably linked with other emerging security issues in a complex web of interdependence, which complicates the security calculus for governments and non-governmental organisations alike. One recent example of the way in which unregulated population movements can impact on security is the fall of the East German state in 1989. As Myron Weiner has observed, here is a salutary example of a state destroyed not by military invasion but by the large-scale flight of its citizens.[37]

The increase in unregulated population movements globally has been quite dramatic over the past two decades. In 1975, the overall number of refugees globally, as measured by the United Nations High Commissioner for Refugees (UNHCR) was still only around 2.4 million. By 1992 there were 18.2 million refugees, rising to 27.4 million in 1995, an increase of over 1000 per cent in 20 years.[38] In addition to those officially categorised as refugees, there are substantial numbers of people displaced within their own countries, principally as a result of ethno-nationalist and tribal conflict, estimated conservatively at around 24 million in 1992.[39] This is not the end of the story. In the same year there were some 20–40 million undocumented or illegal migrants globally, in addition to the 25–30 million legal migrants.[40] Other estimates put the total number of people living outside their borders in 1992 at 100 million, up from 50 million in 1989. In East Asia, at the end of 1994, there were probably between 4–5 million illegal migrants and refugees who represented what former Australian Foreign Minister, Gareth Evans, termed a 'potential, non-military security' threat to the region.[41]

## TRANSNATIONAL CRIME

Turning now to the issue of transnational crime, there is a growing body of literature which asserts that criminality, either of the organised or anarchic variety, is becoming a threat to nation-states and global order, and, by the early part of the twenty-first century, unless checked, will pose security challenges which will rival those of the Cold War.[42] These claims are not confined to academics or officials responsible for law and order. At a conference on global organised crime held in Washington in 1994, the former Director of the United States' Central Intelligence Agency, James Woolsey, said:

the threat from organized crime transcends traditional law enforcement concerns. They affect critical national security interests. While organized crime is not a new phenomenon, today some governments find their authority besieged at home and their foreign policy interests imperilled abroad. Drug trafficking, links between drug traffickers and terrorists, smuggling of illegal aliens, massive financial and bank fraud, arms smuggling, potential involvement in the theft and sale of nuclear material, political intimidation and corruption all constitute a poisonous brew – a mixture potentially as deadly as some of what we faced during the cold war.[43]

As with unregulated population movements, it is the sheer volume and scale of much of today's criminal activities, as well as their transnational nature, which is compelling a major reassessment of the security implications of crime globally. Let me illustrate the scope of the problem today.

- There are some 5700 criminal gangs operating in Russia, who have penetrated virtually every aspect of the Russian economy and society, and who are responsible, by one calculation, for 35 per cent of the nation's gross domestic product. They employ about 100 000 gang members. Another 3 million Russians are thought to be indirectly associated as workers in illegal enterprises.[44]
- The Italian Mafia is richer than 150 sovereign states, based on its narcotics revenue alone.[45]
- In recent years, The US Department of Defense has measured a quantum increase in the number of cases of unauthorised access to its sensitive computer systems by 'hackers'. Many of these 'hackers' are teenagers recruited by criminal organisations which are employing state of the art technology to protect their own communications and to compromise those of their adversaries and intended victims. In one recent incident, 65 000 computer sites in Europe were accessed illegally in one weekend from an attack originating in Australia, which used a compromised system in the US to effect the entries into the European computers.[46]
- One computer expert expressed confidence that with 20 people and US$1 billion he could 'close down' the United States by disrupting its computer-based communication networks.[47]

There are states like Liberia in West Africa, which are besieged and undermined by what Kaplan has characterised as an 'anarchic implosion of criminal violence'.[48] In other cases criminals have corrupted the whole apparatus of government and exercise de facto political and economic control over large areas of territory, effectively becoming a state within a state. This is occurring not only in the impoverished developing states of West Africa, but in relatively advanced countries like Brazil, where, in cities like Rio de Janeiro, drug barons have established autonomy over the poorer areas of the city to such an extent that the inhabitants regard the drug barons' foot soldiers as their protectors, and the police, armed forces and government as the enemy.[49] Rising crime in the Asia-Pacific region has also put at risk the sovereignty and writ of central governments in some countries and made a mockery of border controls, particularly in outlying areas distant from the centres of administration. Examples which come to mind are Cambodia, Myanmar and parts of southern China. Criminals involved in narco-terrorism also employ their own military or paramilitary forces to protect their illicit activities, sometimes outnumbering and outgunning government forces.[50]

The point about many of these new security issues, is that they interlink and overlap in a way which makes them difficult to counter without an integrated policy approach, nationally and internationally. There is probably no better example of this within the Asia-Pacific region than the way in which criminal groups are both fuelling and exploiting Chinese illegal migration. Fundamental economic and social change has created a massive floating population in China of some 100 million people seeking employment opportunities or just a better lifestyle. Until recently, this had been essentially an internal problem for China, largely due to severe government restrictions on overseas travel combined with low incomes. However, rapidly improving incomes and the increasing accessibility of the global telecommunications system to ordinary Chinese[51] has stimulated a new wave of Chinese emigration into the Asia-Pacific region which well organised Chinese gangs, often from Taiwan and the overseas Chinese community, are exploiting. Since 1987, around 500000 illegal Chinese migrants have been moved by criminal networks into the United States,[52] while in East Asia, an estimated 180000 Chinese immigrants illegally entered Thailand, Hong Kong, Japan and Taiwan between 1992 and 1994.[53]

Criminal organisations are probably earning around US$3.5 billion annually from smuggling illegal Chinese migrants to East Asia and the West. This trade is clearly proving an attractive and lucrative complement to their more traditional activities in narcotics and prostitution. In the process, criminally assisted illegal migration is eroding the authority of central governments, calling into question the integrity and inviolability of borders, corrupting officials responsible for law and order, including the armed forces, and posing new threats to national security. Small wonder then that US President Clinton, Indonesia's Immigration Director and the Chief of Thailand's National Security Council have all declared illegal Chinese migration to be a threat to their respective country's national security.[54]

## CONCLUSION

Let me summarise the key points of this chapter so far. I have noted the contested nature of security as a concept, and some of the arguments about its scope, object and the hierarchy and nature of threats – the who and what of security. I have also attempted to provide some insights into the underlying assumptions and patterns of traditional thinking about security, which for most of the past 60 years has privileged the military dimension of security, and seen the state as both the instigator and victim of the security dilemma.

My argument is that the emergence of new kinds of threats, in conjunction with the re-emergence of old threats, in different forms and guises, are fundamentally challenging the way we think about security. When considered against the background of other significant changes in the international security environment, they also raise serious questions about the adequacy of mainstream security paradigms. Thus, realism's traditional concerns with territoriality and the sovereignty of borders may have far less relevance in an era when the majority of conflicts are intra-state rather than between states,[55] and when borders bear little or no resemblance to the realities of natural ethnic, linguistic or cultural boundaries. Examples are legion. In Europe, the Bosnian conflict graphically illustrates the essential meaningless of defining security for any of the protagonists and their innocent victims purely, or even primarily, in terms of defence from the aggression of other states. Where multi-ethnic states predominate, such as in the Asia-Pacific region, ethnic or religious minorities may well see the state as the principal threat to their well-being, rather than a protector or guarantor of basic freedoms and rights. In both cases, internal divisions may become so acute as to deprive conventional notions of national security 'of any theoretical, let alone operational utility'.[56]

Because state-centric notions of security inherently privilege direct challenges to territoriality and sovereignty, there is a concomitant tendency to ignore, or discount, threats which may be more amorphous and less directed, but which may pose equally serious dangers to individual and communal security. Realism is unable to accommodate environmental threats to security, such as global warming or desertification, because they are phenomena which are not necessarily attributable to the actions of any one state, nor are they specifically directed at the core elements of traditional security concerns, such as territoriality or political independence. Yet the consequences of environmental degradation may be more cataclysmic for the security of the planet than any conflict short of a full-scale nuclear war. The environment also needs to be factored into the security equation as a cause of conflict, both within and between states. The same may be said of other non-military challenges to security, of which unregulated population movements and transnational crime are but two. They can pose, in extremis, a threat to security every bit as serious as those of a military or political nature. What can be said about the liberal alternative? It is certainly better structured to cope with the interdependent, transnational and non-military aspects of the new agenda issues. On the other hand, it can be criticised for presenting too optimistic a view of the security enhancing effects of international trade and international institutions. As realists point out, under certain circumstances, unrestrained economic growth and trade liberalisation can actually lead to insecurity, through competition for resources and markets, as well as by contributing to environmental degradation and social dislocation. Democratisation may also exacerbate centripetal tendencies in states, particularly in developing countries where democratic institutions and values may be fragile at best.[57]

It is difficult to escape the conclusion that neither of the existing major international relations paradigms, in either their classical or contemporary formulations, offers a satisfactory overarching framework for dealing with the complex, multifaceted and interlinked security threats which the world community faces in the twenty-first century. This is despite a degree of convergence in thinking about security which is evident in many of the more syncretic recent expositions on the subject by both neo-realists and neo-liberals.[58] What is needed is a more holistic theoretical and policy framework, which can synthesise the still germane and salient elements of traditional security thinking with those of the new agenda. As Henry Kissinger, the arch exponent of balance-of-power geopolitics and elder statesman of the realist school, was once moved to say: 'the traditional agenda of international affairs – the balance among major powers, the security of nations – no longer defines our perils or our possibilities .... Now we are entering a new era. Old international patterns are crumbling; old slogans are uninstructive; old solutions are unavailing. The world has become more interdependent ....'[59]

## POLICY IMPLICATIONS

If one accepts the central argument of this chapter that the way we think about security will have to be broadened to take account of what Gwyn Prins has termed 'threats without enemies',[60] then there are some obvious policy implications. Let me suggest a few:

Security policies will need to become multidimensional in scope and intent, less reliant on military force as the primary instrument for achieving security, and more cognisant of the emerging range of non-military, transnational challenges and threats. Security will also become the concern of a far greater range of actors, domestically and externally, placing a premium on effective coordination and cooperation. The globalising forces which are revolutionising international society will diminish the capacity and prerogative of individual nation-states to determine their security agendas in the twenty-first century.

While some governments' and international organisations have begun to readjust their thinking, policies and structures to accommodate these changes, most have not. One notable exception is the United States. In a significant, but under-reported speech in October 1995, President Clinton urged the United Nations to address the new security challenges of the post-Cold War era. He focused particularly on terrorism, organised crime, drug trafficking and the proliferation of weapons of mass destruction, highlighting the inter-connectedness between these issues and the social, environmental and political conditions in which they flourish. Clinton drew attention to the need for greater international cooperation to combat their spread and proposed a number of concrete countermeasures, many of which will increasingly feature on national and international security agendas in the years to come. The US President's policy response combined inducements and threats. For example, Clinton exhorted other states to bring their banking and financial systems into conformity with 'international anti-money laundering standards. We will help them to do so', he said. 'And if they refuse, we will consider appropriate sanctions.'[61] Whatever the merits and utility of this kind of approach for the rest of the international community, it is clear that the United States is taking very seriously the new security agenda, and is rethinking and refocusing its policies accordingly.

The effects of this rethink are likely to be far-ranging for all sectors of the US security establishment, in which I include those departments responsible for foreign affairs, trade, justice and defence, as well as the intelligence community. Let me quote from a recent press article, to illustrate the kinds of changes which are being contemplated:

> Partly in response to a growing body of conflict analysis asserting the pivotal role of non-military factors in provoking war, Vice President Al Gore has instructed U.S. intelligence agencies to evaluate the degree to which environmental, economic, and social factors influence national and global security .... The Gore initiative marks the first time these trends not ordinarily associated with strategic planning have been retrieved from the background and given serious thought in the councils of war.[62]

The US trends are likely to be replicated, in part at least, regionally and globally. Intelligence collection and assessment priorities will begin to reflect the demand, by governments, for a more integrated analysis of security trends, as well as for specific reporting on the security implications of issues like transnational crime, unregulated population movements and the environment. It may well be, as Simon Dalby has observed, 'that some ecological literacy will become an indispensable part of the intelligence community's tool kit'.[63]

The new security agenda will also, over time, significantly alter the way in which defence forces are structured and operate, in both developing and developed states. Developing Asian states tend to take a more comprehensive approach to security, domestically, because of their concerns with political stability and regime survival. However, they have generally placed less emphasis on the external dimension of security, and are not well equipped doctrinally, organisationally or in resource terms to deal with the new challenges which they face.

The defence forces of the region's developed states face fewer resource constraints but comparable problems of adjustment, doctrinally and organisationally. In countries like Australia, for instance, the defence forces are still principally configured for major conventional warfare against other states. But if the salience of non-military threats increases, then the role and function of the primary instruments of military force – the army, the navy and the air force – will undergo significant change. We may find, for example, the defence forces taking on responsibility for monitoring the health of the physical environment, or using their organisational and technological strengths to assist other agencies in repairing environmental damage as the US armed forces are doing in Europe and elsewhere. Or decisions may be taken to reconfigure equipment like radar, and other surveillance systems, so that they can more effectively monitor the small, extremely fast-moving boats used for transporting drugs and other illegal contraband across maritime borders. Even more fundamentally, as a number of analysts have already warned,[64] the actual nature of warfare and conflict itself may be radically transformed by some of the same political, social, economic and environmental factors which are compelling a reassessment of the meaning and scope of security as this millennium draws to a close. If Kaplan's somewhat apocalyptic vision of a premodern formlessness invading the battlefields of the underdeveloped world is only half right, then future conflict, as well as conflict prevention, will pose demands of a far different order on defence forces and policy-makers everywhere.[65]

NOTES

1. Michael Howard, 'Military Power and International Order', *International Affairs*, vol. 40, no. 3, 1964, p.407.
2. Arnold Wolfers, 'National Security as an Ambiguous Symbol', *Political Science Quarterly*, vol. LXVII, no. 4, December 1952, p.481.
3. Robert Osgood cited in E. Azar and Chung In Moon (eds), *National Security in the Third World: The Management of Internal and External Threats*, (University Press, Cambridge, 1988), p.279.
4. Hedley Bull, *The Anarchical Society: A Study of Order in World Politics*, (Macmillan Press, Melbourne, 1977), p.18.
5. Barry Buzan lists over a dozen definitions of security in his authoritative book on international security studies. See Barry Buzan, *People, States and Fear: The National Security Problem in International Relations*, (Wheatsheaf Books, Sussex, 1983), pp.16–17.
6. United Nations Development Programme, *Human Development Report 1994*, (Oxford University Press, Oxford, 1994), pp.22–3.
7. Joseph A. Camilleri, 'Security: Old Dilemmas and New Challenges in the Post-Cold War Environment', *Geojournal*, vol. 34, no. 2, October 1994, p.131.
8. See, for example, *The Human Development Report 1994*, p.22, and former Australian Minister for Foreign Affairs and Trade, Senator Gareth Evans in 'Cooperative Security and Intra State Conflict', *Foreign Policy*, no. 96, Fall 1994, pp.6–11. Mel Gurtov uses the term 'global humanism' as an alternative perspective of international relations which focuses on 'global human needs'. Mel Gurtov, *Global Politics In The Human Interest*, (Lynne Reinner Publishers, Boulder, Colorado, 1991), p.4.
9. *The Human Development Report 1994*, p.22.
10. Richard Ullman, 'Redefining Security', *International Security*, vol .8, no. 1, Summer 1983, p.133.
11 See Kal Holsti, *The Dividing Discipline: Hegemony and Diversity in International Theory*, (Allen and Unwin, Boston, 1985) chapter 2, for a succinct analysis of post-Westphalian paradigms of international relations.
12. Anarchy, in the sense that there is no supra-national body or organisation which can impose its will over the state. Sovereign, in the sense that national governments exercise exclusive jurisdiction 'over all matters, foreign and domestic, affecting the people within its boundaries.' See Kenneth Waltz, 'Realist Thought and Neorealist Theory', *Journal of International Affairs*, Summer 1990, p.29, and Robert Scalapino in Bunn Nagara and Balakrishnan (eds), *The Making of a Security Community in the Asia-Pacific*, Proceedings of the Seventh Asia-Pacific Roundtable, Kuala Lumpur, June 6–9, 1993, Institute of Strategic and International Studies, Malaysia, 1994, p.45.
13. Hans Morgenthau, *Politics Among Nations*, (Alfred Knopf, New York, 5th edition, 1973), p.5.
14. For example, in what is regarded as the classical exposition of realism, Morgenthau devotes only 11 out of 548 pages of his book to security *per se*, and these 11 pages are devoted exclusively to collective security. *Ibid.*
15. There is a considerable degree of ambiguity associated with the use of the term balance-of-power, but it normally connotes the distribution of power among states

in a zero-sum sense. That is, the accretion of power by one state, or group of states, brings about a proportional decrease in the power of others. See Richard Betts, 'Wealth, Power and Instability', *International Security*, vol. 18, no. 3, Winter 1993/94, p.35, and Hedley Bull, *The Anarchical Society*, p.24.

16. See William Wohlforth, 'Realism and the End of the Cold War', *International Security*, vol. 19, no. 3, Winter 1994/95.
17. Barry Buzan, *People, States and Fear*, p.8.
18. Liberalism is the second great tradition in international relations and differs from realism in believing that security can best be achieved through cooperation, rather than conflict and war.
19. Robert Keohane and Joseph Nye, *Power and Interdependence*, (Scott, Foresman and Company, Glenview, Illinois, 1989), pp.24–5.
20. *North–South: A programme for survival*, Report of the Brandt Commission, (Pan, London, 1980).
21. There is no agreed definition of Common Security, but a comprehensive summation of its features can be found in Geoffrey Wiseman, 'Common Security in the Asia-Pacific Region', *The Pacific Review*, vol. 5, no. 1, 1989, pp.42–3, which remains the best analysis of the concept.
22. Gareth Evans, *Cooperating for Peace: The Global Agenda for the 1990s and Beyond*, (Allen & Unwin, St. Leonards, NSW, 1993), p.15.
23. *Report on Comprehensive National Security*, Comprehensive National Security Study Group, 2 July 1980, pp.19–24.
24. Muthiah Alagappa, 'Comprehensive Security: Interpretations in ASEAN Countries' in Robert Scalapino, et al. (eds), *Asian Security Issues: Regional and Global*, (Institute of East Asian Studies, University of California, Berkeley, 1988), p.55.
25. The case for including such issues under the rubric of security is not without its detractors. See for example Daniel Deudney, 'The Case Against Linking Environmental Degradation and National Security,' *Millennium*, vol. 19, no. 3, Winter 1990; Marc A. Levy, 'Is the Environment a National Security Issue?, *International Security*, vol. 20, no. 2, Fall 1995; and Robert Jervis, 'The Future of World Politics: Will It Resemble The Past?, *International Security*, vol. 16, no. 3, p.64.
26. One of the first to coin the term 'new security agenda' was Fred Halliday, in 'International Relations: Is There a New Agenda'?, *Millennium: Journal of International Studies,* vol. 20, no. 1, Spring 1991.
27. See Charles A. Beard, *The Idea of National Interest: An Analytical Study in American Foreign Policy*, (Macmillan, New York, 1934).
28. Kennedy focuses on the correlation between the productive and revenue-raising capacity of states and their military power. Paul Kennedy, *The Rise and Fall Of The Great Powers*, (Fontana Press, London, 1989), p.xvi. Tai Ming Cheung's otherwise excellent analysis of the relationship between economics and security in China is another case in point. Tai Ming Cheung, 'The Interaction Between Economics and Security for China's External Relations', in Christopher Twomey and Susan Shirk (eds), *Power and Prosperity: Economic and Security Linkages in Asia-Pacific,* (Transaction Publishers, New Brunswick, 1996), particularly p.119.
29. On this point see Alagappa in Nagara and Bala Krishnan, *The Making of a Security Community,* pp.51–2.

30. Richard Rosencrance, *The Rise of the Trading State: Commerce and Conquest in the Modern World*, (Basic Books, New York, 1986), pp.24–5. There is an opposing view, in which 'protectionism and other beggar-thy-neighbour policies are seen as actually contributing to war and conflict'. The critical question is whether the web of expanding economic ties and dynamic economic growth will create a more stable security environment, or will new lines of fracture and cleavage develop which will exacerbate existing tensions and 'define new lines of conflict?'. Zysman and Borrus, in Twomey and Shirk, *Power and Prosperity Economics and Security Linkages in Asia-Pacific*, p.77. See also Paul Dibb, 'Towards a New Balance of Power in Asia', *Adelphi Paper 295*, International Institute for Strategic Studies, Oxford University Press, 1995, p.20. There is a third view – that there is no direct relationship between war and trade at all. Edward Mansfield, *Power, Trade and War*, (Princeton University Press, Princeton, New Jersey, 1994), pp.124 and 121.
31. See Richard Higgott, *The Evolving World Economy: Some Alternative Security Questions for Australia*, (Canberra Papers on Strategy and Defence No. 51, Strategic and Defence Studies Centre, Australian National University, Canberra, 1989).
32. One of the earliest to consider the security aspects of environmental degradation was Richard Ullman. Other significant treatments of the subject include Jessica Tuchman Matthews, 'Redefining Security', *Foreign Affairs*, vol. 68, no. 2, Spring 1989; Michael Renner, *National Security: The Economic and Environmental Dimensions*, Worldwatch Paper No. 89, (Washington, D.C., Worldwatch Institute, 1989); and Norman Meyers, 'Environmental Security', *Foreign Policy*, no. 74, Spring 1989.
33. Robert Kaplan, 'The Coming Anarchy', *The Atlantic Monthly*, February 1994. This article has become mandatory reading for national security staff in the Clinton Administration.
34. *Ibid.*, p.58.
35. *Ibid.*, p. 60. For a thought-provoking analysis on the probability of food scarcity in China, see Lester Brown, *Who Will Feed China*, (Worldwatch Environmental Alert Series, Earthscan Publications, London, 1995). See also Vaclav Smil, *China's Environmental Crisis: An Inquiry into the Limits of National Development*, (M.E. Sharp, Armonk, New York, 1993).
36. Noting that environmentally induced conflicts are likely to be more pervasive and acute in developing countries because of their greater political, social and economic vulnerabilities, Homer-Dixon predicts that environmental pressures, either singly or in concert, will have four 'causally interrelated social effects', which will lead to 'scarcity disputes between countries, clashes between ethnic groups, and civil strife and insurgency'. The four main social effects nominated by Homer-Dixon are 'reduced agricultural production, economic decline, population displacement, and disruption of regular and legitimized social relations'. See Thomas Homer-Dixon, 'On the Threshold: Environmental Changes as Causes of Acute Conflict', *International Security*, vol. 16, no. 2, Fall 1991, p.78.
37. Myron Weiner, 'Security, Stability and International Migration', *International Security*, vol. 17, no. 3, Winter 1992/93, p.91.
38. UNHCR, *The State of the World's Refugees 1993*, and UNHCR, *The State of the World's Refugees 1995*.

39. *The State of the World's Refugees 1993*, pp.1 and 25.
40. *Ibid.*, p.24.
41. Australian Minister for Foreign Affairs and Trade, Senator Gareth Evans, *Australia's Regional Security*, Ministerial statement, December 1989, p.35.
42. See, for example, Louise I. Shelley, 'Transnational Organised Crime: An Imminent Threat to the Nation State?', *Journal of International Affairs*, vol. 48, no. 2, Winter 1995.
43. James Woolsey, 'Global Organized Crime: Threats to U.S. and International Security', in Linnea P. Raine and Frank J. Ciluffo (eds), *Global Organized Crime: The New Empire of Evil*, (The Center for Strategic and International Studies, Washington D.C., 1994), p.137.
44. Claire Sterling, 'Containing the New Criminal Nomenklatura', *ibid.*, p.106.
45. Stanley E. Morris, 'Maintaining the Security, Integrity, and Efficiency of our Financial System in a Global Criminal Market', *ibid.*, p.64.
46. See Garry Dain, '"Hacking" through the Cyberspace Jungle', *ibid*, pp.37–59, especially p.56.
47. Cited in D. Parker, 'The Wild West of NETSEC – Between Warning and Disaster', *ibid.*, p.155.
48. Kaplan, 'The Coming Anarchy', p.49.
49. 'Pulp Future', in *The Cutting Edge*, Australian Special Broadcasting Service Documentary, 26 December 1995.
50. See John McFarlane, 'Transnational Crime and Australian National Security', paper presented to the conference on *Crime and Australian National Security*, Australian Defence Force Academy, 1 December 1995, pp.5–6.
51. Access to international television programmes has sensitised Chinese to the outside world, and also conjured up an idealised image of life in the West.
52. 'Dragons of Crime: Climbing the Golden Mountain', Australian Special Broadcasting Service Documentary, 19 April, 1996.
53. The above analysis draws substantially on Paul Smith's excellent article on 'The Strategic Implications of Chinese Emigration', in *Survival*, vol. 36, no. 2, Summer 1994.
54. *Ibid.*, p.66.
55. In 1992, 29 out of 30 major armed conflicts were occurring within state borders. Gareth Evans, 'Cooperative Security And Intra State Conflict', p.3.
56. Camilleri, 'Security: Old Dilemmas and New Challenges ...', p.136.
57. Jim Richardson, 'Asia-Pacific Security: What Are the Real Dangers?', in Coral Bell (ed.), *Nation, Region And Context*, Canberra Papers on Strategy and Defence No. 112, (Strategic and Defence Study Centre, Australian National University, Canberra, Australia, 1995), p.101.
58. See, for example, Richard Betts, 'Wealth, Power and Stability, p.36.
59. Henry Kissinger, 'A New National Partnership', Speech by Secretary of State Henry A. Kissinger at Los Angeles, 24 January 1975, cited in Keohane and Nye, *Power and Interdependence*, p.3.
60. Gwyn Prins (ed.), *Threats Without Enemies: Facing Environmental Insecurity* (Earthscan, London, 1993).
61. Speech by President Clinton to the special 50th anniversary session of the United Nations General Assembly, 22 October 1995.
62. Mark Sommer, 'Non-military factors bring new meaning to art of spying', *The Jakarta Post*, 15 January 1996, p.5.

63. Simon Dalby, 'Security, Intelligence, the National Interest and the Global Environment', *Intelligence and National Security*, vol. 10, no. 4, October 1995, p.191.

64. Most notably, Martin van Creveld in his book *The Transformation of War,* (The Free Press, New York, 1991) and Alvin and Heidi Toffler, *War and Anti-War: Survival at the Dawn of the 21st Century,* (Little, Brown and Company, Boston, 1993).

65. Kaplan, 'The Coming Anarchy', p.46.

# 5 The Impact of Economics in the New Asia-Pacific Region
Stuart Harris

In 1845, the British government repealed the Corn Laws. The 150th anniversary of that event was celebrated last year by those who see the benefits of liberalised international trade to global welfare as having emerged very significantly from that event. It was also significant for Australia because it was the start of Britain's economic interdependence with Australia, among other producers of agricultural commodities.

It meant of course that Britain became potentially vulnerable to food supplies being interrupted by aggressive action from other countries. With the rise of Germany in the latter part of the nineteenth century, Britain felt the need to strengthen its naval power, eventually building up its fleet of Dreadnoughts. Yet what was, initially at least, a defensive action by Britain did not look defensive to Germany – which saw that those Dreadnoughts could also interdict its sea-lanes. So Germany built up its naval strength. Some scholars now see the outbreak of the First World War as importantly influenced by that classic security dilemma.[1] That episode offers important lessons. One is that vulnerability goes with interdependence; a second is the potential for conflict that mutual insecurities offer; a third is that the indirect consequences of an action may be critical but take a long time to manifest themselves, something that policy-makers ignore not just at their peril, but at ours as well.

Yet it is not easy to find those issues discussed in the numerous histories of the 1914–18 war. It is just as difficult to find economic issues discussed in standard references on the lead up to the Second World War.[2] And it took quite a time for it to be realised that the end of the Cold War came about as much because of the influence of economics as through political or strategic pressures, and that the other two fundamental changes in the region in the second half of the twentieth century (even if both have been exaggerated) have been in the relative economic strengths of the US and China.

Of course, commentators have now become more interested in economics. Geo-economics, globalisation and interdependence became the new buzzwords and the economic inefficiency of war, in the brave new 'Western lookalike' world, the basis for a new peaceful international era. Yet, as the Corn Laws example indicated, economic interactions with security are not new. In case I sound like an economic determinist, however, let me stress

51

that interactions between economic forces and political forces are always present and are what determine outcomes.

Economic exchange reflects the interactions of individual actors who want to trade and so make up a market. Market forces exist in most societies and have throughout much of history. They exist in various forms; queues and shortages in Moscow under the Soviets reflected that as much as do the high prices reported today. And if exchange is voluntary and unhindered, all participants gain.

Governments do not create market forces. But governments can and do influence them for good or ill. And creating the framework within which a market can operate effectively, which is a political and social construct, is normally a state matter. Nationally, that framework includes the security of the state, domestic law and order, the laws of contract, and often some social provisions. What economists look for in international cooperation is the creation of a market framework consisting similarly of rules for international economic exchanges. Hence the GATT, now the WTO, and regional economic cooperation processes such as APEC.

I have discussed elsewhere the interactions between economic and security issues.[3] Their range is very extensive and it grows more so with new items continually being added. Examples include population movements, traffic in military related technologies and drugs (with trade in drugs now larger than any other traded item, and well ahead of oil). In general, however, attention to economic impacts on security in the region has been mainly about economic growth and potential expansion of military capabilities, leading (as with British and German naval reequipment) to a traditional security dilemma – what is defensive to you looks offensive to me.

In the Asia-Pacific region, economic impacts have been wider, and stronger than elsewhere. Economic development, for example, has been pursued by many regional states to reduce threats to regime stability, and links between the military and civil and political society are often close. In the early postwar decades internal discontent which could be used by external powers to undermine the governments in the region – China's aid to communist-led insurgencies – was the major security issue confronting Malaysia, Thailand, Indonesia and the Philippines among others. Economic development overcame those largely poverty-related internal problems, but for those countries, such security concerns remain important motivating factors.

I shall not catalogue here what is in practice a great variety of economic impacts on the security of individual countries, their international relations or domestic politics. Rather, I want to look at the security implications of what is frequently termed the East Asian economic miracle,[4] since basic assumptions about its impact seem to be central to the new security agenda in the Asia-Pacific region.

When we look at the region's security environment, the potential trouble spots are few and economic questions are central to most. On the Korean peninsula, a basic question is whether North Korea's economy might implode, with major sub-regional impacts, including massive refugee flows and economic burdens on South Korea's economy. The China–Taiwan issue primarily concerns sovereignty, but Taiwan's inevitably increasing economic dependence on China makes one wonder about the reality of recent events.

Elsewhere in the region, the security issues mostly involve China – from Burma, with China's sales of military equipment, to its growing economic and other influence in Cambodia and Vietnam. Both the latter we expect to participate in ASEAN, the ostensibly economic grouping of Southeast Asia, and which Australia sees as a counter-influence to China. China is also involved in the South China Sea, and with the Spratly Islands where sovereignty is mixed with resource interests.

Clearly the issues that are high on the new security agenda largely involve China, and now that ideological issues have virtually vanished in Asia, largely emerge as a result of China's growing economic power. This is not to underestimate economic impacts of, or on, Japan or relating to the US regional presence, but these are not new security agenda items.

Public discussion of the East Asian miracle, the high rates of economic growth and the expanding global and regional economic interdependence, on regional security relationships and where China fits, in particular, is often overly simplistic. That is perhaps understandable since the issues are complex and not easily reduced to simple propositions. Nor, for that matter, are there simple conclusions.

The tremendous growth in economic strength has changed the material wealth and industrial capacity of the countries in the region. Expected future growth will lead to further change in the levels and distribution of political and strategic power and the potential for military power and political influence. Theorists argue still about whether it is small or large inequalities of power and capabilities that are more likely to induce or deter conflict. And like many theoretical arguments the answer is yes – or, if you prefer, no – depending on the circumstances. In other words, these issues remain highly contested.

There are many different ways to consider relationships between economic interactions and conflict. I shall discuss four. The first is that states are inevitably conflictual and that power and its distribution is the important question. Balances of power are important for maintaining peace, while significant imbalances cause conflict. Those who argue this way believe such imbalances cause neighbours to see countries such as Japan, China and eventually India and Indonesia as threats. These realists, the Kissingers of this world, give less attention to how this power is achieved than how this power is distributed. Economic growth, of the kind the region has experienced, is likely to be seen as unhelpful and destabilising. Such theorists tend to see the need for power to be balanced and, in the post-Cold War era, for a balance of power – among the US, China, Japan, the EU, perhaps India (and presumably Russia).

A second view argues that a high intensity of trade across nations reduces political tensions, and the likelihood of war. For such liberal thinkers, with a long historical tradition, economic exchange provides a more efficient and less costly means than war for states to gain resources and markets; resources are becoming less important, markets are opening in a multilateral rules-based system and the costs of war are rising exponentially.[5] The opportunity costs that conflict implies in an interdependent world, the severing of ties between trade partners, the forgoing of the gains from trade, will deter states from engaging in hostilities.

A third, contrary, view agrees that the distribution of power is important, but sees countries consciously enhancing their relative power through economic means. While acknowledging the gains from trade, they believe these will be uneven and give disproportionate gains to potential adversaries. These revisionists or economic nationalists, important in US policy thinking today, see countries in the region such as Japan and now China gaining increased power relative to the US by pursuing neo-mercantilist policies. Therefore in the US (or other countries) there should be greater state involvement in determining economic gains internationally.

A fourth view comes from those who argue that yes, higher levels of economic activity and interdependence among states do increase the expected costs associated with using armed force, but power is still important. Economic interdependence, they argue, produces incentives to cooperate but interdependency also creates possibilities of vulnerability. Some go further and argue that while independence brings peoples close together this could equally lead to conflict – what has been called 'the myth of interdependence'.

For some analysts, a potential source of dispute is that although both countries in an interdependent relationship can gain from economic cooperation, countries are more concerned with relative gains than absolute gains; cooperation, in this view, requires one country to gain relative to the other.[6] Since this cannot hold for both countries, it leads to disputes as threats to sever the relationship are used to try to improve a relative position. Overall, conclusions on this fourth view seem to depend upon circumstances.

All told then, answers to whether economic growth and greater economic interaction among countries is conducive to peaceful interaction and cooperation is, at best, two noes, one yes and one don't know.

Why then are we all pursuing policies that encourage countries in the region, particularly China, Vietnam and North Korea, to engage more fully in the international economy and to undertake the economic reforms that will make them so much stronger?

One answer could be: what else can we do? The conditions do not exist to make containment feasible and attempts to do so are likely to be counter-productive. A balance of power that does not include China seems too much like a return to Cold War conditions and, in any case, is unlikely to work in the long run. The region faces what I have called an economic security dilemma, and this is particularly relevant to China. We welcome economic development in China in part because it directs China's attention to domestic matters and to cooperative relations with neighbours. In part, also, China's growth is seen as supporting a process of peaceful evolution in social and political structures that is judged to be conducive to international peace.

The dilemma is that at the same time it makes China increasingly powerful relative to its neighbours. In the short run, the region (and others) gain from China's economic growth; without that growth, political instability in China is likely; and the belief underlying the policy is that by engaging in commercial activities with China (and Vietnam and perhaps in due course with North Korea), the benefits of participating in the international community on a peaceful cooperative basis will become embodied in their thinking to the point that it or they will not want to be aggressive.

Abstract theoretical discussions on these questions either lack an adequate empirical base or draw lessons from past Northern hemisphere experience questionably relevant to Asia. Provided certain conditions are met, I believe the broad assumptions of the engagement policy enable us to be reasonably sanguine in conditionally accepting more of the yes conclusion than that of the two noes and one don't know. I shall look therefore at some of the arguments, for and against, in the light of the specific circumstances of the region.

First, however, we need to have some sense of the magnitudes involved. The economic growth in the region has meant that the Asian countries in APEC now account for a little over 25 per cent of global GNP. That figure will probably grow to over a third of world GNP by the year 2010. The East Asian countries are then expected to account for some 40 per cent of world trade. Outside the US, Japan is now central to the regional economy, but central to future growth is expected to be China. That China could be the world's largest economy by the second decade of the twenty-first century is, of course, why China is at the centre of the new security issues agenda.[7]

Paul Krugman has recently questioned whether the economic growth in the region in practice has staying power, or will we, as he has suggested, look back on current projections for Asia's economic growth as silly.[8] Krugman's arguments are largely that Asian growth has been input-driven – everyone is working harder – rather than productivity driven – everyone is working smarter. His arguments have found few supporters. Most economists argue that he has greatly underestimated the contribution of productivity growth.[9]

It is always possible that downturns in the business cycle or something else will slow the region's growth. The region avoided much impact from the US–European downturn in economic activity of the early 1990s. That may not happen in the future, and other events may slow growth, as the current Japanese situation reminds us, although that too seems to have had little effect on the region's dynamism. Generally, however, the experts see regional growth continuing, and since most Asian governments depend upon their economic performance for their continued legitimacy, in its absence, risks to regional political stability, and hence security, could result.

Let me return then to look at what are normally regarded as liberal arguments under four headings: resource conflicts, interdependence, socialisation and democratisation. Again I shall concentrate on China, although the points have broader generality.

RESOURCE CONFLICTS

Countries go to war for a variety of reasons. In the past, wars were often resource wars – for land, to expand human settlement (*lebensraum*) or for food or other resources.

Sovereignty issues also cause armed conflict – perhaps as important as any – although perhaps less now for outright war. Motives for such conflicts in the region do not for the most part concern economic issues other than the resources – oil, gas, fish – that island territorial disputes involve. The major regional sovereignty issue is Taiwan but the motivation certainly has little directly to do with economics, even if the interdependence of the two economies is a major factor in the relationship. This does not mean that there will not be resource conflicts. They still happen, if we accept that the Gulf War was oil related. Nevertheless, the resource motivations for conquest of the past are less significant now that education, technology and managerial skills are much more substantial sources of wealth. Some in the Chinese military have talked of the Spratlys in resource terms and access to fishing and potential oil areas may continue to spawn armed conflicts even if not wars, although the probability is that, despite China's growing energy import needs, these conflicts will be settled by negotiation.

Japan is more secure now with oil freely available on open markets; to that extent the liberal view is correct that it is less costly and more efficient to gain resources through the market than through conquest. The question of sea-lane security, however, may become more important. Japan now values the defence treaty with the US more, following the Gulf War and the emergence of China, because, among other things, of the reminder to Japan that its economic security remains global, and dependent on global sea-lanes. China will also be increasingly concerned about sea-lane security, as its imports of energy and food supplies grow. While Japan is comfortable with the US as a defender of its sea-lanes, China's view of the US is ambivalent, and potentially a security threat.

Nevertheless, on balance, specific resource-related conflicts are likely to be less.

INTERDEPENDENCE

Associated with the Asian economic miracle has been a growth in economic interdependence. Interdependence encompasses two broad concepts. The first is openness to the international economy as a whole. Thus the countries in the region have almost uniformly become more involved in the global economy (North Korea being a notable exception). Chinese exports as a share of its GDP – now, on traditional measures, 24 per cent – were only 3 per cent of GDP in 1970; Indonesia's exports have gone from 13 per cent in 1970 to 28 per cent today.[10] Apart from North Korea, only in Japan has the export share of GDP not changed in recent years but Japan's overseas investment has grown significantly.

The second aspect of interdependence relates to the dependence for market outlets, imports, investment or technology of one country on another. Thus, North America, mainly the US, takes almost 20 per cent of China's exports, compared with some 6 per cent in 1980.[11] Interdependence enables countries to benefit from the gains from trade; it also makes countries vulnerable to outside pressures. What is important here is not the absolute percentages, but the sensitivity of the dependence. Japan would only be vulnerable to its high reliance on Australia's coal if there were no alternative sources should that supply fail – and of course there are. Nevertheless, countries do lose some of their policy control and autonomy. The liberal argument is that countries in such interdependent relationships have strong incentives to adopt trading and investment strategies for the development and maintenance of cooperative practices in international society. Few ever give up the benefits of interdependence once they have experienced them – but they may try to defend themselves against the vulnerability it implies. Moreover, although interdependence implies a two-way dependency, this is seldom experienced completely in practice. Thus the US is less dependent upon China than China is upon the US, and this gives the US bargaining leverage. Yet, in pluralist societies, leaders who put economic interests at risk face internal opposition from those interests, as the business opposition to the US threat to stop MFN admission of Chinese goods illustrates. So too did the Taiwanese business opposition to some potentially damaging arguments being used in the recent presidential election, and such constraints are not absent in authoritarian societies, as witnessed by the concern expressed by Chinese business interests over the souring of the US relationship.

Growth of interdependence will not prevent conflict. Sovereignty claims, as over Taiwan (as over the Falklands), illustrate that costs are at times considered almost irrelevant. Moreover, in its simplest form, this liberal argument was dented by the events of 1914, and more recently by the wars among the states of the former Yugoslavia.

Nevertheless, while perceptions of threat can lead to conflict through arms expenditure spirals, the greater one country's dependence on another, the greater the costs of conflict and then, other things being equal, the less the likelihood of conflict. Other things are not equal, of course, but if two countries are significantly interdependent then it is less likely that there will be conflict.

The vulnerability of interdependence, however, tempts the exercise of pressure and, there, problems could occur in the economic field not only in the immediate but in the long-term efforts by the country under pressure to reduce its vulnerability, including building up its military. There must be concern, therefore, at unilateral threats of, or imposition of, economic sanctions, now seemingly a standard tool of US policy towards the region. Apart from putting at risk the security gains from interdependence, it is inconsistent to have a long-term policy to encourage North Korea, for example, to open its economy to the world and then to threaten economic sanctions when a problem emerges.

We forget at some cost that the Atlantic Charter and the Bretton Woods institutions reflected beliefs that economic sanctions and embargoes were important causes of tensions and ultimately conflict in the 1920s and 1930s, with long-lasting implications. Hence the importance not just of multilateral rules for international economic exchanges, global or regional, but also multilateral mechanisms for dispute settlement. Hence also the importance of seeing China, with Taiwan, as WTO members.

## SOCIALISATION

A basic assumption of the policies of engagement that we now address towards China (and Vietnam and North Korea) is that a degree of socialisation of those countries is achievable – that there is a learning process possible or underway.

The validity of such an assumption has been illustrated by the success of ASEAN, ostensibly a regional economic body, but which has acted as an effective confidence-building process to reduce security risks among the member countries. Vietnam has now been brought into that socialisation process. China has been participating in the Pacific Economic Cooperation Council (PECC) and the Asia Pacific Economic Cooperation forum (APEC) processes positively and constructively, as it has in other global or regional economic institutions such as the IMF, World Bank or the Asian Development Bank (ADB) where it has at times been a defender of the status quo.

China's participation in the various economic organisations, including the regional organisations, has led it to change fundamentally its view of the international economic environment. An interesting feature concerns the English economist, Ricardo, who was both a major influence on Marx's economics but also developed the concept of comparative advantage – the basis of the liberal trade argument. Intensive study and debate around Ricardo's ideas took place in China in the mid-1980s over the pure theory of international trade, as China changed from a Marxist (or self-sufficiency) to a Ricardian (or trading interdependence) view of the global economic system. Certainly in the economic field, cognitive learning, a fundamental change in basic assumptions about how the world works, has occurred.[12]

## DEMOCRATISATION

That learning of the benefits of cooperative behaviour has occurred in the economics field gives support to the liberal argument. China has generally played a constructive role, consistent (like other countries) with its national interest, in other international organisations.[13] Precisely how far that process of socialisation applies generally to the social and political arenas in the Asia-Pacific region is still not totally clear. The assumption of the liberal approach, however, often implied if not stated, is that continuing economic growth will in a variety of ways, such as through the growth of civil society, lead to greater demands for political liberalisations that will lead authoritarian states down the path to democracy.

Democratisation has commonly followed economic development because of the spread of democratic ideas that comes from increasing economic, and then social and political, interactions. The view that because democracies share common values and understandings of appropriate international behaviour, and given the domestic constraint of public opinion, the probability of war between them is small, is supported by a great body of statistical evidence. Democracies tend to be pretty aggressive but not towards one another. The assumption is that authoritarian states are more prone to conflictual behaviour.

The democratic peace argument is still contested for a variety of reasons.[14] Moreover, authoritarian countries have public opinions that provide constraint, as the Soviets found over the war in Afghanistan. Again, not all countries in the Asia-Pacific region that have pursued economic interdependence have been involved in significant democratic change. Western-type institution-alised democracy is less likely to follow quickly in the footsteps of economic reform in the region for various reasons. Moreover, in contrast to social pluralism, Asian societies value group conformity, collective welfare and deference to authority.[15] Again, in pursuing their objective of nation building, to take their proper place in an international community of states, rather than to pursue the possessive individualism of Western liberalism, individuals in these societies are assessed in terms of 'their compatibility with the task of achieving freedom for the state as an actor in international society'.[16]

This might be seen as a fatal flaw to those relying on the liberal idea of 'peaceful evolution' to a democratic system. Apart from the excessively simple conception of democracy that is commonly involved, the evolution of an international system with cooperative international behaviour is seen by some, such as Francis Fukuyama, as requiring homogenous political forms (that is, democracy).[17] Yet the early protagonists of the idea of international society, such as Immanuel Kant, did not believe that was necessary.[18] Democracy was preferred, but cooperative discourse between democratic and non-democratic forms of government was quite feasible, and so was a peaceful international community. As we have argued, China has followed the norms and rules of the large number of international organisations to which it belongs. Given a learning period, there is no reason why this should not apply to Vietnam as well, in principle at least, even eventually to North Korea.

Therefore, the flaw may be less of a problem than critics of liberalism believe. The case is not necessarily as strong as that for the argument that democracies do not fight democracies, although the evidence is stronger when a market economy variable is included in the statistical analysis.[19] It is symptomatic, however, that compared with the numerous empirical studies of democracy and peace, studies of liberal markets and peace have been relatively few.

## CONCLUSIONS

The logic of all these arguments depends upon the application of rational minds. Not all the international actors are rational and the normally rational are not always so. History has many examples of people losing wars they thought they could win, and events often emerge from happenstance and misperceptions. Yet, to paraphrase Allan Taylor, the Western world, and presumably the Eastern world, is committed to the proposition that rational human beings will in the end prove stronger and more successful than irrational beings.[20]

What then does it all add up to? Let me stay with China although much will also apply to Vietnam, Indonesia and others in the region. China's domestic motives for maintaining economic reforms, and the associated opening up of the economy, remain strong for various reasons including the government's legitimacy, its domestic needs and the objective of nation building as a basis for gaining or developing equality and respect internationally. Our hopes for the future come substantially from a view that China (and others) have shown themselves capable of learning and of cooperating constructively in economic institutions and, for the most part, in other organisations as well. They also come from the absence of any signs that the learning of the benefits of international cooperation has diminished significantly.

Nevertheless, if learning is possible in one direction, as I have argued, then it can also be experienced in another. It is from this point that one can be worried. Realists maintain conflict comes from insecurity and countries believe other countries to be aggressive and ready to attack them unless they are themselves strong. Our example of the First World War reflected the fact that both Britain and Germany felt threatened by the other. Hence the need argued for confidence-building measures in the military security field. But China now sees its security based on its economic and technological capabilities. Its major security concerns are what it fears are attempts by the outside world to undermine its economic development.[21] The possibility does exist that US attempts to press for commercial advantage or to threaten economic sanctions under a variety of unilaterally determined conditions will be seen as a threat to China's security and could encourage conflict, or at least support the views within China of the Pat Buchanan sound-alikes that international cooperation weakens rather than strengthens the country.

It is customary to look at how China should respond to the international community in respect of its economic activities. Gary Klintworth and I have argued elsewhere that how the rest of the world responds to China, including avoiding the double standards that are currently widely present, may be just as important an influence on how it develops in the long-term future.[22] This applies no less to economic issues than to other security issues.

## NOTES

1. Avner Offer, *The First World War: An Agrarian Interpretation,* Oxford: Clarendon Press, 1991.
2. An example of how little attention is given to economics can be seen in Peter Calvocoressi and Ben Wint, *Total War: Causes and Courses of the Second World War,* London: Penguin, 1974.
3. Stuart Harris, 'The Economic Aspects of Security in the Asia/Pacific Region', *Journal of Strategic Studies,* 18(3), 1995, 32–51. For a more theoretical viewpoint, see Stuart Harris, 'Conclusion: the Theory and Practice of International Cooperation', in Andrew Mack and John Ravenhill (eds), *Pacific Cooperation: Building Economic and Security Regimes in the Asia-Pacific,* Sydney: Allen and Unwin, 1994, 256–69.
4. Including by the World Bank in its *The East Asian Economic Miracle: Economic Growth and Public Policy,* New York: Oxford University Press, 1993.
5. For a careful discussion of the costs of war and related questions see James Richardson, 'The declining probability of war thesis: how relevant for the Asia Pacific?', paper to Northeast Asia Program workshop on Economic-Security Interactions in the Asia Pacific, Australian National University, December, 1995.
6. Joseph Grieco, 'Anarchy and the Limits of Cooperation: A Realist Critique of the Newest Liberal Institutionalism', *International Organisation,* 42, 1988, 485–507.
7. Charles Wolf et al., *Long Term Economic and Military Trends 1994–2015: The United States and Asia,* National Defense Research Institute, Rand, Santa Monica, 1995.
8. Paul Krugman, 'The Myth of Asia's Miracle', *Foreign Affairs,* 73(6), 62–78.
9. Peter Drysdale and Yiping Huang, 'Technological catch-up and productivity growth in East Asia', paper to the 24th Conference of Economists, September, 1995.

10. World Bank, *World Development Report 1995*, New York: Oxford University Press, 1995, Table 9.
11. Asia-Pacific Economics Group, *Asia Pacific Profiles 1995*, Australian National University.
12. Stuart Harris, 'The WTO and APEC: What Role for China', paper to an IISS Conference on China Rising: Interdependence and Nationalism, San Diego, June 1996; Harold Jacobsen and Michel Oksenberg, *China's Participation in the IMF, the World Bank and the GATT: Toward a Global Economic Order*, Ann Arbor: University of Michigan Press, 1990.
13. Ann Kent, 'China, International Organisations and Interdependence: the ILO as a Case Study' (unpublished paper), Department of International Relations, Australian National University, March 1996.
14. Christopher Lane, 'Kant or Cant: The Myth of the Democratic Peace', *International Security*, 19(2), 1994, 5–49.
15. Steve Chan, 'Regime Transition in the Asia/Pacific Region: Democratization as a Double Edged Sword', *Journal of Strategic Studies*, 18(3), 1995, 52–67.
16. Christopher Hughes, 'China and Liberalism Globalised', *Millennium*, 24(3), 425–45.
17. Francis Fukuyama, *The End Of History and the Last Man*, London: Penguin, 276–84.
18. John Macmillan, 'A Kantian Protest Against the Peculiar Discourse of Inter-Liberal State Peace', *Millennium*, 24(3), 1995.
19. Edward Mansfield, *Power, Trade and War*, Princeton: Princeton University Press, 1994.
20. A.J.P. Taylor, *Rumours of War*, London: Hamish Hamilton, 1952, 262.
21. You Ji, 'Interdependence and China's Economic Security', paper to Northeast Asia Program Workshop on Economic-Security Interactions in the Asia-Pacific, Australian National University, December, 1995.
22. Stuart Harris and Gary Klintworth, 'Conclusion: China and the Region after Deng', in Stuart Harris and Gary Klintworth (eds), *China as a Great Power: Myths, Realities and Challenges in the Asia-Pacific Region*, Melbourne and New York, Longman and St Martin's Press, 1995, 357–66.

# 6 Environmental Scarcities and Conflict: Assessing the Evidence in the Asia-Pacific Region

Philip Howard

A debate now rages over the importance of evidence collected by researchers in the field of 'ecological security', an area of enquiry which examines the role of ecological factors in a growing number of conflicts around the world. A significant body of literature, consisting mostly of case studies, has been produced by research projects around the world; each has in some way addressed the methodological problems of exploring a question of 'causation' in a situation involving both complex ecological and social systems. The best of these case studies are careful to explain that ecological factors in conjunction with other political and economic factors are responsible for creating situations of conflict. Still, the most common critique of the field of 'ecological security' is that too much emphasis is placed on the 'ecological'. Given the wide range of methodologies employed, it is also hard to gather together evidence for easy comparison. These uncertainties can be addressed with careful use of the recently developed 'environmental scarcities' rubric and a contextual weighing of ecological, economic and political elements causing conflict.

This chapter will review the origins of the field of ecological security, summarise the common critiques of the ecological security field, and introduce a helpful conceptual framework that can capture some of the complexity of socio-ecological systems. Then, a series of brief case studies of environmental scarcities in the Philippines, Indonesia and China will suggest the potential for this framework for testing out a hypothesis that ecological factors can cause conflict, suggesting the need for further research in the Asia-Pacific region.

## THE EVOLUTION OF THE SUBJECT

It has been over a decade since scholars began to explore the connection between environmental degradation and security. Most of this early exploration focused more on expanding the definition of 'security' for nation-states than studying the specific connections between environmental degradation and conflict between combatants.

The first step came in acknowledging the impact ecology has on economic productivity: when scholars began to examine global economic interdependence, one observation was that ecological catastrophe in one area could have economic consequences for the rest of the world. Furthermore, environmental degradation was shown to slow down economic development by presenting itself as general economic loss. For example, fuelwood shortages, dams ruined by silt collection, fouled drinking water or salinised irrigation systems have direct economic impacts. Human population growth then adds to the demand on a deteriorating resource base. These ideas informed foreign policy strategies designed to better plan overseas development assistance.[1] That conflict might spring from environmental degradation seemed self-evident because resource scarcity often caused economic hardship, which often caused conflict; since environmental degradation was likely to increase, so too were incidences of violence.

However, there is no clear and simple correlation between poverty and violence, and the second step came in acknowledging the complexity of socio-ecological systems. When researchers began looking at specific cases of conflict with a possible ecological component, the complexity of the connection between environmental degradation and conflict became increasingly evident. Socio-ecological systems are dynamic, robust, flexible, irreducible, spontaneously mobile, and largely self-regulating. Thus, successful policy-making must build on the synergy between the emergent properties of elements in the system when its self-regulating mechanisms break down; and more importantly in the long run, try to restore the self-regulating mechanisms. For example, most small agricultural producers know the techniques of sustainable agriculture most suitable for their habitats. Often they are forced to use slash and burn techniques because only intense swidden agriculture can meet the critical short-term needs of family on land resources they have no vested interest in maintaining.

First it was found that most relevant cases were instances of sub-national conflict, rather than conflict between nation-states. Second, since most of the strife in the world occurs over arable land, freshwater supplies and forest resources, the focus of research narrowed from resources in general to renewable resources; in this way the research was charting a new course away from the accepted connection between conflict and scarcities of resources such as oil and mineral wealth to a controversial connection between conflict and the decreasing quantity or quantity of renewable resources for human communities. This was easier to trace in many cases, though it quickly became apparent that social institutions could mitigate, exacerbate or even concentrate the harmful impact of environmental degradation within their communities. The complex interaction between social institutions and ecological systems requires a careful methodology to assess the importance of ecological factors without denying the role of other political and economic factors.

Our research found that under certain circumstances, scarcities of renewable resources, such as cropland, forests and water, produce civil conflict and instability, but that these scarcities act mainly by generating social effects, such as poverty and migrations, that analysts often interpret as conflict's immediate causes.[2] Environmental scarcity is caused by the degradation and depletion of renewable resources, the increased consumption of these resources, and/or their inequitable distribution. Evidence from several cases suggests that these three sources of scarcity often interact and reinforce one another. Environmental scarcity often encourages powerful groups to capture valuable environmental resources and encourages marginal groups to migrate to ecologically sensitive areas. These two processes in turn reinforce environmental scarcity and raise the potential for social instability.

Societies can adapt to renewable resource scarcity either by using their indigenous environmental resources more efficiently or by reducing their dependence on these resources. In either case, the capacity to adapt depends upon the level of social and technical ingenuity available in the society. If social and economic adaptation is unsuccessful, environmental scarcity contributes to impoverishment and migrations, weakens state capacity, sharpens distinctions among groups and enhances their opportunities to participate in violent collective action. Ethnic conflicts, insurgencies and *coups d'état* are often the result.[3]

COMMON CRITICISMS

There are several themes common to the literature which have emerged in opposition to the findings of the field of environmental security. Some critics argue that humankind has been fighting over land, water, and other resources for centuries and that there is nothing new about analysis that links resource scarcities to violence. Others dispute the independence of ecological factors as causes of conflict, arguing that they are usually only a byproduct of political or economic or social trends, and are at most a distant and indirect cause of conflict. Still others argue that where scarcities occur, they are almost always redressed by market responses which encourage conservation, substitution and technological innovation. Finally, there are those who argue that the countries in which conservation, substitution and innovation fail to redress scarcities are invariably among the poorest countries in the world, and are therefore unlikely to cause security threats to their neighbours. It is possible, however, to address these concerns with a careful methodology that respects both the direct ecological causes of conflict and those indirect ecological causes of conflict which are actually the result of socio-economic activity.

## DESIGNING A USEFUL COMPARATIVE FRAMEWORK

A useful methodology for studying the importance of environmental degradation in shaping the character of conflict should lay out the possible interactions between social systems and ecological systems while providing a framework for comparison with other cases. Such a framework was recently developed by the Project on Environment, Population and Security at the University of Toronto. The project studied conflict in places as diverse as Rwanda, South Africa, Pakistan, Gaza, and Chiapas, Mexico, by assessing 'environmental scarcities' – resources made scarce by a number of different social and ecological processes.[4] With the framework as a guide, not as an imperative, researchers found that comparisons between cases could be productive and that the causes of conflict in many specific cases could be set into sharp relief.

A demand-induced scarcity occurs when the number of people using a resource increases, or when consumption of the resource increases on a per capita basis. Rapid population growth due to high fertility rates in a community, or rapid, unplanned in-migration from neighbouring regions can raise the demand for local land, forest and water resources. Also, the consumption habits of developing societies often changes, raising demand for the specific ecological resources needed to produce goods. To satisfy a growing demand for beef products, for example, a society must devote vast areas to pasture land.

A supply-induced scarcity occurs when ecological conditions diminish or deplete the resource used by a population. This can be the result of either human abuse of the local ecology or natural disasters. Land degradation in the developing countries usually begins with the rapid removal of forests for commercial profit, continues with intense farming for little more than three or four years, then ends when overgrazing by cattle, sheep, and goats removes the last protective roots and grasses from the soil.

A structural scarcity occurs when the resource is not equitably distributed within a population. Good land can be quantitatively scarce because some families control large estates, while others have small land holdings or no legal titles at all. It can be qualitatively scarce because some families have secured large tracts of the most ecologically valuable lands, leaving for others land that is less productive agriculturally. Structural scarcities exist for resources whenever powerful groups control the use of land, forest and water resources and less powerful groups suffer with inadequate supplies.

These natural resource scarcities often occur together, and the compounded effects in a social system can be described as the processes of resource capture and ecological marginalisation. Resource capture occurs when powerful groups see that natural resources are becoming scarce, and manipulate the state's property laws and development plans to secure a supply of resources for themselves. This process results in large areas of forest, land and water resources being set aside for the use of powerful groups in society. Ecological marginalisation occurs when large numbers of people react to a severely inegalitarian resource regime, and migrate to more ecologically fragile areas in search of relief from scarcity. Living at the edge of forests or at the edge of great urban centres, migrant populations can grow quickly in density and damage local environmental resources, which effectively deepens their poverty.

Many methodological issues raised by critics can be addressed using this framework: sub-state conflict over renewable resources, not studied by a simple political economy perspectives, can be clearly identified; the causal independence of ecological factors from social factors can be better understood; the interaction of ecological factors with population growth, distributive problems, market malfunctions, government weakness and elite interests can be mapped out. In several cases, states dealing with internal environmental scarcities have violently suppressed civil unrest, become more authoritarian, and tried to deflect internal criticism by intimidating and threatening neighbouring countries. Even though sub-state conflict is the most frequent outcome of severe environmental scarcities, a hardening of the regime can have implications for international security.

## ENVIRONMENTAL DEGRADATION AND CONFLICT: THREE CASES IN THE PACIFIC

The Pacific Rim region has experienced rapid yet uneven economic growth among its states. Some nations have put the wealth towards raising the education, health and welfare standards of their people, and others have consolidated the wealth among elite groups. The example of the Philippines was chosen for its long history of conflict due to the scarcity of good quality land; the case of Indonesia was chosen for the recently violent conflict over the scarcity of forest resources; the case of China was chosen because experts now realise that the scarcity of water may lead to conflict in years to come. Each case provides brief illustrations of how environmental degradation, in conjunction with other political and economic factors, can lead to civil strife.

## Environmental Scarcity in the Philippines: Persistent Conflict

The project of development in the Philippines has largely been based around the export of its natural wealth. From fish stocks to timber, the state has unabashedly extracted resources, leaving many local inhabitants to struggle with subsistence agricultural production. But because the Philippine economy is primarily an agricultural economy, centuries of use and abuse have consumed much of the lowland soil nutrients, and the increased use of irrigation, fertilisers and pesticides has only brought temporary relief from decreasing overall soil productivity. Currently, 13 out of 72 provinces are considered 'severely eroded', due largely to improper farming practices.[5]

In a scenario repeated in many places, population growth in the resource-rich lowland areas has forced a migration to the uplands and into urban centres. In the uplands, migrants join with communities trying to farm on steep slopes, cleared of forest cover, that have soil erosion rates of 300 to 400 tons per hectare per year and a yearly indigenous population growth rate of 2 per cent.[6] This demand- and supply-induced scarcity of land couples to diminish agricultural productivity on a per capita basis. In the Philippines, large populations of migrants in urban centres still make demands of municipal infrastructure and unrest has been increasingly frequent; large populations of migrants in the uplands have further impoverished communities there, making them more receptive to insurgent ideologues.[7] The Philippines have had many peasant rebellions, liberation movements and violent protests in its history, some of which were related to the history of resource capture and ecological marginalisation in the islands.[8] However, the most recent examples of violent conflict over environmental scarcities in the Philippines include the death of more than 100 people in disputes over land loss to the Chico River Basin Project in Kalinga-Apayao, and the violent nation-wide protests over illegal logging activities on the island of Mindanao.

## Environmental Scarcity in Indonesia: Recent Outbreaks of Violence

Many parts of Indonesia currently suffer from a shortage of forest resources, and from the indirect effects of mismanaged forest resources. Because of high population densities and diminishing agricultural productivity, state 'transmigration programmes' move people from degraded areas to new sites carved out of other forests, which, in the end, provide only a few years of healthy cropland from the rich but thin tropical soils.

There are three broad types of forest in Indonesia: the tropical rainforests of Sumatra, Kalimantan and West Papua; the monsoon forests of Java and other Inner Islands; the dry forests of Nusa Tengara. These diverse forests contain a range of commercially valuable woods and biologically valuable species. Most estimates of the rate of forest conversion since 1950 are in the range of 1 million hectares of forest annually.[9] In other words, each year 1 million hectares of forest was lost to selective and clear-cut logging for commercial sale or burning to create cropland. The island of Sumatra, where many people from Java have been relocated, has the largest total area of what the government calls 'critical land': 2.3 million hectares of land that is so degraded that it cannot even sustain subsistence agriculture or serve its natural function of absorbing water. Supply-induced scarcities of forest resources make the extraction of commercial timber, rattan and medicinal plants fiercely competitive. At the same time, the demand for forest land by farming communities, cattle ranchers, logging concessions and the coal mining industry – which wants to get at the vast deposits of coal under the forests – is rising quickly and even the Chair of the National Development Planning Board realises that the forest production targets of the Sixth Five-Year Development Plan are beyond Indonesia's supply of forests.[10] Moreover, all of these interests are in conflict with those who promote the expansion of nature reserves. Serious structural scarcities also exist in many places because 30 years of granting timber concessions to a small selection of private and state enterprises and undermining community harvest rights has meant poverty for many. Communities living in and adjacent to the forest are often denied access to the forest, and rarely benefit from the profit generated by forest wealth since the resources have been captured by state elites. This ecological marginalisation and resource capture has spurred conflict between local communities and logging concessions in Lampung, Maluku, East Kalimantan and South Sumatra which has been particularly violent in recent years.

**Environmental Scarcity in China: A Potential Source of Conflict?**

China currently experiences a demand-induced scarcity of water, with 1.2 billion people drawing from the nation's freshwater supplies in 1994. In urban centres the legal and illegal use of the water supply is high because of the significant water consumption of modern appliances; illegal migrant communities also strain the water supply infrastructure, threaten local hygiene conditions, and make hydrological planning very difficult.[11] Thus, the per capita consumption of water is higher in urban centres than rural areas. Demand for water resources in China will grow significantly since its population, even if the one-child policy is maintained, will increase by at least 25 per cent or 300 million people in the next 20 years.[12] At the same time, supply-induced scarcities of water appear in regions with particularly high residential waste and industrial growth. In 1991, 80 per cent of China's 30 billion cubic metres of industrial waste water was expelled without treatment, 66 per cent of the rest was pre-treated, and only 27 per cent of this was pre-treated to government standards.[13] Because of drought and pollution, the catch of the Yangtze river's four major fish species dropped from 20 billion in the 1970s to 1 billion currently,[14] and half of China's towns are said to be without potable water.[15]

Table 6.1: *Economic and Environmental Contrast Between Rich Coastal and Poor Northwestern Provinces, 1988*

|  | Coastal Provinces | Northwestern Provinces | Regional Difference (%) |
|---|---|---|---|
| Grain Output (kg/capita) | 375 | 300 | +25 |
| Meat Output (kg/capita) | 21 | 11 | +90 |
| Gross Agricultural Output (Rmb/capita) | 740 | 380 | +95 |
| Gross Industrial Output (Rmb/capita) | 2600 | 1100 | +235 |
| Average Population Growth (%) | 1.23 | 1.49 | −20 |
| Average Precipitation (m³/capita) | 4000 | 2700 | +50 |
| Average Soil Erosion (t/ha) | 15 | 45 | +300 |

Source: Vaclav Smil, 'Environmental Change as a Source of Conflict and Economic Losses in China', Table 1, p. 17. Rmb stands for the Chinese Renminbi currency.

There is growing concern that water scarcity in China's burgeoning urban centres and dry northwestern provinces will touch off fierce competition for water resources because of the structural scarcity of water within the Chinese polity. It is estimated that at least 50 million people in the northern rural areas – Shandong, Hebei, Shanxi, and most of Shaanxi, Gansu, Ningxia, Nei Monggol, Qinghai and Xinjiang – live with a very limited supply of water for irrigation, drinking and industrial use, a supply which was severely depleted during the droughts of the 1980s.[16] With economic disparity between the coastal and Northwestern states on the rise, severe degradation of the already strained water supplies could make the relative disparity between regions a source of conflict (see Table 6.1), though it is more likely that conflict would occur between families and within local communities over the use of water wells.

## CONCLUSION: WHEN DO ENVIRONMENTAL SCARCITIES CAUSE SOCIAL CONFLICT?

The three cases studies cited here are not meant to offer an exhaustive assessment of ecological damage and must be understood within the political context of each regime. However, there is evidence that conflict over natural resources has been increasing around the world. Given the probable rise of environmental scarcities in Southeast Asia, it is likely that civil strife will also spread there. In the Philippines, years of soil erosion have made good land more precious, and this good land has been the focus of years of struggle. In Indonesia, the competition for forest resources between the logging concern and displaced, impoverished communities has grown increasingly fierce. In China, the scarcity of water and its attendant health and economic problems is expected to be the source of civil strife in years to come. What can be concluded about the circumstances under which environmental scarcities cause social conflict?

While each country has had environmental scarcities for some time, countries such as China have remained relatively stable. Conflict (as distinct from crime) only occurs when individuals form challenger groups in the hope that collectively expressing grievances will be successful. Such groups form along clear social cleavages such as ethnicity, religion or class, though violence is not necessarily the outcome of growing social cleavages. If the grievances can be addressed by democratic and legal means, then recourse to violence is not taken. Serious civil strife does not occur unless the political structures prevent challenger groups from expressing their grievances legitimately, making a peaceful resolution impossible. In such a situation, groups must assess their opportunities for violently expressing their grievances, by assessing the capacity of a state to respond repressively. The opportunity for violent conflict arises when, for example, the state is burdened by corruption, diminishing revenues or factionalised elites. A state trying to undertake liberal economic reform can also leave itself unable to manage violence as its ability to coopt or repress its constituents.

A necessary part of civil strife is the 'cognitive liberation' of group members. Effectively organised leaders can inform a group on how its strategic position is evolving, making members aware of any change in the opportunity structure for expressing grievances through legitimate or violent means.[17] The insurgent consciousness is made of an awareness of the economic, social and ecological forces that entrap the group. When the grievances become great, the social balance maintaining peace can be tipped (Figure 6.1). The political and economic conditions pertaining to each case remain crucial because they determine the way in which the state and other social groups respond to scarcities. In this sense, a state's capacity to respond to environmental scarcity can be the intervening variable that prevents social fragmentation developing into conflict. The Philippines has not had the state capacity to relieve the pressure of environmental scarcities on its people, resulting in protests, riots and insurgency. Indonesia's transmigrations have successfully relieved this pressure in some places and worsened conditions in others. In contrast, China has done well in managing its resource use internally, but it remains to be seen if China's state capacity can manage ever-increasing environmental scarcities in the future.

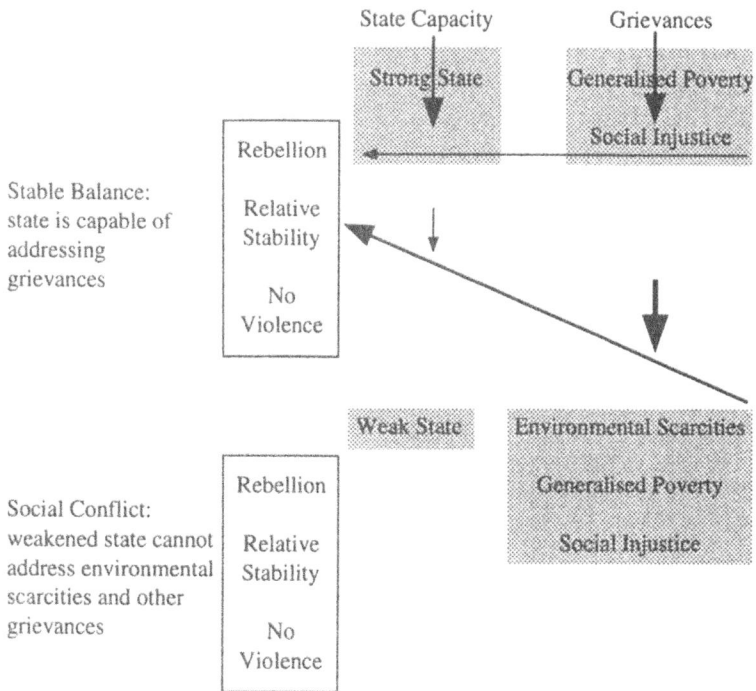

*Figure 6.1: Tipping the Balance: Environmental Scarcities in the Context of Diminishing State Capacity and Increasing Grievances*

Environmental scarcity significantly both adds to community grievances and diminishes the state's ability to meet social needs by damaging infrastructure such as dams, roads, irrigation and sewerage systems, and impoverishing those who live in ecologically marginal areas. Extending or even maintaining services to migrants at the edge of urban centres or in the countryside becomes an extra drain on state coffers. By interfering with wider economic productivity, environmental scarcities decrease the resources available to the state, and in many cases, can upset or strengthen power alliances between state elites while reducing the state's managerial, bargaining and coercive power to maintain stability. Deprivation also reduces the state's legitimacy, and violence such as insurgency, ethnic conflict, and riots remain one of the few tools for the impoverished to express their grievances against the state. Environmental scarcities result in conflict when they significantly add to the grievances of a population and, simultaneously, diminish the state's ability to address these grievances.

## NOTES

1. See Janet Welsh Brown, *In the US Interest*, (London: World Resources Institute, 1990).
2. See Philip Howard and Thomas Homer-Dixon, 'Environmental Scarcity and Violent Conflict: The Case of Chiapas, Mexico', Occasional Paper for the Project on Environment, Population and Security, University of Toronto, April, 1996.
3. See Thomas Homer-Dixon and Val Percival, 'Environmental Scarcity and Violent Conflict: Briefing Book', University of Toronto: Occasional Paper for the Project on Environment, Population and Security, May, 1996. This project gathered, evaluated and disseminated existing data among population growth, renewable resource scarcities, migration and violent conflict. It produced several thematic papers and case studies on Chiapas, Mexico, Gaza, Pakistan, Rwanda and South Africa and was supported by the Pew Global Stewardship Initiative of the Pew Charitable Trusts.
4. See Thomas Homer-Dixon, 'Environmental Scarcity and Violent Conflict: Evidence from Cases', *International Security* 19(1), Summer 1994.
5. Celso Roque, 'Economic Inequality, Environmental Degradation and Civil Strife in the Philippines', *Occasional Paper for the Environmental Change and Acute Conflict Project*, p.27.
6. A sustainable rate of erosion is considered to be between 3 and 4 tons per hectare per year.
7. Thomas Homer-Dixon, 'On the Threshold: Environmental Changes as Causes of Acute Conflict', *International Security* 16(2), p.32.
8. See Benedict Kerkvliet, *The Huk Rebellion: A Study of Peasant Revolt in the Philippines.* Quezon City, Philippines: New Day Publishers, 1979.

9. The range of estimates is from 600000 to 1.3 million hectares per year because there has been no accurate forest inventory or adequate reporting of harvest levels. Charles Secrett, 'The Environmental Impact of Transmigration', *The Ecologist*, Vol. 16, No. 2/3, 1986.

10. H. Suharyanto and G.N. Munthe, 'Tropical Forests: National Treasure Trove', *Indonesian Business Weekly*, 10 June 1994, p.4.

11. It has been estimated that between 10–33 per cent of the population in China's major cities do not have residential permits. Dorothy Solinger, 'China's Urban Transients in the Transition from Socialist and the Collapse of the Communist "Urban Public Goods Regime"', in *Comparative Politics* (January 1995), p.128.

12. Vaclav Smil, *China's Environment* (Armonk, NY: M.E. Sharpe, 1992).

13. *East Asian Executive Reports* (April 1994), p.14.

14. *World Resources 1994–95* (New York, NY: Oxford University Press, 1994), p.76.

15. Dr Tad Homer-Dixon interview with Nanjing Academy of Sciences official, Nanjing, PRC, 27 June 1995.

16. Vaclav Smil, 'Environmental Change as a Source of Conflict and Economic Losses in China', *Occasional Paper Series, Project on Environmental Change and Acute Conflict*, (Number 2, December 1992), p.14.

17. Doug McAdam, *Political Process and the Development of Black Insurgency 1930–1970* (Chicago: University of Chicago Press, 1982).

# 7 Beyond Armageddon? The Shape of Conflict in the Twenty-First Century

Stewart Woodman

If one was to look back at strategic planning in the 1990s perhaps 50 years hence, there would probably be two key elements in that caricature. The first would be the furrowed brows of senior strategists as they seek to come to terms with that frightening word 'uncertainty'. They cannot quite put their finger on what the problem is, nor can they find enough props to give them greater confidence. But, it is their responsibility, to use Sir Michael Quinlan's words, to guard against 'the possibility that matters do not go well'.[1] And in the world of the 1990s, there are many 'worst case' scenarios that cannot be completely set aside.

The second part of the caricature would almost certainly be a pile of glossy brochures and magazines jam-packed with advertisements for new high-tech weapons systems and designed to seduce the world's armed forces across the threshold in the new age of information warfare. Little space would be devoted to the van Crevelds and Tofflers in the debate – those who have actually taken the time to step back to try and assess just how fundamental the changes occurring in warfare really are.[2] It is not that their ideas aren't considered worthy of noting but that they keep getting pushed aside by 'real' security problems such as an emerging China, the dangers of anarchy on the borders of Europe, or demands for a 'peace dividend'. The immediate agenda for many is to halt the free-fall – not to let the known foundations of defence planning crumble.

## COPING WITH UNCERTAINTY

In many respects, this caution is quite understandable. Not only is the current strategic outlook extremely complex but the changes that are taking place are generally subtractions from the old strategic constructs of the Cold War. There are few clear leads as to the direction of, or time scales for, any future transformation of the security environment – and the leads that do exists are not ones that can provide a confident focus for national defence planning. The lessons of the Gulf War, for example, remain fraught with ambiguity. On the one hand, it can be dismissed as a quite unique clash of political, military and technological capabilities. On the other, it can be portrayed as revealing fundamental weaknesses in conducting conventional military operations unless one is able to master the new dimensions of warfare highlighted in what has become known as the 'revolution in military affairs'.[3]

What does need to be understood, however, in an environment characterised by complexity and fluidity is that how planners interpret developments is conditioned very much by the strategic lens through which they view them. In this respect there can be no doubt that the current approach of most developed nations is shaped by two key elements. The first is the well established practice of planning on the basis of what specific threats could emerge within particular time frames. Even those who have moved away from specific threat-based planning in the aftermath of the Cold War generally remain preoccupied with the components of threat – geography, capability, instability, and possible motives for the use of military force.[4] They tend to discount the other elements in the new security agenda.

The other element is a very traditional approach to what the use of military force is all about. Reduced to the bare minimum, it is the belief that, along the continuum of conflict, the ultimate justification for possessing a defence capability is to be able to prevail head-to-head in sustained, joint intensive operations.[5] In reality, a lack of resources means that many fall short of that goal but that does not generally negate it as an important principle in their defence planning construct. It will most often appear in the guise of 'the expansion base' or concepts of inter-operability and alliance.

The critical question is whether the problems planners are encountering in coming to terms with the current and prospective strategic environment can be put down simply to the absence of a threat or whether they reflect a much more fundamental strategic change which challenges the very analytical assumptions on which overall security planning is based. If it is the former, the current approach of 'steady-as-she-goes' – of seeking greater efficiency dividends, guarding against the advance of technology, while basically waiting for a new order to emerge – would appear prudent. But if that is not the case, and defence planners are confronting a major shift in their strategic paradigms, then there are significant costs and risks in continuing with a business-as-usual approach.

Most analysis to date has unfortunately done little to illuminate this issue. It has been content to speculate about alternative political futures, justifying either an optimistic or a pessimistic outlook on the relative weight given to economic linkages or military technologies.[6] Neither argument, however, is wholly convincing and, in the absence of authoritative guidance, defence planners are tending to fall back on the enduring features of conflict as it has evolved over the last few hundred years. Indeed, it can be argued that the competition for ascendancy between liberal and realist interpretations is diverting attention from more thorough and open-minded analysis of the strategic trends that are occurring.

How then can one meaningfully talk about the shape of future conflict? The crux of the problem is, I believe, to recognise the failure of the current debate to come to terms with just what is meant by 'uncertainty'. All too often it is equated, almost nostalgically, with little more than the absence of threat. But if one scratches beneath the surface, what is going on is in reality far more complex. The real strategic challenge is that fundamental shifts are occurring concurrently in both the envelope within which the use of military force will be considered appropriate in the future and in the means for pursuing conflict. It is the combination of these factors, far more than any speculation as to possible future scenarios, that will determine the role which military force is to play.

In attempting to sketch a portrait of what conflict will be like in the future, it is of course unrealistic to expect that it will fit every situation like a glove. There will always be some exceptions to the rule. The United States, due to its economic strength, the size of its military forces and technological leadership, will be able to absorb change and continue on its traditional path far more easily than others. The differences between regions in terms of economic development, technological development and existing strategic frictions mean that there will inevitably be variations as to the extent and timing of any changes.

The critical need in current circumstances is to be able to step back from the details of what is happening in individual countries or in particular weapons systems in order to identify the essence of the change that is occurring. This identification of the core elements is vital not only because of the danger in a fluid environment of starting at shadows, of imbuing small strategic shifts with major significance. It is also important because many security planners are currently craving some sort of certainty to grasp onto. In areas such as advanced technology and the role of the major powers, there are many false gods decorating the strategic horizon that are comfortable because they are familiar rather than because they are necessarily correct or thought through.

## REDEFINING THE CONFLICT ENVELOPE

What, then, are the factors that are shaping the envelope within which conflict might occur in the future? These encompass not just the factors that could be considered most likely to give rise to the use of military force. They also include the context within which those military dynamics operate – the changing nature of the relationship between states, the means available to regulate those relationships and the ways in which security and strategic importance are conceived. They may be divided into five main categories.

The first is that there is a definite shift in what might be termed the focus of conflict – that is, the range and type of issues to which military force might be realistically applied. Much of current strategy is shaped by the use of force to take and hold territory or at least to deny the effective use of an actual or potential battlespace to an adversary. That situation is now changing. With a few notable exceptions such as the Middle East and the Korean Peninsula, the new strategic space in which nations are competing is not amenable to occupation and control in the traditional way.

There are several elements to this new space. First, there is the recognition that maritime areas have a strategic value in their own right as distinct from being simply a linking medium between the territory of sovereign states. Control of maritime surrounds not only provides a strategic buffer zone but those areas are now recognised as a potential source of national wealth and, increasingly, as a measure of the strategic weight and influence of particular nations. The significant difference from a security planning perspective is that national interests in those areas remain a form of qualified sovereignty. This is due to:

- the absence of the normal instrument that a state is designed to protect (for example, people, land, industry);
- the widespread acceptance of certain common values, such as freedom of movement and navigation under the United Nations Convention on the Law of the Sea (UNCLOS); and
- the incapacity of most states, with the tools at hand, to exercise sovereignty or presence in a comprehensive way.

In these circumstances, the exclusion of others from some degree of activity is impracticable (except in a grand coalition) and, if exercised for more than a brief period, can be retaliated against in other distant locales and is likely to damage the interstate linkages that most states are themselves increasingly dependent upon. To the extent that sea-bed resources are at stake, the difficulties of extraction, reliance on international technologies and the vulnerability of associated infrastructure and support make denial strategies in many situations inappropriate and unsustainable.

The second new area of this conflict space is that of increasing internal competition for control of either the territory of a state or at least the means to exercise control within it. It is the type of conflict that flashes across television screens from Africa, the Balkans or other areas of a disintegrating

Soviet empire. Importantly, it is not of itself a direct challenge to the integrity of neighbours, although the violence may spill across borders, but competition for political domination and the capacity to protect and/or enforce certain social and cultural values. While the weapons of war being employed in such circumstances may become increasingly sophisticated, their use is oblivious to and generally destructive of the wealth and material welfare of the state itself, alienating political and economic support from outside.

It is also a space in which traditional warfare is by no means the only, and certainly not a complete, solution. Whether in terms of intervention from outside, or the efforts of the victorious to rebuild the apparatus of nationhood, it requires a full range of policy instruments among which the use of force should, as far as possible, be minimised. The merging of civilian and military life, the dual value of targets, and the generally indirect nature of conflict make such situations not amenable to traditional solutions which hinge on applying the maximum firepower at the point of decision. The constant danger is that the costs of success in war will deny a regime the means to win the peace.[7]

This new focus for conflict does not, of course, by itself rule out the prospect of more direct military clashes between nations. What it does suggest, however, is that for many nations their priorities are likely to shift away from the physical defence of their borders and from direct force-on-force engagements as the primary determinant of their defence capabilities.[8]

The second factor shaping the conflict envelope of the future is that this shift is being reinforced by the changing nature of the interrelationship between states themselves. That change too is occurring on a number of planes. The most prominent in the strategic debate has been the growing importance of economics as nations move through each stage of development. Not only is there a shift in production profiles as countries move offshore to find cheaper sources of labour or more profitable investments or move away from industry into a post-industrial phase dominated by information, ideas and technology. There is also the need for the more advanced echelon to maximise the return on their new-found expertise by distributing the benefits or opportunities back to those on the development rung below.[9]

These enhanced economic interactions have been accompanied by other significant changes. They have fostered a shift away from command economics to more liberal economic and trading systems which even authoritarian regimes have had to accommodate.[10] They have been accompanied by the impact of global communications (not just electronic but also the movement of people) which are increasingly setting the pace and nature of interactions, but which are also shaping perceptions of events and of other peoples, making comparisons possible and often odious for those who lag behind.

At the same time, control is passing out of the command of the state to those very vehicles which the liberal democratic state sees as essential to its success, the large corporations. Those corporations themselves are, of course, becoming ever more multinational with the capacity to shape tastes, interests and opinions both within and across nations.[11]

What these trends do mean is that the relative strategic weight of powers is changing away from an exclusive focus on military force. Judgements on both the value of engaging particular nations and the areas of engagement are now much more multifaceted. One only needs to look at the new US East Asia Strategy statement with its emphasis on economic interests as being the primary justification for continued engagement,[12] or the trade tensions between the United States and Japan, to appreciate the new complexities.[13]

Furthermore, not only are the grounds for engaging others changing but the vehicles of interaction are as well. While the state can, through its legislative processes, still control some of the boundaries of interaction, the substance has been largely ceded to private industry – with whom state-centred national interests, no matter how important, are balanced by other interests, not the least of which is a suitable profit margin. This dependency is in turn leading to a more qualified concept of sovereignty, the state having to accommodate increasingly the interests of the companies, whose wealth and lines of production are essential to the national well-being. As these corporations become more multinational, they shape both the national economies (by where they invest and who they interact with) and what the substance of interstate exchange is.[14]

Several important strategic conclusions emerge from these developments:

- there has been a shift away from formal alliance structures based on military force to more transient marriages of convenience on specific issues;
- there are different tools of strategic leverage available to nations and any decision to resort to the use of military force will be increasingly influenced by more complex cost benefit analyses and by the interests of non-state actors; and
- many nations have a growing investment in maintaining the means of communication and exchange.

This does not mean that there will not be war. Economic competition between the 'haves' and the 'have nots' has always been an important source of international tension,[15] but there are significant forces working to constrain its impact. The costs of major conflict are increasingly beyond the point that it is worth pursuing.

The downside of these developments is that the new interactions between states have also provided a vehicle for other types of security problems to emerge – most notably the activities of international crime and drug syndicates. These create particular security problems, partly because they can be disguised under the cloak of corporate respectability but also because their scale allows them to acquire significant political leverage and military capabilities. The latter will often be well beyond the ability of traditional domestic security arrangements to handle. An effective counter may well demand some of the resources and the skills and capabilities previously dedicated to the prospect of external military attack.

Third, and closely related to the changing relationships between states, definitions of security are becoming much broader. There is a growing body of literature, both official and academic, which interprets national security as encompassing not just the military instrument but also issues of sustainable national development, environmental protection and assured access to resources, particularly energy supplies.[16] While it is possible to interpret these as little more than an attempt to fill the vacuum when no menacing military force bestrides the horizon, and to extract from them only possible causes for future conflict, their impact is in fact much more fundamental and enduring.

There are two reasons for this. First, they reflect what might be called the changing middle-ground definitions of statehood. An increasing number of international players have won their independence the hard way – imposing political stability and maintaining the state's legitimacy and resilience on the back of economic development. And it is these vulnerabilities that shape their strategic outlook.

At the same time, if one projects forward into the future, there are a range of challenges which for many nations are much more real and certain than the emergence of a military threat. These vary from area to area but include:

- the impacts of environmental degradation and climatic change, especially for those less well endowed with natural resources; and
- for the larger and more developed nations, the burning question of resources, particularly energy supplies, to feed their future development.

It is an area in which the 'security' interests of the developed and developing nations are beginning to coalesce.

This is not to suggest that military force is still not an important instrument of state. The course of history would make nations feel extremely naked without it. But it does reflect a growing recognition that military force is only one among a number of instruments of state policy and that it addresses only part of a state's vulnerability.[17]

The other important implication of these broader definitions of national security is that the issues they raise are not necessarily amenable to unilateral, and especially military, solutions. When considering the impact of industrial pollution, over logging, or the fishing out of marine resources, countries face a genuine alternative as to solutions. They can cooperate or compete. Even if one looks at some of the prospective oil and gas reserves, such as the South China Sea, both technologically and in terms of location, the win–lose approach of military conflict is unlikely to provide a sustainable solution. Similarly, when assessing the implication of damming a river and its impact on neighbours, a country must balance the national benefit of resources against an unstable environment and international opprobrium which may impact adversely (as global resources dwindle) on other aspects of sustainable national development.

Perhaps not surprisingly, given this new focus, traditional security concerns have shifted to areas where issues of common good and independent national interest intersect, such as the control of maritime areas and, most recently, the protection of sea lines of communication. One only has to look at Japan's preoccupation with the safety of maritime trade or the operations to maintain the flow of seaborne resource trade during the Iran–Iraq War to realise not only how important these issues have become but the speed with which these are translated into problems requiring military solutions.[18]

Before taking these arguments too far, however, one has to be careful to look at what is militarily and politically possible in terms of interdiction without the risk of direct retaliation and significant detriment to a national trading system. Most nations lack the comprehensive array of capabilities necessary to conduct and sustain the interdiction of trade or to enforce an exclusion zone in a particular area. Even within maritime focal areas, there is seldom only one country with a stake in maintaining freedom of movement. That is not to say that such actions could not occur – the rational actor model is always a dangerously narrow approach to determining security prospects – but much more thought needs to go into their likelihood, location and the comprehensive response strategies available. There is a great danger in military competition over resources, such as fresh water, of denying the subject to all.[19] Yet the scope for lose–lose situations is undoubtedly diminishing.

The fourth element shaping the envelope within which conflict might occur in the future is what might best be termed the resurgence of regionalism. The Cold War's globalisation of security dynamics on the one hand, together with the internal focus of developing nations on the other, between them left little scope for a true sense of regional or sub-regional identity to emerge in many parts of the world. Stripped of that overlay, many nations are beginning to appreciate the advantages of enhanced cooperation with neighbours in both ensuring greater freedom for independent national decision-making and in the cooperative management of common problems, particularly those related to development and the impact of the global economy.[20]

The potential benefits, which vary from region to region, include:

- maximising economic potential through attracting external investment, creating growth triangles, and sharing production and technology;
- developing mutually supporting national infrastructures which underpin the development potential of the region as well as that of individual nations;
- establishing mechanisms for political accommodation and conflict resolution; and
- presenting a unified stance in wider international fora on issues of common concern.

The latter is particularly important to smaller nations now that the Non-Aligned Movement, which articulated their interests during the Cold War, has lost some of its focus.

There can be no assurance that these arrangements will prevent disputes arising and possibly leading to the use of military force. Many will continue to experience tensions between the advantages of engaging external powers independently or as a regional grouping, a factor becoming more important with the emergence of major regional powers with greater room to manoeuvre.[21] But with the implementation of concepts like the European Union, NAFTA, AFTA and the emerging bilateral and trilateral development zones, together with the decline of traditional insurgencies:

- borders are becoming a less absolute asset;
- other players within a region have a direct investment in issues not blowing out of control; and
- the costs of overt military aggression are increasing.

The introduction of such regional arrangements is generally accompanied by a growing number of mechanisms to discuss or negotiate disagreements and there is probably less opportunity for external power involvement to derail regional or sub-regional processes. The sheer frequency of ASEAN meetings, for example, makes it less likely that potential frictions will not be addressed at an early stage and continually reinforces the concept of negotiation across many areas of public life even when substantive progress is often not being made.

There are undoubtedly a number of regions in the world where the potential for conflict will continue to have a very high currency, but even there there are growing, albeit grudging signs of interdependence. This was reflected in relations between Israel and the Arab states during the Gulf War and the subsequent moves towards a peace settlement; in the prospects for Japanese investment in China and Siberia, and in growing China–Taiwan economic linkages despite continued political distancing. The accommodations will sometimes be fragile but, rather than divergence or cohesion being reflected in different (and often imposed) political ideologies or international alignments, it is the basic or natural synergies that are being addressed.

The critical factor is that these developments not only substantially change the scope for external linkages to override individual regional dynamics, but they also change the tools of engagement or points of interaction between regions. The instruments of interaction are no longer primarily political alignments or military force which may force countries to choose between regional and broader linkages and on which it would be harder to gain consensus. Instead they are markets, tariffs, quotas and technologies. They are not issues in relation to which military force has much utility. Regionalism, of course, does not stop wars but it does serve to raise the threshold for conflict and puts significant constraints on uncontrolled escalation.

The final element that needs to be taken into account is the old chestnut of international law. In the past, this has been seen as a very weak reed in the management of security relations between states. While its provisions are interpreted by the International Court of Justice, its authority lacks a consistent and effective enforcement mechanism. Unless states voluntarily comply with its rulings, it is only in those more extreme cases where a political consensus is forged in the United Nations that a more robust response might occur. Furthermore, widespread support for its provisions has generally arisen only after a conflict has rawly exposed the depths of man's inhumanity.

There are still, however, a number of ways in which, by its moral and political rather than its legal suasion, international law is beginning to constrain the envelope of future conflict. For years, it has been nibbling away at the extremes of the traditional security spectrum, particularly the instruments of war (nuclear, chemical and biological), the treatment of civilians and the use of inhuman weapons such as land mines. Today, its moral force is enhanced by the greater transparency of modern conflict and the role of the global media.

Secondly, while the UN itself has tended to flounder on the handling of peace-keeping, the new scope for progress beyond the Cold War has been highlighted by the steps towards a comprehensive test ban treaty, continuation indefinitely of the Nuclear Non-Proliferation Treaty, and moves to outlaw chemical and biological weapons. Progress has also been made with the UN Registrar of Arms Transfers. These moves reflect not just a resurgence of idealism but a recognition from the major powers of the levelling up of military potential globally and the advantages of containing any future blow out. Indeed, the major powers are attempting to introduce agreed measures of their own, such as the Missile Technology Control Regime designed to limit the spread of the knowledge and systems necessary for strategic missile capabilities.[22]

Furthermore, within the broader definitions of security now being propounded and the new foci for conflict, international law measures are carrying greater weight. By far the most pertinent at this stage is the Law of the Sea Convention which has provided a useful regime for negotiating marine and sea-bed interest disputes. In the process, it has created a climate in which nations both have an alternative means of dispute resolution and are forced to consider the political acceptability of their actions – potentially broadening any challenge into a questioning of agreed global values – and in the process preserving freedom of the seas. It is an important caveat on the ability of nations to exercise complete control over their maritime surrounds. More comprehensive environmental regimes are also in the wind but may be more difficult to negotiate because of great discrepancies in levels of development in different parts of the world.

Where initiatives to manage these broader aspects of security are starting to have an effect is at the regional level. Indeed, what is perhaps the most significant development in this area is the emergence of complementary actions by regional organisations in attempting to control the impact of some of these new security challenges. Good examples include pollution control and anti-piracy measures and the gradual introduction of a range of nuclear-free zones in the southern hemisphere.

Obviously, while each of these trends has the potential over time to bring about a fundamental change in the future strategic order, just how far and how fast they will progress is not yet clear. To this point, their individual impact is not yet dramatic enough to push security planning from its traditional perch. What they do represent is a gradual chipping away at the freedom of nations to use military force and the value of doing so. They certainly do not rule out conflicts occurring, nor, indeed, that some of those might be quite intense. But they do point to the location and purposes of warfare being increasingly different in the future and they tend to rail against the likelihood of large-scale planned aggression or of conflicts escalating uncontrollably once they have begun.

## THE CHANGING TOOLS OF WAR

Where the changing political and economic context for conflict assumes much greater significance, however, is when it is taken in conjunction with the no less profound changes occurring in the traditional tools for waging war.

In an organisational sense, substantial question marks hang over the future role of military alliances, as the political and ideological constructs that underpinned them are being swept away. They imply a formality and a commitment that few would feel confident in making in the current fluid environment. NATO's attempts to reinvigorate the alliance by emphasising out-of-area commitments and challenges from the periphery have a rather hollow ring. It is also not clear what role, apart from confidence building and a stable periphery, an expanded organisation to include the former states of communist Eastern Europe is to play.[23]

Similarly, the United States' second-phase agenda in the Asia-Pacific region with its emphasis on promoting democracy and human rights has a much more intrusive, internal focus with more tenuous links to shared interests in stability. It is already being compromised, at least in relation to China, on the holy grail of economic expediency. US official policy towards the western Pacific continues to emphasise burden sharing but exactly what that security burden is remains undefined apart from vague references to the past. It sits rather uncomfortably with US assertions that its continued presence in the region reflects its own economic interests. On the other side of the equation, the teeth of communist regimes are being drawn by the moves towards more free market economics and an external orientation which does not fit comfortably with past images of darkness and light.

The shift both in Europe and Asia is towards more cooperative regimes whose success hinges on their inclusiveness rather than exclusivity. The fortunes of the ASEAN Regional Forum in tackling the more serious security issues and making substantive progress on defence cooperation[24] and the debate in NATO over the inclusion of the former communist regimes in Eastern Europe, while not offending Russia,[25] illustrates clearly the difficulties of coordination and focus in these new arrangements. Yet, amid the current rhetoric, who would have confidence in the resilience of these organisations should a major power flex its muscles on their boundaries? The focus has shifted more to ad hoc coalitions and marriages of convenience on specific issues. The more sustainable and consistent linkages now belong to the world of economics.

Even more fundamental, however, are the changes going on within military capabilities themselves. The current glut of weapons systems on the international arms market, and their snapping up by countries not previously in possession of advanced conventional capabilities, has been reflected in some fairly pessimistic prognoses of arms races and instability.[26] But that would appear to be a bubble very much set to deflate as arms manufacturers internationally are converting to a broader civil production base. The new capabilities are also ones which many of the recipients do not yet have the technological skills, educational levels and national infrastructure to exploit effectively in combat.

If one steps beyond these short-term contradictions, however, it is possible to identify a number of underlying trends which will shape military acquisitions and capability specifications in the future. The most talked about are undoubtedly the range of new technologies that are being introduced. These might be divided into five broad categories:

1. Those new technologies such as stealth designed to push conventional capabilities beyond the range of current countermeasures. They are limited in number and extremely expensive if done well because they are not add-ons but require a complete redesign of the weapons system.
2. The advanced intelligence, surveillance and reconnaissance systems designed to allow reliable, early location, identification and engagement of targets. The high end is dominated by space-based capabilities, advanced AEW&C and the JSTARS system, but others are more affordable, including unmanned aerial vehicles and phased-array radars.
3. The improved command, control, communications and computing capabilities to ensure more reliable communications and response with much greater data handling, organisation and dissemination capabilities.
4. Closely related to this, the new world of information warfare and cyberspace with the capacity to disable a sophisticated adversary without a shot being fired. This could be either tactically on the battlefield or by 'strategic' strikes against the electronic communications and economic infrastructure of the adversary.[27]
5. Finally, there is the increasing proliferation not only of precision-guided munitions but also of medium- to long-range ballistic missile systems with much greater accuracy and lethality. While some systems feature older technologies, they remain effective because they are difficult to counter. In response, missile defence systems like Patriot have jumped to the top of the agenda in countries such as Japan and Israel.[28]

While many of these trends can be relatively easily translated into images of the high-tech battlefield of the future, their impact on the shape of future conflict is in fact much more complex. On the one hand, they:

- provide the capacity for the much more accurate and controlled application of military force (an important consideration in both politico-military conflicts and before the eyes of the global media);
- have the potential to equip many nations with greater strategic reach without the need for substantial power projection capabilities (thus overcoming some of the primary logistic and geographic qualifications on the use of force); and
- can significantly limit battlefield casualties, an increasingly important consideration for developed nations in sanctioning the use of force.

On the other hand, the new technologies are making larger conventional platforms and formations much more vulnerable and rapidly escalating their costs beyond both the value of their potential missions and the capacity of many nations to afford them.

The obvious panacea of light, agile forces with advanced capabilities able to apply precision firepower over considerable distances – the sharp rather than the blunt instrument – is, however, by no means the comfortable solution that it first appears. Significant question marks hang over both its affordability and its usability.

There are fundamental changes occurring in defence manufacturing and production.[29] Most companies are converting significant capacity to civilian production. Many are currently prepared to sell technology and research and development skills to achieve sales. Multinational projects and company mergers are becoming more common. Full military specifications – the hallowed ground of past procurements – are being supplanted by the new civil technologies available to perform similar functions, especially in combat support areas.[30] At the same time, market leader the United States has moved to give much greater emphasis to research and development, while cutting production numbers of advanced equipments. This is pushing the costs of the technological edge of the next generation of capabilities well beyond the means of most countries.[31]

The impact of these changes will be several fold. Not only will there be a levelling out of capability but the emphasis will not be on technology edge per se but on whether that capability is able to be deliverable for its primary missions. The operational edge will come from a nation being able to exploit its environment to the full, thus shifting the emphasis away from firepower differences to key combat support areas – especially $C^3$, surveillance and intelligence, mobility and operational maintenance.[32] It will become much more expensive to support and deliver the same level of combat capability, albeit more effectively, and the size of forces will shrink. Finally, few will be able to afford balanced, conventional defence forces as currently defined, with the possible exception of geographically small but technologically advanced states like Singapore.

As military capabilities are reshaped in this way, it is important to consider just how usable many of the advanced weapons systems will be. There is clearly the question of cost – where platforms are simply too expensive to be put seriously in harm's way – a major question already in relation to larger surface combatants. But it is not just a question of cost. While many were mesmerised by the effectiveness of advanced systems in the clear battlefield of the Gulf War, one has to ask how appropriate they will be in situations of either more limited hostilities or more confined geographic locations. Furthermore, conventional power projection is being squeezed out on the one hand by the option of longer-range missile systems and cheaper, unmanned systems like UAV and, on the other, by the potential of information warfare to cause substantial damage to the communications and economy of another nation without firing a shot.

The other question which hangs over these future capability visions is whether the new technologies are in fact outrunning the human dimensions of warfare. Many nations have begun to identify the need to attract and maintain sufficiently highly skilled manpower in defence, including in competition from civil industry, but that is only the thin end of the wedge. There is:

- the question of the national technical capacity to support the new weapons systems and the need to have the trained operators;
- the question of whether nations are really able to exploit all the improvements (for example, the massive data flows) and whether warfare will any longer – if it ever did – fit predetermined moulds that artificial intelligence and automatic response systems can cope with;
- the major dilemma of training for command. The skilled technician will seldom have the breadth of experience and the wider adaptability to progress to the top. The operational commander who has learnt in the field will need to master a completely new set of doctrine and options. Yet all the technological advances in the world could be negated if nations are increasingly forced to conduct warfare by committee.

The concept of conflict as currently reflected in the defence planning and military capabilities and doctrine of most developed nations is thus under siege. The challenge is rather deceptive because no individual trend is so stark or so immediate in its impact to jolt strategic planners from their established paradigms. Yet the cumulative impact of the changes that are occurring is no less profound. And it is not a challenge that will simply disappear if one closes one's eyes, accepts certain worst case scenarios, and hopes the storm will blow over. Even the emergence of a threat – that wonderful certainty that a traditional strategic lens leaves planners craving for – would probably do little more than prolong the agony. The essence of the problem is that both the political and economic context within which conflict might occur and the very tools for conducting warfare have all been tossed up in the air at the same time. Conflict is being attacked from both the outside and the inside. Unfortunately, security planners have virtually no experience in handling this complex interaction of factors and their existing policy constructs serve to mask rather than illuminate the significance of the changes that are occurring.

THE SHAPE OF FUTURE CONFLICT

How then are security planners to make sense out of the new strategic dynamics and to establish future policy directions? Or do they simply toss a coin?

The key to finding an effective solution lies in not being mesmerised by the immediate detail of what is occurring, particularly in the technological area, but stepping back far enough to see how this convergence of political, economic and capability trends will affect the shape of future conflict. What then becomes very clear is that there is occurring a significant and growing disjuncture in the traditional continuum of conflict which has dominated security planning in the twentieth century.

Previously, the approach of many defence planners has been to see warfare as a series of graduations ranging from the lowest level of hostilities up to the conduct of sustained joint intensive operations (see Figure 7.1). And it was the latter, worst case prospect that ultimately set the framework for planning in the developed nations. The only break in the continuum occurred when one stepped beyond that into the use of nuclear weapons. It was a break that related not just to the different means by which military force was projected (and the difficulties of countering this) but also the extent to which the impact of nuclear 'means' threatened to outrun the desired 'ends' of the conflict.[33] The trauma which NATO planners faced in the 1950s when attempting to develop concepts of limited nuclear war bears stark witness to the different considerations applying on each side of the nuclear divide.

The break in the spectrum of conflict will in the future occur at a much lower level (see Figure 7.2). At the lower end of the spectrum, there will continue to be a range of limited conflicts. They will encompass:

- traditional low-intensity, counter-insurgency and peace enforcement type operations;
- possibly extend to some quite intense conventional military confrontations over specific issues, not least in maritime areas – but these will generally be limited in time and geographic spread as well as confined in their purpose; and
- they are likely to be pushed out further by the complexity and possible sophistication of threats posed by non-state actors.

Whether or not the latter task falls to the established military forces or other state security bodies will depend on national circumstances.

Where the break will occur in the continuum of conflict in the future is in the assumptions as to how these might escalate in terms of major state-on-state confrontations employing large forces for a protracted period and over a wide geographic area. Most countries have tucked away in their planning cupboards concepts of expansion and national mobilisation for sustained joint intensive operations – that insurance policy should strategic circumstances deteriorate markedly.

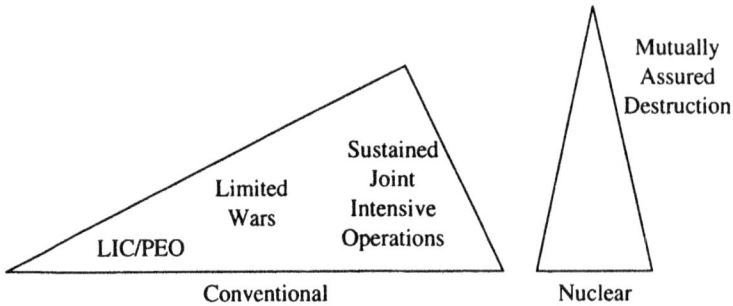

*Figure 7.1: The Present Continuum of Conflict*

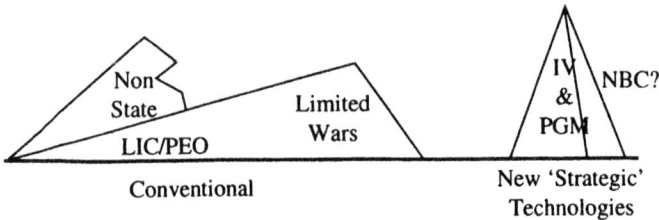

*Figure 7.2: Conflict in the Future*

The critical question is whether that is any longer a viable option for most nations:

- not only would national mobilisation imply huge, and for most unsustainable, costs in resource (financial and human) terms; but
- it is not clear if the state continues to have independent control over the means for promoting such expansion;
- what grounds would make it worthwhile given the certain disruption, or damage, to other key elements of the new broader definitions of national security?; and
- even if the state could overcome these obstacles, could it do so in a timely enough fashion?

The bottom line is that there are now much cheaper and controllable military tools available to an increasing number of nations which can be delivered over long distances within short time frames and, at this point in time, are extremely difficult to provide comprehensive defence against. These tools are primarily medium- to long-range precision guided missiles and, increasingly, information warfare capabilities able to exploit the global communications network. Even if larger conventional forces could be deployed, their effectiveness is questionable and their vulnerability increasingly high.

Military force will not in the future, except in certain time and geographically limited scenarios, be about significant head-to-head confrontations with high expenditure of munitions and attrition of platform numbers. Rather:

- it will be about light, agile forces able to accomplish particular tasks with great precision and the minimum of engagement;
- numerically, force elements will be relatively small; they will not be seeking to hold ground on a continuous basis; and operational success will be determined primarily by the quality and synergy of combat support elements;
- many tactical actions are likely to be loaded with significant political implications, both compressing the scope for independent military doctrine and pushing more fundamental decisions down to lower levels of command;
- the primary determinants of success will be knowledge, speed, flexibility and the blending of force with a controlled political impact strategy.

There will, however, be significant questions as to just how much capability and technology can be justified (and, indeed, afforded) for these more limited scenarios. There may also need to be trade-offs between quality and quantity if defence forces are expected to take an enhanced role in low-intensity conflict, peace enforcement, and the combating of the activities of non-state actors. Should a conflict outrun resolution by this range of capabilities and develop into a major, protracted stand-off, increasingly the only option for many states will be to jump the break in the conflict spectrum and rely on selective strategic strike capabilities.

While the greater precision of targeting and controlled lethality of warheads demonstrated in the Gulf War appear, on the surface, to make this an attractive option, the apparent triumph of technology masks some major difficulties.

First, the control of escalation will be much more difficult. There will be limited options for a gradual increase in the intensity or spread of hostilities. The fight will be taken directly to either the adversary's own military infrastructure or to the heart of its political and economic system. The national costs will be potentially much greater than the loss of a few combat units and it could quickly swing both protagonists into offensive strategies. The 'soft option' might be to employ offensive information warfare strategies but, perhaps even more than conventional warfare, the danger would be their spiralling out of control – not the least because they too are invisible tools of warfare – and causing even greater damage to the national well-being of either or both parties to the dispute.

The second problem is the extent to which this new upper segment of the conflict spectrum tends to bring nuclear capabilities back into the fold of strategic deterrence. Certainly, in the area of ballistic missiles and precision strike, the difference is primarily in the warhead, not the delivery system. That potential ambiguity will almost certainly force opponents to react earlier rather than later, albeit at a level rather less than that of mutually assured destruction. There will be huge difficulties in getting proportional retaliation right, pushing many countries towards either longer-range anti-ballistic missile defensive systems or, if that is unaffordable, a small number of nuclear warheads.

The third difficulty is that escalation would no longer be synonymous with expansion. Technically, it could occur very quickly and, rather than being catered for with reserve personnel and capabilities, it would have to constitute a significant element in the force-in-being of a nation pursuing that strategy. Yet this operational imperative clashes directly with the growing economic and political interdependence which would point to such capabilities only being used when national survival is at stake.

## TOWARDS A DANGEROUS WORLD?

The lessons that emerge from this brief glance at the shape of future conflict are thus quite profound. On the one hand, it spells the demise of larger-scale conventional military operations and with it condemns to irrelevance so much of the doctrine, structures and capabilities that underpin current defence planning. It is not just a question of tossing the expansion base, national mobilisation and reserve forces on the rubbish heap of history. Training and command structures need to be rethought while operational effectiveness will depend on the performance of combat support capabilities – surveillance, intelligence, command and control, and mobility assets in particular – rather than the volume of firepower at the point of decision.

Perhaps ironically it will be the larger powers that will have the most difficulty coming to grips with change. It is they that have the greatest investment in the current way of doing business and have sufficient resources to attempt to cope with the new dimensions of warfare within traditional strategic paradigms. It is, however, an agenda which sits very comfortably with the changing nature of sovereignty and the political and economic relationships between states.

Unfortunately, the other side of the coin is much more disturbing. For all the tantalising attractiveness of the new defence technologies – of precision guided munitions and information warfare – in contributing to relatively bloodless and controlled conflict, their real strategic impact may be very different. The danger is that their proliferation across a range of nations will foster a new era of competitiveness and substantially increase the strategic importance and the destructive power of the upper peak in the conflict spectrum. But that upper peak is the very area:

- where the complexities of new technologies make human control much more difficult; and
- which is potentially unstable because it is not tied to other aspects of the conflict continuum.

The very chilling question which must be asked is whether, despite the greater levels of global and regional interdependency and the prospective demise of the military dinosaurs of the past, current trends are dragging many nations towards a replay of the Cold War in microcosm? The only difference would be that the trigger can be pulled at a much lower level and that there are many more players who could pull it.

It is not an inevitable future, it is probably an avoidable future. But defence planners have no chance of tackling it until they can escape from their traditional strategic lens and look seriously at the shape of future conflict. And if they do not do it soon, it will probably be too late.

NOTES

1. Sir Michael Quinlan, 'A United Kingdom Perspective', *Journal of the Royal United Services Institute of Australia*, Vol. 12, No. 2, October 1991, p.18.
2. Their thought-provoking analyses of war in the future are captured in M. van Creveld, *The Transformation of War*, The Free Press, New York, 1991 and A. and H. Toffler, *War and Anti-War: Making Sense of Today's Global Chaos*, Warner Books, London, 1995.
3. For a discussion of the revolution in military affairs and its potential impact, see D. Jablonsky, *The Owl of Minerva Flies at Twilight: Doctrinal Change and Continuity and the Revolution in Military Affairs*, Professional Readings in Military Strategy No.10, Strategic Studies Institute, US Army War College, Carlisle Barracks, Pennsylvania, April 1994 and Admiral W. Owens, 'The Emerging System of Systems', *Military Review*, Vol. LXXV, No. 3, May–June 1995, pp.15–19.
4. This is reflected, for example, in the Major Regional Contingencies (MRCs) which are at the foundation of the United States' 'Bottom Up Review' and the Australian concept of 'credible contingencies' which, Paul Dibb notes, 'is essentially designed to reduce risks by planning for the more credible threats and to assist planning judgements by narrowing the range of geographical and military contingencies'. *Planning a Defence Force Without a Threat: A Model for Middle Powers*, Strategic and Defence Studies Centre, Australian National University, Canberra, 1996, p.24.
5. US Army doctrine (FM100-5) continues to insist that: 'The Army must be capable of achieving decisive victory. The Army must maintain the capability to put overwhelming combat power on the battlefield to defeat all enemies through a total force effort.' Jablonsky, *The Owl of Minerva*, p.29.
6. R. Betts, 'Wealth, Power and Instability', *International Security*, Vol. 18, No. 3, Winter 1993/94, pp.37ff.
7. This dilemma is graphically illustrated in the problems the United Nations is facing in coming to terms with the new peace-keeping agenda with the need for multidimensional and protracted commitments to restore the apparatus of a state, but often in circumstances where the use of force is necessary either to institute or protect that process. A. Roberts, 'The Crisis in UN Peacekeeping', *Survival*, Vol. 36, No. 3, Autumn 1994, pp.93–120.
8. The American experience after Vietnam when the military were so reluctant to adjust to a new and much less direct style of warfare highlights how difficult this transition is likely to be. L.B.Thompson (ed), *Low Intensity Conflict*, Lexington Books, Lexington, Massachusetts, 1989, pp.6–15.
9. As Stuart Harris has argued: 'It is not just that, as in the past, economic strength and technological capacity determine a nation's relative power and influence but that such strength and capability now depends upon competitive participation in the international economy'. *Journal of Strategic Studies*, Vol. 18, No. 3, September 1995, p.33.
10. As Frank Frost has noted in relation to Vietnam: 'The policies of economic "renovation" have sought to decontrol major areas of the economy, create a substantial role for private economic activity, revitalize the state sector and encourage foreign investment.' *Vietnam's Foreign Relations: Dynamics of*

*Change*, Pacific Strategy Papers, Institute of Southeast Asian Studies, Singapore, 1993, p.3.

11. For an interesting exposition of the challenges to the modern state, see M. van Creveld, 'The Fate of the State', *Parameters*, Spring 1996, pp.4–18.

12. Department of Defense, *United States Security Strategy for the East Asia-Pacific Region*, Washington, February 1995. The new dimensions of US national security strategy are assessed in J. Conklin, *Forging an East Asian Foreign Policy*, University Press of America, Lanham, Maryland, 1995.

13. For an analysis of the importance of economic interests in US foreign policy beyond the Cold War, see F. Bergsten, 'The Primacy of Economics', *Foreign Policy*, No. 87, Summer 1992, pp.3–24.

14. Mel Gustov, *Global Politics in the Human Interest* (2nd edn, Lynne Reinner, Boulder, 1991), notes that: 'The prominence of global corporations in world politics can be further gauged by noting their market dominance and size. About 500 TNCs (Transnational Corporations) (of over 10,000 worldwide) account for about 80 percent of total world production. A mere fifteen of them, and in most cases only three to six, control world trade in all basic commodities from food to minerals. When their total output is matched against that of states, TNCs ... occupy 41 of the top 100 places.'

15. Max Singer and Aaron Wildavsky, in a provocative study of *The Real World Order. Zones of Peace. Zones of Turmoil* (Chatham House Publications, Chatham, New Jersey, 1993), foresee a world divided between the developed democracies and the developing world where conflict will continue to be prevalent.

16. See, for example, G. Prins, 'A New Focus for Security Studies' in D. Ball and D. Horner (eds), *Strategic Studies in a Changing World: Global, Regional and Australian Perspectives*, Canberra Papers on Strategy and Defence No.89, Strategic and Defence Studies Centre, Australian National University, Canberra, 1992, pp.178–222.

17. Paul Kennedy, *Preparing for the Twenty-First Century* (Fontana Press, London, 1994, p.336), notes that: 'Unlike traditional threats to security, these dangers are less obvious and therefore less likely to induce a unified, determined response. In addition, the usual mechanisms by which nation-states respond to threats seem inappropriate to some of the challenges posed here.'

18. Harris, 'Economic Aspects of Security', pp.40–1.

19. J.R. Starr, 'Water Wars', *Foreign Policy*, No. 82, Spring 1991, pp.17–36.

20. A. Hurrell, 'Explaining the Resurgence of Regionalism in World Politics', *Review of International Studies*, Vol. 21, No. 4, October 1995, pp.331ff.

21. This can be seen particularly in the way a number of the countries in Southeast Asia are currently seeking to balance their membership of ASEAN with the desire to maintain a stabilising US presence in the region while keeping their options open for the future bilateral engagement of China, Japan or India.

22. A range of these new arms control initiatives are discussed in depth in J. Brown (ed.), *New Horizons and Challenges in Arms Control and Verification*, VU University Press, Amsterdam, 1994.

23. D. Allin, 'Can Containment Work Again?', *Survival*, Vol.37, No.1, Spring 1995, pp.53ff. The UK *Statement on the Defence Estimates*, 1992 (HMSO, London, July 1992), makes the interesting admission that: 'It remains a key security interest to sustain the present network of multinational Western co-operation and to avoid any reversion to nationally-driven defence.'

24.  For a detailed analysis of the strengths and weaknesses of the ARF concept, see
     M. Leifer, *The ASEAN Regional Forum*, Adelphi Paper No.302, International
     Institute of Strategic Studies, Oxford University Press, 1996.
25.  The complexities of redefining the European security agenda are discussed in
     H. Brown, 'Transatlantic Security in the Pacific Century', *The Washington
     Quarterly*, Vol. 18, No. 4, Autumn 1995, pp.77–86.
26.  D. Ball, 'Arms and Affluence: Military Acquisitions in the Asia-Pacific Region',
     *International Security*, Vol.18, No.3, Winter 1993/94, pp.78–112.
27.  'A Survey of Defence Technology', *The Economist*, 10 June 1995, pp.5–20; R.
     Molander et al., 'Strategic Information Warfare: A New face of War', *Parameters*,
     Vol. XXVI, No. 3, Autumn 1996, pp.81–92.
28.  R. Manning, 'Futureshock or Renewed Partnership? the US–Japan Alliance
     Facing the Millennium', *The Washington Quarterly*, Vol. 18, No. 4, Autumn
     1995, p.94.
29.  M. Hewish, 'Redirecting the defense R&D pipeline', *International Defense
     Review*, Vol. 26, July 1993, pp.555–6.
30.  J. Gansler, *Defense Conversion, Transforming the Arsenal of Democracy*
     (Twentieth Century Fund, MIT Press, Cambridge, Massachusetts, 1995, p.88)
     has argued that: 'It is essential that future weapons systems be explicitly designed
     to use commercial subsystems, components, software, and materials ...' and (p.92)
     'The equivalent military parts are significantly more expensive, less reliable,
     and two to three years later in state-of-the-art performance.'
31.  Martin Edmonds notes in relation to the new US advanced technologies that:
     'These American objectives and developments are beyond the purse and, in
     several areas, the technological capabilities of the UK or its European partners.'
     *British Army 2000, External Influences on Force Design*, Occasional Paper No.
     21, The Strategic and Combat Studies Institute, 1996, p.46.
32.  Secretary of Defense William Perry has stated that: 'the U.S. advantage in this
     new military technology is not in components, but in systems, training, and
     operational experience'. Gansler, *Defense Conversion*, p.97.
33.  M. Howard (ed.), *Restraints on War*, Oxford University Press, Oxford, 1979,
     p.8.

# 8 The Emerging Strategic Architecture in the Asia-Pacific Region
Paul Dibb

The world of the 1990s faces a dramatically new strategic situation. The ideological confrontation and tensions of the last half century have gone but it is far from certain what will replace them. The very fact that, more than four years after the end of the Cold War, the conditional phrase 'the post-Cold War era' is still being used indicates how uncertain we are of our present strategic situation. Perhaps such words as 'the era of uncertainty' better describe the contemporary strategic condition. In my view, today's uncertainty is itself strategic in nature and this demands an unprecedented degree of flexibility in strategic thinking.[1]

This does not necessarily imply, of course, that the strategic outlook is pessimistic: the general consensus amongst most defence planners is that global nuclear conflict is now a remote possibility and that war between the major powers is improbable. But it is far from certain that the next one or two decades will see a peaceful and cooperative world. The now commonly held view that economic power has replaced military power as the central element of international affairs is greatly overstated.[2] And the early expectations of a 'new world order' after the disintegration of Soviet communism and the Warsaw Pact were quickly dashed on the battlefields of Kuwait, Bosnia-Hercegovina and Chechnya, as well as in Somalia, Rwanda and Lebanon.

If the sudden collapse of the Soviet Union should have taught us anything about strategic analysis, it was to expect the unexpected. And yet many international relations scholars are talking, with a great deal of certainty, about a new interdependent world order in which economic factors will succeed in bringing about a less conflictual world – if not a brave new world of cooperative liberal democracies averse to the very idea of war.[3]

Much of this is a little too simplistic: it smacks of a new strategic orthodoxy at a time when there is an urgent need to challenge comfortable assumptions about a threat-free world. Straight-line extrapolations from our recent experience are not necessarily a dependable guide for the future. We live in an era of great change where there is the potential for stark discontinuities. The world is not approaching the 'end of history' in the sense that an era of permanent global peace lies ahead.

Practically all the theories of international relations are contested and yet we are being asked to accept unquestioningly that a revolution has now occurred in the way in which mankind behaves. According to this thesis, the end of military conflict between states is in sight because of: the triumph of liberal democracy and free enterprise; the emergence of a new era of inter-dependence through open trade, transnational financial markets and the exchange of information; the peaceful settlement of territorial disputes; and the declining importance of the state and the growing salience of multilateral institutions – such as the Asia-Pacific Economic Cooperation forum (APEC).

Most often, these ideas are advanced by international relations theorists and by economic rationalists. They have little acceptance in the world of strategic studies nor in most defence ministries.[4] It is true that some foreign ministries were initially attracted to optimistic views of a reordered world but the practical experience of the Gulf War and United Nations operations have shaken their faith. In many parts of the world a sense of caution is setting in: the free-fall in defence budgets is coming to an end as governments seek to cope with a more fluid and complex world that has to encompass a wider range of possible policy outcomes. Wilsonian optimism is being tempered with Hobbesian realism.

## THINKING ABOUT STRATEGY IN THE ASIA-PACIFIC REGION

It might be asked, what is the relevance of all this to strategic developments in the Asia-Pacific region? The answer is: a great deal. It has become very fashionable in certain parts of the region to proclaim that the 'Pacific century' has arrived and that Asia's economic success and cultural values have found a new path to regional cooperation and the resolution of disputes without using force.[5] These claims tend to come more from Southeast Asia than from Northeast Asia, where ideological and territorial disputes, historical animosities and the dangers of military conflict are much more in evidence.

Of course, Asia's economic success has been remarkable and the region promises to be the focus of world economic growth well into the twenty-first century. Historically, however, economic prosperity and growing interdependence have not seen the avoidance of war. The society of states in Europe in the second half of the nineteenth century experienced an unprecedented period of prosperity, economic interdependence and technological innovation and yet the end result was the First World War. The breakdown of the balance of power in Europe, and the challenge of Germany's rise to power, may have some future lessons for how Asia copes with China's aspirations for great-power status.[6]

It is very important, of course, to recognise the differences between Asia now and Europe in the nineteenth century. Nuclear deterrence is an overwhelming inhibition to military confrontation between the major powers. Moreover, most economists argue that the scale of economic interdependence in the region is now such that the costs of war would be prohibitive.[7] And although it is true that Asia lacks any formal security mechanism, such as the European Union, it has developed in recent years impressive multilateral organisations such as APEC and the ASEAN Regional Forum (ARF).

Even so, strategic thinking about the Asia-Pacific region needs to challenge some of the conventional wisdom about the inherent stability of the region.[8] This is not to argue that the Asia-Pacific region at present is inherently unstable – although the tensions currently between China and Taiwan, between India and Pakistan, on the Korean peninsula, and in the South China Sea, as well as the insurgencies in Sri Lanka, Cambodia, the Philippines and Papua New Guinea, are cause for concern. Rather, the problem is that a rather unreal sense of 'peace in our time' is descending on some quarters of the region, just as the balance of power is changing. Some of the ASEAN countries seem to believe that they have discovered a new formula for peace, called consultation (*musyawarah*) and consensus (*mufakat*). It is true that ASEAN has been enormously successful in developing informal methods of cooperation and in avoiding conflict or confrontation. But to believe that it is possible to translate such an impressive – albeit diffuse – arrangement to the wider region is problematical: the strategic issues in Northeast Asia, as well as in South Asia, are much more serious and they are on a very much larger scale.

Asia has not had much experience with handling a multipolar balance of power. Neither is it comfortable, as yet, with conflict resolution agreements, or with formal arms control and military transparency measures. Since the creation of the ASEAN Regional Forum, however, progress is undoubtedly being made with confidence building.[9] Transparency in military matters – which became an accepted part of the Cold War relationship between the United States and the USSR through the use of national technical means of verification – is viewed by much of the region with great caution. Progress in this highly sensitive area will be slow.

Another difficult area is territorial sovereignty. In Asia there are a large number of unresolved territorial claims. Desmond Ball has identified some two dozen issues involving competing sovereignty claims, secessionist movements, and territorial conflicts in East Asia alone.[10] This list does not include the half a dozen or more unresolved territorial disputes or secessionist movements in South Asia.[11]

These disputes vary greatly in intensity, but from the point of view of regional order the most serious concern is that some of them involve acute ideological, territorial, or religious differences (China and Taiwan, North and South Korea, India and Pakistan), and more than one-third of the disputes are over maritime boundaries and offshore territorial claims. In contrast to the trend elsewhere in the world, which is towards conflict within states, these territorial disputes in Asia involve the potential for conflict between states, threatening neighbourhood stability. There is the ever-present danger of miscalculation and escalation – particularly where the military forces of rival claimants operate in close proximity to each other, as they do on the Korean peninsula, across the Taiwan Strait, in Kashmir, and in the South China Sea. Any of these territorial disputes could be used as an excuse to escalate tension if political relations in the region should deteriorate. The Stockholm International Peace Research Institute's survey of major conflicts shows that Asia accounts for more disputes than any other region in the world, including Africa.[12] And unlike Africa, where the majority of disputes are over the form of government, most conflicts in Asia are over territory.

Associated with these territorial disputes is a tendency to strong nationalism. At a time when it is being claimed that the role of the state is diminishing and that territorial differences are unlikely to lead to conflict, much of the region is seemingly heading in the opposite direction. Politically, and with few exceptions, Asia is characterised by strongly nationalist governments. Moreover, democracy is not – and is not likely to be – the prevailing political system in Asia any time soon, even though impressive progress is being made in some countries. Whilst economic growth may bring about demands for greater political participation, many regimes in the region are experiencing an unstable transition period. Regimes in transition to political pluralism – and particularly authoritarian regimes – can be prone to dangerous transitional instability, in which resort to the external use of force could occur.[13]

Asia has many countries potentially in this category: China, Russia, Vietnam, South Korea and Taiwan are currently undergoing great political and social change, and North Korea and Myanmar are obvious future candidates. It cannot be said that democracy has strong roots yet in most of the Asia-Pacific region. Authoritarianism of one sort or another still prevails.

The imperatives of the information revolution will bring about more open societies: but some regimes will prefer state control over the free flow of information, even if that means diminished economic success. The experience of China has shown that there is no necessary correlation between greater economic well-being and a better human rights record or political freedom.

Some of these freedom of information considerations may well affect the international competitiveness of certain Asian countries in the longer term. And others, such as human rights, will impinge more immediately on the relations of Western democracies – and particularly the United States – with the region.

In terms of the emerging strategic architecture in the region there will be other risks: there is a danger that the strong sense of nationalism that prevails almost everywhere in Asia will inhibit the development of a regional security community – other than in the rather limited sense of dialogue in such multilateral forums as APEC and the ARF. In Asia it is power balancing and economic growth that are the main security variables and not arms control regimes or multilateral security organisations. However, the Asian states' penchant for strong leaders, the view that ideological and human rights issues should not hinder interstate relations, and their intense sense of the priority of the national interest would seem well suited to geopolitical realism. Asia's soft authoritarianism emphasises order, a strong state and pragmatism in interstate relations. These values broadly support power balancing interests. Moreover, contact between Asian states is rapidly increasing as external influences broaden and economic necessities become the driving force.[14] This should help to moderate tension in the region and make for a more cooperative atmosphere.

But the proliferation of nuclear weapons, and other weapons of mass destruction, in Northeast Asia (China, Russia, North Korea) and South Asia (India and Pakistan) is a matter of grave concern. So is the spread of advanced conventional weapons, which is now endemic in Asia. Defence spending has been forging ahead in the region, supported by strong economic growth: Asia now spends more than US$135 billion on defence or more than three times the defence expenditure of the Middle East.[15] The Asian region is the only strongly growing defence market in the world: defence expenditure increased by 23 per cent in real terms between 1985 and 1994. In 1985, Asia spent 58 per cent as much as NATO Europe on defence, whereas by 1994 the proportion was 81 per cent. This trend suggests that by the year 2000 Asia will have outstripped NATO Europe in terms of the amount of money it spends on defence.

Not too much should be made of these comparisons: neither Europe nor the Middle East is in a competitive position with Asia strategically. But the rapid growth in Asian defence spending is a matter for concern in itself because it is occurring independently of the collapse of the USSR and without any palpable military threats. The explanation lies with other variables within the region itself. As Desmond Ball has noted, some of the most significant factors are entirely non-military, such as the availability of economic resources arising from strong economic growth and the perceptions of prestige deriving from the acquisition of high-tech platforms (such as advanced fighter aircraft).[16] There is also a distinct trend towards a gradual proliferation of locally produced arms and the transfer of technology that will enhance the ability of regional countries to build the next generation of weapons themselves.[17]

An arms race, as such, does not yet exist – although there are distinct elements of arms racing in Northeast Asia and South Asia. Rather, a competitive arms acquisition process permeates the region: the sense of risk is enhanced by the fact that (as mentioned earlier) throughout the region there are unresolved ideological, territorial and historical disputes. Increasingly, most countries in the region – including many middle powers – will be able to afford a quite comprehensive range of defensive and offensive military capabilities, albeit in limited numbers. Such expended capabilities will widen the range of military options available and increase the scale and intensity of combat that can be sustained.

It is quite clear from this brief review of thinking about Asia strategically that laying the foundation for security in the region will require more than just continued economic growth and the spread of its political and social benefits. There is no evidence to support the theory that economic interdependence necessarily leads to peace.[18] Economic institution building alone does not have the ballast to sustain security cooperation in Asia. Considerable uncertainty lies ahead as old alignments and alliances are changing and there is no real prospect of a collective security organisation or regional security community emerging in the foreseeable future. Progress in the area of establishing multilateral security mechanisms – and conflict resolution procedures – will not be easy given the disparate nature of the Asian region, the range of security issues that require resolution, and the fact that there is little tradition of successful security cooperation on a multilateral basis. This leads to the conclusion that, far from the Asia-Pacific region developing a comfortable regional order in which the great powers will play a coordinated or collusive role to maintain stability, separate national interests will underscore an uncertain and basically competitive strategic outlook. This will be enhanced by the intensity of economic competition, which will increasingly characterise relationships in the region.

## THE ROLE OF THE GREAT POWERS IN SHAPING REGIONAL ORDER

Traditionally, the great powers have played a dominant role in shaping international society. That role can be either responsible or predatory. Asia is evidently at the beginning of what will be a protracted process of adjustment among the great powers. There are two new powers emerging in the region – China and Japan – with no clearly articulated roles and considerable suspicion of each other, and a third country – India – that, so far, has an unrealised potential as an Asian great power. Russia has, at least temporarily, lost its power base in almost every dimension, although it could re-emerge in the longer term as a disruptive power in the Asia-Pacific region. The United States is the one actor that truly possesses all the attributes of power but there is questioning in the region about whether it will hold the balance of power.

Any new strategic balance in Asia will likely rest upon the relationships among the five great powers.[19] A five-power balance presupposes not only a continuous system of diplomacy, providing the players with intelligence about the moves of all other players, but also the means to act upon moves that threaten the balance. Such means have to include a sense of regional order comprising a system of collaboration and self-restraint, as well as the restraint of others.

The question is whether the security architecture of the region is ready yet for such a sophisticated and intricate concept of order. The answer is that it is not, but that the self-preservation of the great powers, and the anxiety of the middle powers, will probably push events in the next decade or so in the direction of a positive balance-of-power collaboration. This is because the chief function of a balance of power is the preservation of the existing local system of states, for which there is strong support in Asia. There is nothing automatic, however, about a balance of power – states will have to choose constantly between devoting resources and energy to preserving or extending their relative power and devoting resources and energy to other ends, including pressing domestic problems. There will have to be a constant balancing between nationalist and internationalist impulses.[20]

It is not a requirement of a five-sided balance of power that the players be equal and politically equidistant from each other. Neither does a balance have to rest on a common Asian culture. Rather, a new system of order in Asia can encompass a less hierarchical structure than the traditional balance of power, tolerating a greater inequality of military power and a broader diffusion of influence and levers of power in the post-Cold War era. In Asia, the presence – and indeed growing significance – of the middle powers limits the political position of the great powers, which will seek accommodation and alignment with key secondary players as junior partners in the emerging system of regional order. The growing political strength of the ASEAN countries and the reluctance of key middle powers, such as South Korea, Vietnam and Indonesia, to be subordinated to any concert of the great powers will serve at least as a partial check on hegemony. The fact that each of the great powers possesses different types of power, and in differing degrees, and that there is a growing overall rough equality in political power among them, will also encourage a more stable balance in the near term.

In the longer term, however, the relative strengths of the great powers will be very different in 2010 from what they are today. The strategic potential of regional powers is changing rapidly. Strategic potential means the combination of economic strength, technological capability, population and educational level, and natural resources that determines the capacity to develop and employ armed force. Nations with great strategic potential have the capability to expand their forces relatively quickly. In Asia, the armed forces of many countries are well below their strategic potential.

China, in particular, promises to be a more powerful country and both Japan and India have the potential to play much stronger roles in the new regional order. The United States' power may consolidate or it may proceed to decline gradually: but America has by far the greatest strategic potential of any power – now or foreseeably. Russia has a latent capacity to regenerate its military power and exert great-power status in Asia. These very uncertainties are a cause for concern because almost all significant possibilities for future order in the region are left open.[21]

The changing economic power of the Asian states will affect the hierarchic order and the distribution of power in the region. According to Kennedy, the power disposition of the leading nations in the world over the past five centuries has closely paralleled their relative economic position.[22] The historical record also suggests a very clear connection, in the long run, between a great power's economic rise and fall and its military growth and decline.[23] Uneven economic growth leads to cycles of rise and decline among states. Gilpin has observed that periods of rapid change within and among nations create dangerous uncertainties and anxieties that can lead political elites to miscalculate.[24] Arguably, Asia is now undergoing such a period of sustained growth and rapid political and social change. It would be a mistake to be complacent about the underlying social stability of significant actors in Asia or about the potential for tension between America and newly emerging Asian great powers.

Several key Asian countries are entering a period of political uncertainty because the leadership is about to change (for example, China), or where there is considerable domestic political turmoil (for example, Japan). China's system of government is under pressure as China becomes a modern industrial state undergoing huge economic and social change. Significant evolution of Japan's political system also seems likely. Korea may well become unified, introducing a new strategic element into Northeast Asia. Vietnam faces major challenges as it adapts its political system to the demands of the modern world and the way it does so will determine whether its economic potential is realised. Indonesia will undergo an important transition in leadership at a time of rapid growth and social change. The relationship between China and Taiwan is evolving in response to political change in both countries, and in a direction that is causing widespread unease in the region about China's military intentions.

The geopolitical structure of Asia has already changed significantly in response to the end of the Cold War and the collapse of Soviet power. The predictable geopolitical alignments of the last two decades have disappeared. In the past, the Sino-Soviet split between Asia's two great continental powers; the hostile relations between Japan and the Soviet Union; suspicions between China and Japan; the dominance of US military power; and the clear alignment of several other regional countries either with America (for example, South Korea, Taiwan, the Philippines, Thailand) or with the USSR (for example, Vietnam and India) made the geopolitical architecture of Asia relatively predictable.

As Jim Rohwer observes, this was an unusual coincidence – which has probably disappeared for good – of factors that made for a stable balance of power in a complex and inherently unstable neighbourhood.[25] This relatively stable correlation of forces is about to change. The balance of power in Asia is likely to be less predictable in the future than in the past: international uncertainty and changing structural conditions, whereby the relative power of key actors is likely to change quite rapidly, heralds a new strategic architecture in Asia.

Assessing the relative power of the great powers over the next 10 or 15 years is no easy task. There is insufficient space here to address all the possible permutations, and future trajectories, of great-power interaction.[26] It is sufficient for our purposes to note that there is considerable disagreement even amongst experts on the likely nature of the future power of China and the United States in particular. There seems to be a broad consensus that neither Japan nor India is likely to play a leading role in the new regional order in the next decade or so but there is uncertainty about Russia's potential to regain its great-power status.

Japan is a country with enormous potential, including militarily, but until it demonstrates a greater sense of political maturity it is highly unlikely that the region will easily dispel doubts about Japan's unfortunate past. Even so, there are clear indications that – for the first time since the Second World War – Japan is devising a security policy of its own: one that is not just a reflection of US policy, as has been the case for the last 50 years.

Japan's relations with China promise to be the key strategic uncertainty in the new regional order.[27] There is the potential for intense strategic competition – if not tension and hostility – between these two giants whose history is characterised by hostility and mutual distrust. From the perspective of regional security, a Sino-Japanese relationship that is moderately competitive is preferable to any form of collusion or partnership, which other powers in the region would see as fundamentally threatening because it would undermine the entire strategic balance in the region and effectively promote a major confrontation with the United States. There are probably sufficient historical, cultural and other differences between China and Japan to preclude this.

Short of such an unlikely strategic alignment, China and Japan must come to terms with each other if a sense of order is to prevail in Asia. For this to occur, China has to accept a far more active Japanese role in regional affairs. Japan, however, seems unable to decide how to apply its power in support of regional security. As we have seen in recent crises with regard to North Korea and China–Taiwan, Japanese policy is hesitant and gives its ally the United States no confidence that Japanese military support would be forthcoming in the event of a major regional crisis. Japan still has no clearly defined concept of its national interest and responsibilities in the post-Cold War era. This makes it an unpredictable actor in the emerging regional order.

India is in many ways 'the odd man out'. It has relatively little influence beyond the subcontinent. In the past, its alliance with the USSR and its socialised economic structure left it out of the mainstream of economic advancement in the region. It is now preoccupied with reforming its economy and diversifying its external economic relations. India's economic reforms promise a much more successful economy in the long run and one that – unlike China's – is based on an established democratic, judicial and financial system. However, a long, hard road of reform lies ahead.

The inevitable expansion of China's power will attract India's attention and cause it to look east, to Southeast Asia, for influence. India needs to look at new alignments and the most interesting prospect is for an improvement in relations with the United States: the two largest democracies in the world have never taken each other very seriously, but the challenge of a powerful, authoritarian China might change all that. India must, however, not only reform economically if it is to became a truly great power; it must rise above its obsession with Pakistan, which has narrowed its geopolitical vision for almost half a century.

Unless India can devise a new form of strategic engagement with the wider Asian region, as well as successful economic reforms, it will not play a broader role in the new strategic order in Asia.[28] Serious internal ethnic and religious problems and security preoccupations on the subcontinent threaten to constrain India's potential to play a wider security role. There is a danger that India could become an isolationist and insecure state.[29]

India has no historical international role in Asia to draw on, at least in recent times. Although India is strategically weaker than the other Asian great powers it does not – unlike them – confront any serious challenges to its immediate regional position. This means that, even though strategically weaker than the other large Asian powers, and even though plagued by domestic instability and insecurity, India has greater potential as a power of influence than its indicators would suggest. It could emerge as a useful player in a multipolar Asian balance but it will have to overcome the political and economic constraints that have limited its horizons in the past.

Opinions are highly divided about Russia's future. None of them envisage a Russia emerging any time soon as a major player in the new regional order in Asia. Russia's domestic political and economic problems, as it attempts to make the transition from communism to some form of democracy, will be a major preoccupation for many years. In the longer term, an economically successful Russia, enjoying a participatory democracy, would be a positive force in the emerging new strategic balance in Asia. Its values and basic objectives might then be closer to America's than to those of China.

But if Russia fails in its political and economic reforms it could re-emerge onto the world stage seeking to recover its lost status and influence.[30] It could then, once more, disrupt the peace in Asia by reasserting its historical hostility to Japan, aligning itself with an anti-Western China, and reclaiming its lost territories in Central Asia. Such a revanchist Russia would present a much greater challenge to regional order than China. And yet the possibility of another fundamental challenge emerging from Russian military power scarcely rates a mention in most strategic analyses of the region.

The argument here is not that Russia is likely in the short term to be a putative challenger to regional order but that, in our longer-term planning, such a contingency cannot be dismissed because of its potentially grave consequences. Russia's educational and technological capacities, as well as its natural resource base and geographical spread, would make it a much more threatening power than China – including globally – were it to seek once more the role of challenger to the status quo. Traditional Russian nationalism and xenophobia have always supported strong military forces.[31]

If events go badly in Russia over the coming decade and the autocratic state revives, the passing of the Cold War may only be a short interregnum to a new era of tension and confrontation. For Asia, a powerful, nationalist Great Russian state that sought to reclaim its 'rightful' role in the region as the greatest Eurasian power would pose a fundamental challenge to regional order.

In the medium term, however, it is the future of China and the United States that generates most discussion. The current security debate in the region embraces a wide range of both optimistic and pessimistic views about the roles and influence of these two key players. China is seen variously as both an expansionist, ambitious power and an essentially defensive country that will continue to give priority to economic modernisation. The United States is sometimes viewed as a power in relative decline that is in the process of withdrawal from the region, or, alternatively, as the only superpower remaining in the world and one which intends to maintain a forward-based military presence in Asia to defend both its growing economic interests and its alliances. Clearly, such different views cannot all be correct but the fact that these extremes of analysis exist about the two most influential powers in Asia only serves to underscore the uncertain strategic outlook.

There is no more important question in Asia than the future role of China. Almost nothing is so destabilising as the arrival of a new economic and military power on the international scene. There can be no 'Pacific century' until China, now increasingly the central preoccupation of the region, emerges in a new political form and behaves in a manner that instils confidence.

China's influence will grow over the next decade or two, as its economic strength develops. The Chinese leadership does not shy away from the idea of China soon being a world power and it naturally expects to play a leading role in Asia. China is not a status quo power: it seeks a greater role for itself in world affairs and it does not fully accept the legitimacy of the present international order.

Estimates vary considerably about the size of China's economy, but China seems to be rapidly returning to the position it held in the eighteenth century, and for most of recorded history, as the world's largest economy. It is generally considered that China's GNP is greatly understated by official statistics. On the basis of purchasing power parity, the International Monetary Fund calculates that China's economy is at present only slightly smaller than Japan's. Some internationally respected experts are suggesting that China's economy will eventually surpass that of the United States.[32] All seem to agree that by 2010 China will have Asia's largest economy.

If these predictions are correct – and if we assume the continuing integrity of the Chinese state[33] – they herald the emergence of a new international power. An economically powerful, unified China (which will include Hong Kong and, eventually, Taiwan) will bring about a remarkable shift in the international distribution of power. Whatever the precise calculations of China's future economic size, the growth of China's economic power will affect all the other Asian powers. No contemporary issue is more important than the rise of China. Yet the international community is giving inadequate consideration to the arrival of a powerful China and to whether China's current attempts to expand its influence reflect aggressive intentions or are simply the natural consequences of rising power.[34]

China is the one power with the potential to contend eventually with the United States for leadership in the region. An economically powerful China will introduce new challenges, as well as new opportunities, into Asia. What sort of challenge will the region face from China? Will China be largely benign and cooperative, or will it present a military threat? Will the United States and Japan perceive China as aiming for strategic dominance of the region?

These questions are difficult to address because fundamental economic, political and social changes are still occurring in China. Coping with China's growth is as much a problem for China's rulers as it is for outside powers. But as China moves towards attaining great economic power the political implications of its potential for displacing Japan (and, in the longer term, the United States) are enormous.

China is evidently a state in transition, oscillating between confidence and insecurity. The sense of confidence is growing because, for the first time in centuries, China faces no palpable threat. As a result, it is becoming more assertive. China has a starkly realist approach to its key international interests, as demonstrated recently in its attitudes to Taiwan, the Spratly Islands and nuclear testing. China does not have to become a militarily expansionist country in order to be able to exert influence, through a local preponderance of power, in neighbouring Northeast Asia and Southeast Asia.

Whether China will be peaceful or aggressive in the next decade or two is far from certain. What is clear, however, is that the security dynamics of Asia will be transformed dramatically by the emergence of China as a power. Even a peaceful China will be able to exploit access to its huge market for political purposes.

A stable, secure and unified China is essential for regional peace. To ensure regional balance, the constructive engagement of China in the emerging regional order must be encouraged.[35] But, with the prospect that a strong China with considerable military power will emerge within the next decade or two, the middle powers in the region will want to see power balanced in the region – hence their interest in a continuing US presence.

America, however, is undergoing a process of profound change. At home, it faces enormous social and economic problems, and its foreign policy lacks an overarching vision. The popular and elite consensus that existed about the threat from the Soviet Union has gone. In many ways, Americans are returning to the divisions and debates about their role in the world that are as old as the Republic itself. However, Americans have no evident threat on which to focus their energies.

President Clinton's agenda, which gives priority to restoring economic competitiveness and promoting democracy and human rights overseas, is not a recipe for successful leadership in Asia. America's friends and allies in Asia fear that the United States has got its priorities wrong: that it is basing its foreign policy on the idea of 'a democratic zone of peace', the spread of human rights and a concept of economic interdependence that will render impossible serious security competition or great-power challenges.[36] If this is the case, the United States will not be prepared with a realistic strategy to advance its interests in Asia's emerging multipolar great-power competition.[37]

At the same time, there is general recognition almost everywhere in the region (except for China and North Korea) that America is the single most important player in ensuring that strategic equilibrium is maintained. A precipitate withdrawal of US forces from Asia or a marked worsening of US–Japanese relations would have serious security ramifications. It would greatly accelerate the current arms build-up in the region and undermine regional confidence in US ability to support balance-of-power norms.

Yet, at the same time, a rising sense of Asian identity also makes reliance on the United States less attractive. Asia's security environment will be shaped in the future more by the strength of the large Asian powers than by America and its allies.

In the long run it may be difficult for the United States to retain its current level of forces in Asia, particularly if Korea unifies. Southeast Asia is now of reduced security concern to America. Traditional US interests in Europe and its preoccupations with Russia and the Middle East, as well as UN peace-keeping, are obscuring Asia's importance. The United States will remain the dominant global power well into the twenty-first century, but it will have difficulty in responding to the diverse strategic challenges of the post-Cold War era while also attending to its pressing domestic problems.

It is far from certain that the American alliance system in Asia will decay, but America's alliance partners perceive that they will need to do more militarily for themselves. The concept of a global Western strategic community led by the United States has largely gone. Continuing US engagement in Asia now depends on American recognition of the importance of local strategic issues rather than grand ideological containment.

America's stance on trade issues, labour laws and human rights, however, threatens to tear the fabric of the friendship it has with Japan, Thailand, Malaysia and Indonesia, as well as its relations with China and Vietnam. And yet a realist approach would recognise – for example – that a Vietnam that has a good relationship with the United States could be a useful contributor to the regional balance.

The perception of US strength and a continuing American commitment to the security of the region are central to middle-power expectations that a great-power balance can be secured in Asia. As Henry Kissinger has observed, however, at no time in history has America participated in a balance-of-power system.[38] It now needs to take more seriously than ever before great-power challenges in Asia and the distribution of power in the region.

The United States has certainly not reached the point of decline in its military strength relative to other potential contenders in the balance. Many decades will elapse before America's position of military predominance is eroded. Asia without America would be a highly uncertain and dangerous place in which the rivalry between China and Japan might be unleashed. America's friends need to encourage the United States to develop a more robust, realist policy, including militarily, in response to the strategic challenges arising from the new regional order in Asia. And they need to do more to contribute to alliance burden sharing.

## THE RISKS OF STRATEGIC DISCONTINUITY

What, then, are the dangers of a breakdown in the regional order, as a new balance of power is asserted in Asia? This is a difficult question to address because of the great number of different permutations that are possible in a five-power balance and because of different assessments of the future strengths (and weaknesses) of the major powers. The previous part of this chapter illustrated the divergence of views that exist about the rise of China and Japan (and perhaps India) and about the relative decline of Russia (and perhaps the United States). The emergence of strong middle powers – such as a unified Korea, Taiwan, Vietnam, Thailand, Indonesia and Pakistan – is a further complicating factor in any consideration of future regional order. The potential for a chain reaction of events unfolding in a part of the world where there are deep-seated historical enmities and distrust; outstanding territorial, religious and ideological differences; and growing military capabilities, is another factor.

These central security issues need to be seen, first of all, against the prevailing norms of order in Asia. Most Asian leaders have a genuine interest in securing a prolonged peace in which the prosperity of their countries can be developed free from external (and internal) threats. The Asian approach to regional security and dispute settlement is not, however, to resort to European or American models of legal agreements strengthened by concepts of military transparency. The preference is for informality, setting difficult disputes to one side for later resolution, and achieving consensus in negotiations. In terms of the future balance of power in Asia, this style may well result in a less structured approach to multilateral security. Harry Harding has described this as employing a 'polite balance of power'.[39]

It is quite possible that such informal arrangements might lead, in the Asian context, to a set of tacit understandings to refrain from particular types of action that do not comply with regional norms of behaviour. In any event, a five-sided balance provides for numerous checks and balances and for changing alignments on particular issues. There are sufficient major players in a five-sided balance of power to ensure that a regional hegemon does not emerge. This does, however, require flexibility in alignments and the resolve to resist aggression, territorial expansion and the use of military force. There has to be some doubt whether these attributes exist yet in the region.

In particular, the region has first of all to deal with some serious and unresolved security problems where the use of force could alter the regional balance of power or undermine its stability. These serious unresolved problems include the Korean peninsula, Taiwan and Kashmir. There are other areas of potential dispute in Asia, but none of them risk the involvement of one or more of the major powers or pose the danger of escalation and the use of large-scale force in the same way.

In none of these cases are there agreements for conflict prevention or confidence-building measures in place or even any comprehensive and reliable early-warning systems for conflict avoidance. In each of these examples armed force has been used, or threatened, in the past and generally on more than one occasion. In the cases of the Korean peninsula, Taiwan and Kashmir the risk of attack with little or no warning is perceived as ever present. Until these tensions are resolved the prospects of a stable region remain uncertain. In these three cases one or more of the great powers might use military force on a large scale and risk escalation of conflict – including the use of tactical nuclear weapons.

None of this leads to a cataclysmic view of the region: war between the major powers is improbable. Barring miscalculation in key trouble spots such as Taiwan, the Korean peninsula and Kashmir, the use of military force is likely to be confined to the outbreak of lower level conflict between and within states and in contested maritime areas, such as the South China Sea.

The use of instruments short of armed force, however, may well increase. Patterns of dominance and dependence may emerge, as well as the use of coercive levers, as the great powers accrue more power and multilateral institutions prove to be weak in the face of regional crises. Where states manifest an asymmetry of interests, and there are no strong regional security mechanisms in place, it will be very difficult to construct multilateral security regimes that are workable. Under these conditions, the balance of power will be the main security determinant of Asia for the foreseeable future. The danger is that there will be no agreed norms to regulate the growing strength of the Asian great powers in the twenty-first century.

The most important question here for the middle and smaller powers will be how to avert a slide in regional order (by this is meant not only the use of military force but any tendency to threaten or demonstrate the use of force, as well as the use of coercive measures – such as blockade). A breakdown in regional order could be heralded by actions challenging international norms of behaviour such as these. It could also be ushered in by one or more great powers becoming used to the idea that, short of the use of force, it could use its political power and economic leverage to effectively make neighbouring smaller powers comply with its point of view. A fundamental strategic aim for the middle powers in Asia, in this respect, is to avoid the region as a whole – or particular sub-regions such as Southeast Asia – being dominated by any one great power.

Such an occurrence could be abetted by any one of a number of strategic discontinuities, which appear improbable at present but which are not unthinkable. Some examples that come to mind are set out in Table 8.1. This is by no means a comprehensive list of various contingencies, but it illustrates a spectrum of potential future events. Such an indicative list is helpful in thinking about, and ascribing probabilities to, the risks of strategic discontinuity in an era of uncertainty. In this way, likely theatres of conflict can be identified, along with plausible objectives and strategies of protagonists.[40]

The aim should be to identify what Paul Davis calls unscheduled uncertainties in the form of potential shocks to the regional order: he identifies these as potential developments that are quite plausible, but that would never make it onto a list of approved best-estimate threats.[41] The approach here, first, is to encourage a broad view of the regional security environment rather than one focused on one or a very few threats. Second, it should encourage an attitude of environment shaping rather than the more passive attitude of seeking to react to threats as they arise.[42] Third, the approach is especially helpful for breaking out of standard mind-sets and encouraging non-linear, unorthodox thinking.[43]

The dominance of uncertainty in Asia's strategic outlook means that priority must be given to shaping the strategic environment rather than searching for particular threats. The creation of a more cooperative and transparent strategic community in the region, together with a policy of deterring any challenges to acceptable norms of behaviour, should be key elements in any such shaping policy. In defence planning terms, the dominance of uncertainty will mean that planners will want to hedge their bets: deterrence against potential shocks to the regional order will mean planning a base force larger than one designed only for one or two credible contingencies and creating a reconstitution base that produces high-readiness reserves.[44]

*Table 8.1: Potential Discontinuities*

---

- the re-emergence of an anti-Western, powerful Russia, possibly aligned with China;
- an expansionist China;
- a unified Korea;
- the United States is asked to leave Japan and Korea;
- an isolationist America;
- war between India and Pakistan, possibly involving the use of nuclear weapons;
- war between North and South Korea, involving America and its allies;
- a Chinese military blockade of Taiwan;
- conflict in the South China Sea, involving China and one or more ASEAN countries;
- Russian military operations in Central Asia, possibly involving conflict with Iran and, perhaps, China;
- conflict between India and China;
- limited territorial conflict between China and Russia, Russia and Japan, South Korea and Japan, China and Japan, or some of the ASEAN countries;
- major upheaval in an ASEAN country – for example, Indonesia.

---

In the longer term, however, shaping the regional strategic environment will need to consider more formalised mechanisms for regional arms control and conflict resolution. An Asia that depends solely on a balance of power (however 'polite') and on the defence preparations of individual states will not necessarily be a stable region that manages strategic change in an orderly manner.


A NEW STRATEGIC ARCHITECTURE?

The only realistic alternative to a balance of power is some form of strategic community. This can be highly structured and formal, as in the case of the NATO alliance, or it can be loose-knit and informal, as with ASEAN. Strategic communities can give firm commitments to mutual assistance in the event of armed attack or, more commonly, they provide for consultation. For example, the ASEAN Treaty of Amity and Cooperation, in Chapter IV, says that the contracting parties agree to refrain from the threat or use of force to settle disputes and instead resort to the consultative mechanisms provided by the Treaty.

The current strategic architecture of Asia is, however, very varied and there is no unifying organisation or mechanism, other than APEC (which is primarily an economic multilateral organisation, but excludes Russia, Vietnam and India) and the ARF (which is a more inclusive political security organisation that is developing dialogue and confidence building but not, as yet, conflict resolution or arms control mechanisms). These two organisations, as promising as they are, will take some considerable time to develop a sense of cohesion and confidence before they can embark on concrete security related measures – as distinct from declaratory statements of good intentions.

In the meantime, the security architecture of the region will continue to consist of a complex interweaving of unilateral defence policies, bilateral alliances and agreements, plurilateral arrangements (such as the Five-Power Defence Arrangements involving Malaysia, Singapore, Australia, New Zealand and the United Kingdom), and multilateral organisations (such as ASEAN, the ASEAN Post-Ministerial Conference and the ARF). This complex strategic architecture is likely to persist for some considerable time given the uncertain strategic outlook in the region. Sovereign states are unlikely to change substantially their self-reliant defence policies or proven bilateral alliances in favour of some loose multilateral organisation that does not provide for their security. The strategic diversity of Asia will work against any collective security organisation: and the history of collective security organisations in the region – for instance SEATO – has hardly been encouraging.

The tendency to favour an approach that includes cooperation at all levels of interstate relations in part reflects the fact that the region is in an era of transition 'in which it is felt that there is no need to choose any or only one mode of cooperation'.[45] As the Asia Society has observed correctly, this emphasis on unilateral, bilateral and multilateral approaches to the security of Asia reflects the realities of a region in which countries jealously guard their national sovereignty and where bilateral relationships (particularly in Northeast Asia) have, at least for the past 50 years, been some of the strongest in the world.[46] Regional multilateralism along the lines of the European Union is not a foreseeable prospect.

Rather, the emerging geostrategic architecture of the region will be a complex amalgam of great-power balancing, bilateral alliances (some of which may decline in importance), unilateral defence policies (which will increase in importance) and emerging multilateral mechanisms. The latter may offer the best prospect for shaping the regional security environment in the longer term. But too much should not be expected too soon: a formal collective security structure is not at all likely. Instead, the region will develop, in the Asian way, a form of loose, informal and ad hoc multilateralism. Preserving the existing international order – against the shifting relative power of the major powers and of key middle powers – will be the main aim. Clearly, such an objective will be problematic in view of the potential for large strategic shifts – if not shocks and discontinuities – in the regional strategic balance. The ARF may eventually have the power to solve concrete security problems, such as the resolution of border and territorial disputes. This is not likely to occur any time soon. In the meantime, Asia will undergo a potentially dangerous transition period as a new regional strategic balance unfolds. In these circumstances, the priority for middle powers, such as Australia, will be to manage the strategic environment so that a slide in regional order does not occur.[47]

## NOTES

1. See also Richard L. Kugler, 'Nonstandard Contingencies for Defense Planning' in Paul K. Davis (ed.), *New Challenges for Defense Planning* (RAND, Santa Monica, 1994), pp.165–96.
2. Joseph S. Nye, 'Conflicts after the Cold War', *The Washington Quarterly*, Winter 1996, p.9.
3. See, for example, Francis Fukuyama, *The End of History and the Last Man* (Free Press, New York, 1992); Samuel P. Huntington, *The Third Wave: Democratization in the Late Twentieth Century* (University of Oklahoma Press, Norman, 1991); and James L. Richardson, 'Asia-Pacific: The Case for Geopolitical Optimism', *The National Interest*, Winter 1994/95, pp.28–39. For an Asian view, see Muthiah Alagappa, *Democratic Transition in Asia: The Role of the International Community* (East-West Center, Honolulu, 1994).
4. See Australia's Defence White Paper, *Defending Australia* (Australian Government Publishing Service, Canberra, 1994), especially chapters 1 and 2.
5. See Kishore Mahbubani, 'The West and the Rest', *The National Interest*, Summer 1992, pp.3–12; 'The United States: Go East, Young Man', *The Washington Quarterly*, Spring 1994, pp.5–23; and 'The Pacific Impulse', *Survival*, Spring 1995, pp.105–20; also Yoichi Funabashi, 'The Asianisation of Asia', *Foreign Affairs*, November/December 1993, pp.75–85.
6. See Francois Heisbourg, 'Old Tensions and New Risks in the Asia-Pacific Region', Second Asia-Pacific Defence Conference, Singapore, 24 February 1994; and David D. Hale, *Global Economic Integration After the Cold War* (Kemper Financial Companies Inc, Chicago, September 1994), pp.12, 20–6.
7. Stuart Harris, 'The Economic Aspects of Pacific Security', *Asia's International Role in the Post-Cold War Era*, Adelphi Paper No. 275 (Brassey's for the IISS, London, 1993), Part I.

8. The Asia-Pacific region is defined here as South Asia, Northeast Asia, Southeast Asia and the Southwest Pacific. It includes the United States.

9. Gareth Evans and Paul Dibb, *Australian Paper on Practical Proposals for Security Cooperation in the Asia-Pacific Region* (Department of Foreign Affairs and Trade and Strategic and Defence Studies Centre, Canberra, 1994).

10. Desmond Ball, 'Arms and Affluence: Military Acquisitions in the Asia-Pacific Region', *International Security*, Winter 1993–94, pp.88–9.

11. Raju G.C. Thomas, 'Secessionist Movements in South Asia', *Survival*, Summer 1994, pp.92–114.

12. *SIPRI Yearbook 1993* (Oxford University Press, Oxford, 1993), pp.119–30.

13. See Christopher Layne, 'Kant or Cant: The Myth of the Democratic Peace', *International Security*, Autumn 1994, pp.5–49; Edward D. Mansfield and Jack Snyder, 'Democratization and War', *Foreign Affairs*, May–June 1995, pp.79–97; Edward D. Mansfield and Jack Snyder, 'Democratization and the Danger of War', *International Security*, Summer 1995, pp.5–38; and Lucian W. Pye, *Asian Power and Politics: The Cultural Dimensions of Authority* (Harvard University Press, Cambridge MA, 1985).

14. Robert A. Scalapino, *The Last Leninists: The Uncertain Future of Asia's Communist States* (Center for Strategic and International Studies, Washington DC, 1992), p.79.

15. *The Military Balance 1995–96* (Oxford University Press for the IISS, London, 1995), pp.265–9.

16. Ball, 'Arms and Affluence', p.103.

17. *Strategic Survey 1993–1994* (Brassey's for the IISS, London, 1994), pp.41–2.

18. Layne, 'The Myth of the Democratic Peace', p.48.

19. Paul Dibb, *Towards a New Balance of Power in Asia*, Adelphi Paper No. 295 (Oxford University Press for IISS, Oxford, 1995), p.23.

20. For a comprehensive discussion of British and German policies in this regard in nineteenth-century Europe, see Carsten Holbraad, *The Concert of Europe* (Longman Group, London, 1970).

21. Richard K. Betts, 'Wealth, Power and Instability', *International Security*, Winter 1993–94, p.36.

22. Paul Kennedy, *The Rise and Fall of the Great Powers* (Fontana Press, London, 1989), pp.xxvii, 693–8.

23. *Ibid.*, pp.xxiv, 566–7.

24. Robert Gilpin, *War and Change in World Politics* (Cambridge University Press, Cambridge, 1981), chapter 3.

25. Jim Rohwer, *Asia Rising* (Nicholas Brealey Publishing Ltd, London, 1996), p.305.

26. For a longer study see the author's *Towards a New Balance of Power in Asia*, especially pp.26–38.

27. *Ibid.*, pp.31–2; see also *Asia's Global Power: China-Japan Relations in the 21st Century* (Australian Department of Foreign Affairs and Trade, East Asia Analytical Unit, Canberra, 1996).

28. *Ibid.*, p.34.

29. Shekhar Gupta, *India Redefines Its Role*, Adelphi Paper No. 293 (Oxford University Press for the IISS, Oxford, 1995), p.65.

30. See Georgi Arbatov, 'Eurasia Letter: A New Cold War?', *Foreign Policy*, Summer 1994, pp.90–103; and William C. Bodie, 'The Threat to America from the Former USSR', *Orbis*, Autumn 1993, pp.509–23.

31. Mary C. Fitzgerald, 'The Russian Military's Strategy for "Sixth Generation" Warfare', *Orbis*, Summer 1994, p.476, argues that there is a strong civil-military consensus reflecting a continuing, disproportionate emphasis on military power as the basis for Russia's international status.

32. See Nicholas R. Lardy, *China in the World Economy* (Institute for International Economics, Washington DC, April 1994); and William H. Overholt, *China: The Next Economic Superpower* (Weidenfeld & Nicolson, London, 1993).

33. This chapter does not address the issue of an unstable, fissiparous China. For a discussion of this possibility, see Gerald Segal, 'Tying China into the International System', *Survival*, Summer 1995, pp.60–73 and *China Changes Shape: Regionalism and Foreign Policy*, Adelphi Paper No. 287 (Brassey's for the IISS, London, 1994).

34. See Nicholas D. Kristhof, 'The Rise of China', *Foreign Affairs*, November/December 1993, pp.60–1.

35. Richard L. Grant, 'China and Its Asian Neighbours: Looking Toward the Twenty-first Century', *The Washington Quarterly*, Winter 1994, p.68.

36. Layne, 'The Myth of the Democratic Peace', pp.45–9.

37. *Ibid.*, p.49.

38. Henry Kissinger, *Diplomacy* (Simon & Schuster, New York, 1994), p.22.

39. Harry Harding, 'A Chinese Colossus?', *Journal of Strategic Studies*, September 1995, pp.24–32.

40. Paul K. Davis, 'Protecting the Great Transition' in Davis (ed.), *New Challenges for Defense Planning*, p.135.

41. *Ibid.*, p.136.

42. *Ibid.*, p.137.

43. *Ibid.*

44. *Ibid.*, p.151.

45. *Prospects for International Cooperation in Northeast Asia* (Asia Society, New York, 1996), p.7.

46. *Ibid.*

47. For a discussion of an appropriate security policy for middle powers in a changing balance of power, see Dibb, *Towards a New Balance of Power in Asia*, pp.56–69.

# 9 'Enlitening' China?
Gerald Segal

The rise of China poses perhaps the most far-reaching challenge to the international status quo. While there is much that can be done to engage China, it is unclear what policies might constrain China's undesired activities. China is, and increasingly will be constrained by the need to become interdependent with the outside world, but interdependence is not enough. In the long-term the only effective constraint on great powers is a wider process of liberalism that turns them into Lite powers. If China is to be 'enlitened', then it will be both through some of the features of interdependence, but also through a firm constraint on its unwanted activity while it is in the long and uncertain process of turning Lite.

## LEARNING TO ADAPT

There are a number of different ways in which we can attempt to understand Chinese behaviour. Alastair Johnston's struggle with the distinction between 'learning' and 'adaptation' in Chinese policy is a valiant attempt to tackle what is essentially the question of whether China has come to see the common sense of real interdependence, or whether it has merely been forced to adjust to superior force while it is still relatively weak.[1] There are, of course, a number of problems in any such attempt to divide Chinese action into 'learning' or 'adaptation'. It can be argued that even those states who now seem to embrace the postmodern sense of interdependence and reduced sovereignty did so initially out of a sense of the futility of confronting superior force. Do the states of the Atlantic like having their economies swept by the force of the global financial markets and do they not wish they could restrain those forces? Do they enjoy being Lite powers who can barely use military power, even in their own backyard? It is far from clear that the states of the developed world accept their postmodern condition because they have learned to see that it is a better system.[2]

What seems most likely is that the developed world has learned to adapt to seemingly inexorable realities. Modern great powers have become Lite powers in the sense that they have undergone deep structural change because of powerful social, economic and political forces. They adapted to the forces of change in advanced capitalism and pluralist democratic systems. If they were to prosper and remain free, they had to open their economies and social systems to outside influences and surrender key aspects of control over their economic, social and foreign policies. These changes are not just manifest in open trading economies or global media companies, but it is also evident in the aversion to the use of military force and the development of small, professional armed forces. The former heavyweight powers of the Atlantic world (and Japan) have become Lite powers in what looks like the inevitable path of development for rich and free people.

This apparent digression is relevant to China. The most obvious connection is the conclusion that if other great powers eventually learned to adapt and became Lite, then we should expect no less from China. It is unlikely that China will embrace the powers of economic interdependence and enjoy the loss of sovereignty that is part of the process, but in the long term it cannot have prosperity without becoming Lite. If China wants to become rich it will eventually not only be forced to adapt to interdependence, it will also become enlitened.

Before the critics erupt in cries of 'Western determinism' and denounce this view as 'pidgin scholarship', let us acknowledge that each country adapts somewhat differently to the process of modernisation and democratisation.[3] As Francis Fukuyama has noted, some 20 per cent of the character of the modern political economy of developed states is probably the result of 'culture'.[4] But the overwhelming determinants of the character of developed states are the result of the deep structural forces of modernisation and democratisation. The lesson for China, as it was for Japan, is that if it is to modernise, it will democratise, and as it does both, it will be forced to adapt to the international system.

Nevertheless, it may be that China, by virtue of its size and grand traditions has a greater ability to change the international system as it joins, and therefore a greater ability to resist the deep structural forces.[5] When Japan, with its population a tenth the size of China, became a major player in the global economy, it accounted for less than 10 per cent of world GDP. As China joins the international economy, it is somewhat larger, although still roughly the size of the modern Japanese economy (in purchasing power parity terms). In terms of military power, China is far less impressive than the Soviet Union when it tried, and failed, to transform.

## ADAPTATIONS SO FAR

The clothing worn by Chinese leaders and many of the Chinese people has changed out of all recognition in the past 20 years. The days are long gone when China could be described as the 'nation of blue ants'. Also long gone are the days when the 'Mao suit' was *de rigueur* for Chinese leaders and even many others in the developing world.[6] Although we should avoid the temptation to get carried away with the significance of these sartorial adjustments, they do signify a degree of surrender to forces of global socialisation. To be sure, there still are some world leaders, most notably in the African and Arab worlds, that turn up at international gatherings in local dress, but East Asians (less so in South Asia) have more or less abandoned the practice. The batik shirts on display at the APEC meeting in Bali were so much derided because they were obviously unconvincing symbols of a supposedly common Asianness (and informality). The standard dress for these leaders, whether around a conference table or on the golf course, is best described as mid-Atlantic in origin. When Chinese leaders choose, as they still do from time to time, to wear a 'Mao suit', they are well understood to be making a statement about conserving basic values, usually of a Marxist kind. Thus the change in dress is still symbolically important, still resisted in some quarters, and yet still unavoidable for Chinese leaders in the modern world.

The standard dress for Chinese in China is probably less explicable in such overtly political terms. What seems to have happened is that urban Chinese are more able to break the once rigidly applied strictures of a Communist Party state. As their incomes rise, and they come into greater contact (mostly through the media) with the outside world, they seek to express their individuality in their clothes, and they have the income to afford new attire and hairstyles. The process is far from universal in China, for the majority of the people still live in the countryside and their habits (although perhaps no longer their tastes) in clothing have barely changed. But what is clear is that there is a process of modernisation in the way the Chinese people appear, and it is in the direction set by the forces of globalisation.[7]

One hastens to add that because so much of developed East Asia has already adopted these styles, most Chinese think of the styles as more modern Asian than derived from the Atlantic world. Indeed, the strength of the process of modernisation is probably attributable to an important extent to the fact that other Asians are more easily accepted as role models and that these wealthier Asians have no particular problem in wearing designs set in some distant way by the fashion houses of the global market economy (including the designers of Tokyo). In short, as Chinese modernise, they become more like the rest of us in the developed world. At least as far as clothing is concerned, they do it because they want to, not because they are forced. Such is the power of the forces of global society.

A second adaptation is the extent to which China has opened itself to international tourism. China is now the world's most popular tourist destination, and even though there has been much exaggeration about the impact of tourism on local culture, there is a steady drip of influence from constantly seeing richer and very different people behaving in distinctive ways. Most tourism is packaged, and often tightly, so risks of 'contamination' are reduced. The activities of tall, bearded, big nosed foreigners may be dismissed as zoological oddities, but the swarms of ethnic Chinese visitors who behave like other middle-class big noses makes a greater impact in the long term. When the ethnic Chinese visitor speaks in support of economic choice and political pluralism, it is harder for mainland Chinese to dismiss the powerful forces as decadent Western exports.

Is China forced to accept tourists? In truth they willingly did so because it was a way to attract foreign investment. Deng Xiaoping was not terribly worried about the 'flies' that come in through open doors, and he was persuaded of the financial benefits of investments in the service sector. Building better hotels and allowing more 747s ensured that the even more important business investors would be happier to come to China. Foreign investment does not depend on tourism, but it is part of the climate that makes foreigners confident about China. If China were to suddenly restrict the numbers of tourists, the business climate would be adversely affected. In that respect, China, with all its grand history that is so attractive to foreigners, had to open up to tourism if it wanted to modernise.

A third, essentially social transformation, is China's relative openness to foreign culture. Of course, China is much less open than OECD countries, but then openness, even in developed countries, is relative and still the subject of much debate (for instance, France or Japan). Nevertheless, in comparison to 20 years ago, Chinese can see more foreign films, television, music and art. As we have already suggested, the impact is perhaps greatest from the portion of foreign culture that comes from modernised and wealthy Asians, and especially those who are ethnically Chinese. Canto-pop is more popular than heavy metal. But even the hedonism of modern East Asian Chinese culture undermines authoritarian values and Marxist economics.[8]

The power of the challenge posed by foreign culture is well understood in Beijing, even if the nature of the challenge is harder to grasp. Hence the periodic efforts to clamp down on the Chinese artistic scene, including dissident writers and film makers. Hence also the attempt to restrict access to the Internet or to limit satellite broadcasting. Even economically developed states like Singapore still try to restrict the power of external cultural influences. While some restrictions are possible, especially if Chinese authorities can work with the foreign broadcasters (such as Rupert Murdoch), the long-term trend is that the process is unstoppable and powerful. Beijing can succeed in bumping BBC Television news from foreign satellites, but *Baywatch* and soap operas are let through and in the end are far more corrosive of authoritarian values.[9]

Was China forced to accept such limits on its ability to determine the culture and values of its citizenry? To a large extent the answer is yes. The Internet is increasingly a necessary tool for companies operating in the global economy or intellectuals keeping abreast of global trends, ideas and data. Access can be restricted, but not for long or with an effective comprehensiveness. Satellite broadcasters can be stopped from making much money if they are unable to work with local cable companies and arrange for payment. But where foreign broadcasts can change local tastes, for example in southern China that receives Hong Kong and Taiwanese influences, the local broadcasters must respond to popular demand. As these 'pernicious' demands spread to neighbouring and eventually most other major cities, then local broadcasters do become anxious to strike a deal with foreigners. These forces worked in Eastern Europe and the Chinese autocrats are right to fear that they are no more successful in limiting the power of foreign ideas and values.

Despite the signs that China's civil society is gradually changing under the relentless pressure of these foreign forces, progress in entrenching deep structural change is often uneven. One key area is the possible emergence of new legal systems. In some technical areas, such as methods of accounting and measurement, China has made good progress in reaching international standards. There are often serious reasons to doubt the reliability of Chinese data and the inclination to 'cook the books' and produce bogus figures is clearly very high. Chinese officials know that foreign investors want reliable indicators of results, productivity and profit. They need a real sense of trends in inflation, unemployment or the money supply. There can be little doubt that China has become more transparent in this respect, but there is still a long road to travel. China's inflation figures do not add up, even using official data. Corruption has grown so rife that international rankings of such ills now put China among the top three.[10]

The cheekier economists will tell you that corruption can be seen as merely a useful market mechanism at a time of major economic transformation. But foreign investors are increasingly worried that there is much more sham than reality to China's supposed move to a more regular international legal standard. Compare India and China. Both are well known for official corruption, but at least Kentucky Fried Chicken in India had recourse to the courts to reign in corrupt or arbitrary officials, while

McDonald's in Beijing had to succumb in a system essentially without recourse to law.

The key test of China's adaptation to international legal norms is not so much whether they adopt Western laws, for other East Asians have adapted legal systems in much more subtle ways. The real test is whether there is blind justice – whether there are clear rules objectively adjudicated. In this respect, China has so far resisted significant change. Where it has adopted foreign rules and norms, it has clearly done so because that is what is required by foreigners to do business. China has been forced to adapt, but there are still severe limits to the process of adaptation.

Of course, China has become far more open to international trade. In the first decade of reform, from 1978, China's foreign trade more than tripled (GNP increased by 250 per cent). Total trade in 1995 was ten times that in 1980. Trade as a ratio of GDP roughly doubled since the economic reforms began in earnest 15 years ago. Whether or not the ratio of trade to GDP continues to increase depends primarily on the extent to which barriers to internal trade come down fast enough to allow China's internal market to develop. So far, it has often been easier, especially for coastal provinces, to trade with the outside world than with the rest of China.[11]

Total foreign investment in 1978–82 was about US$1 million, and increased to US$4 million in 1991. But by 1993 the level of foreign investment also increased ten-fold, with some 85 per cent coming from ethnic Chinese outside China. For much of the 1990s China received more foreign direct investment than any other developing country, and in 1995 it ranked second in the world to the United States as a host country for foreign investment. Foreign-funded enterprises account for more than 14 per cent of total Chinese industrial output (1994) and they produce 40 per cent of Chinese exports. According to the Chinese Ministry of Trade, nearly half the Chinese economy is 'related to the international market'.[12]

China was not forced to open up to international trade in the sense that it was in the Opium Wars. But China has grown to understand, in large part because of the trends in its home region in East Asia, that autarky could not be a route to prosperity. China was not compelled to learn that lesson or draw those implications (as was North Korea and for a time Albania), but once it decided that it wanted greater prosperity, it was 'forced' to open up. There was no necessary recipe for how, or how much it would open itself to international trade and finance.

It is important to remember that the degree of connection with the outside world varies a great deal in different parts of China. The growth in GDP and trade and investment are far from synchronous, with some regions doing well with relatively less foreign investment. The decentralisation of economic policy has meant that different parts of China have different degrees of commitment to interdependence, and those who are interdependent, are tied to very different trade partners. Thus it makes little sense to discuss the impact of interdependence on China without understanding that in many important respects, there are different Chinas and different forms of interdependence.[13]

The results of these economic reforms, the new foreign connections, and the decentralisation are well known. Coastal China grew faster than the hinterland, setting up major disputes over resources and uneven prosperity. Different regions integrated more closely with their foreign neighbours and in some cases trade grew faster with the outside world than with other Chinese provinces. Central government lost important levers of economic control as regions and entrepreneurs were newly empowered by their access to the outside world. These risks of decentralisation are sometimes exaggerated, but what is clear is that they result from an economic reform strategy that was necessary in order to effectively open up to the outside world. Beijing is reaping what it sowed. Although Beijing tries to portray itself as in strategic control of this process and working to a blueprint, in reality it is often merely pretending to rule.

Few can doubt that the opening of China to the global economy has had far-reaching consequences for the way in which China is governed. Important elements of sovereignty have irrevocably slipped from the grasp of a once far more centralised authoritarian government. Beijing has serious difficulties controlling the money supply, fiscal policy, reform of state-owned industries and various other key aspects of policy because of this decentralisation. China's foreign policy is also affected, for Beijing cannot implement international accords, such as on intellectual property rights, because it does not control those parts of the economy. For the time being, it still pretends to make such solemn agreements (as do foreigners), even though all concerned know that China cannot make them reality. Neither China, nor even the outside world, seems ready to start dealing with a China that has changed shape.[14]

This is not so much China learning to lose sovereignty, as a China that is not yet ready to acknowledge the consequences of having lost sovereignty by virtue of its decision to engage in economic reform and to open to the global market economy. This is evidence for neither learning nor formal adaptation, but rather an attempt to pretend that it can have the benefits of openness without the consequent loss of control. Real learning and formal adaptation will come later.

In the security sphere China has also made some far-reaching changes of policy. But a change is not necessarily the same thing as accepting the constraints of interdependence. Take for example the issue of China's cessation of support for revolutionary movements. This change of policy is often considered a sign of China's acceptance of the constraints of interdependence. But the evolution of Chinese policy can be read in a different way. China used to support revolutionary movements around the world, and especially in Southeast Asia. When China improved relations with the capitalist world because of its fear of the Soviet Union, it began to dump old revolutionary comrades. The initial motive was geostrategic and only secondarily reinforced by an appreciation that the benefits of international economic relations were unlikely to come if Beijing was trying to foment revolution in its neighbours. It might also be recalled that none of these revolutionary movements were on the brink of success and therefore their abandonment carried few costs. Also, at a time when China was reforming its own view of markets and capitalism, it was illogical to be supporting 'Maoist' radicals.

The change in Chinese policy was in fact far more an assertion of China's new-found faith in a system of sovereign states. Support for revolutionary movements had been an expression of a Marxist world view. The problem with China's conversion to nineteenth-century state sovereignty was that this modernism was increasingly anachronistic in a postmodern world where sovereign states were said to be of fading importance. To be sure, many other states in East Asia which had only recently gained full sovereignty, were (and still are) loathe to move into the postmodern world.[15] But the truth remained that the abandonment of revolutionary movements, as beneficial as it undoubtedly was, was not so much a sign of the acceptance of the constraints of interdependence, as it was the precise opposite.

What about arms control? It is said that China is learning to accept the constraints of interdependence and the need to surrender sovereignty because it has signed important arms control agreements. China joined the NPT, the Chemical Weapons Convention, the Biological Weapons Convention, takes part in the United Nations Conventional Arms Register and signs confidence-building measure agreements with India and Russia. Is China learning that true security is interdependent and that it must agree to international inspections and in fact a surrender of sovereignty?

Alastair Johnston's careful study of this issue revealed little in Chinese behaviour that could be accurately described as learning.[16] Of course he found much evidence of Chinese adaptation to the realities of power in international security. China will sign arms control agreements with neighbours when the agreement is in its favour. India accepted the line of control as China had wanted. Where Russia and China have reached agreement, it has been on Chinese terms. Nothing surprising or difficult here.

Less tractable territorial disputes have not been the subject of arms control agreements. In the South China Sea, China refuses to accept international arbitration or even to accept that anyone else has a claim to sovereignty. The notion of shared sovereignty is nowhere to be found. This is a situation where China feels it has the power to take what it wants, and will do so in time. In 1995 it made more explicit commitments to apply the UN Law of the Sea to the South China Sea, but this was done while asserting that UNCLOS terms would only be applied on the basis of Chinese assertions of sovereignty.[17] And then of course there is Taiwan, where China refuses to contemplate any form of sovereign status for the island. Once again, the picture is of a nineteenth-century approach to sovereignty.

China's signature on multilateral arms control accords offers more support for the notion that Beijing is learning to see security as divisible.[18] For example, the NPT imposes real restrictions on Chinese behaviour. Is this learning, or just China seeing, in good old-fashioned balance of power terms, the virtue of being inside rather than outside the NPT system? What was most notable about the timing of China's decision to join the NPT or to join a moratorium on nuclear weapons testing, was that it was the last of the declared nuclear powers to do so. Is it too cynical to suggest that China did not want the opprobrium attached to being the only power seen to be standing in the way of arms control? If so, things could be worse. China could decide to stand outside the system no matter what – that would be the action of a confident non-status quo power. But China is less confident and more worried about being seen to be a bad citizen. That is not a wholly admirable spirit, but it is better than sheer cussedness.

This sullenly pragmatic spirit of accommodation to the flows of international power is also apparent in the way China comports itself on the United Nations Security Council. Being a supporter of the Victorian value of sovereignty China does not like the notion that the international community, through the Council, can intervene in the domestic affairs of states. When the Council sanctions such intervention, China regularly grumbles, does not participate in the detailed discussions, and then does not block the action through its veto. It regularly expresses qualifications and makes it plain that the international community should not take such intervention as a change in the definition of acceptable international practice. The conclusion could not be more obvious: China is the rear-guard great power when it comes to the erosion of state sovereignty. Nevertheless, China does follow where others lead, for fear of being left behind. Amid the cynicism, there should be reason for some optimism about China's ability to change when given no other option.

AN AGENDA FOR INTERDEPENDENCE

The story so far is of a China that has changed in very important ways because of its far-reaching decision to seek prosperity through economic reform. But that need for economic reform has also required growing inter-dependence with the outside world. This is also a story of reluctant change, for China has resisted the constraints imposed through interdependence. Chinese leaders know full well that the changes they are forced to make are changing Chinese society and the way China is governed. And yet they seem to be locked into a process that requires increasing concessions to the outside world, even as China grows rich. As is the case with already much more Lite powers, China is finding its state power weakens, even though it is growing more prosperous. Chinese leaders had long assumed that as they grew wealthy they would grow stronger in their ability to resist the outside world. It has been the experience of all other modern great powers that eventually they grow to be Lite powers bound by the constraints of being a democracy and living in an interdependent world. The challenge for the non-Chinese world is to ensure that China follows the same path of enlitenment.

The key to enlitening China is a determination to continue to urge China down the path that will lead to economic, social and political liberalisation. Chinese leaders often complain that the West keeps changing the 'goal posts' for acceptance into the international system. Beijing asks (to change the metaphor) for a road map. What follows is a sketch of a road map that should lead both to China's further acceptance into the international community, and the enlitenment of China. But as we work our way through the map, it is important to remember that should China stray from that path, then it will need to be constrained. If China is left unconstrained, it is more likely to undergo the dangerous nationalist stages of enlitenment as seen in earlier phases of German or Japanese power.

## ECONOMIC CHALLENGES

The main method of enlitening China has been, and will continue to be the lure of economic prosperity. A weak and weakening Communist Party knows that it needs to produce the economic goods for its essential legitimacy. China knows that it cannot sustain economic growth without continuing to open up to the outside world. It needs access to foreign markets on favourable terms that comes, for example, from membership in the World Trade Organisation. China must export to the developed world in order to pay for imports of technology, and increasingly the imports of vital food and fuel.[19]

An organisation aspiring, as the WTO does, to be a 'World' body, can see the virtue of Chinese membership. But if only because of the scale of the potential Chinese economic challenge, it is obvious why the developed world wants China to join the WTO under a strict set of rules with an effective dispute settlement mechanism to ensure that China is more changed by the rules than the rules are changed by China. Therefore a key starting point for the enlitening of China is the desire to see China reduce its current average tariff level from 23 per cent to at least 16 per cent (the average level for developing countries).[20] But this is not a one-time concession to the West, the WTO or even to common sense. The opening of the Chinese economy is an ever-demanding and perhaps even never-ending process. As the nature of the Chinese and global economies change, the pressure will always be there for further opening to the outside world. Indeed, it may be that one of the reasons for the seeming softening in the Chinese desire to join the WTO is the recognition that a deal is not a one-time negotiation and the pressure to reform will be constant and intense, even when it is inside the WTO. For those Chinese leaders who feel that concessions to the outside world are just short-term necessary evils, the WTO issue begins to look increasingly like a major trap. Chinese planners are beginning to make more explicit their desire to see international trade bodies, including APEC, as 'non-binding'.[21]

There are already plenty of signs that China is increasingly torn between the need to bend to the global economy and the desire to make the outside world bend its knee to China in order to enjoy the benefits of the Chinese market. Consider the question of the restrictions China imposed in early 1995 on the operations of providers of global financial information such as Reuters and Bloomberg, or its attempts to restrict use of the Internet.[22] China may have been merely trying to ensure that Xinhua reap the profits of such services, or this might have just been a foolish decision taken at a relatively low level, but even if these were the more benign explanations (rather than a desire to censor the outside world), then it is a clear violation of WTO rules. It is either a sign that China is determined to resist the logic of economic interdependence, or that, as Hu Yaobang once said, 'the main foe of the Chinese communists is their own ignorance and their main task is to overcome that ignorance'. Whether the explanation is greed, ignorance or political fear, the result is resistance to the strategy of opening China up to external constraints.

The free trade in financial service information is merely a recent prominent example of a much wider problem concerning China's attempt to resist the power of the global economy in shaping China's domestic system. Similar motives lie behind China's imposition of quotas on items which can be imported and even on the number of companies who can import specific goods. Therefore a key challenge is to reduce the myriad (formal and informal) regulations on how foreigners can access the Chinese market. Many of these regulations are subject to arbitrary and changing rules by corrupt officials.[23] A China that joins the international economy will find all these activities subject to intense external scrutiny. As the Chinese economy continues to grow, and its exports continue to do well in American, EU and Japanese markets, the pressure will increase, not decrease, for further reform.

A related challenge for China is the need to move to a fully convertible currency. By remaining outside the stormy seas of the global financial markets, China believes it can avoid the buffeting of national policy by international pressures. China was only too aware in 1994–5 how the Mexican economy was forced to conform to external dictates and China can see how even developed economies in Europe or East Asia are upset by the power of the global market economy. It is therefore not surprising that China has slowed its move to a full convertible currency. China seems most likely to accept a convertible currency for current account transactions (that is, trade in goods and services) in the near future, but will resist full convertibility (including for capital account transactions). Full convertibility is probably not sustainable without far-reaching reform of the dinosaurs of state-owned industry, and reform of state-owned industries obviously requires far more progress in building a welfare system and in breaking through powerful political logjams.[24] In short, China recognises that opening its economy to the constant and powerful scrutiny of the international money markets will reduce the power of the Chinese state, help push China down the road to being a Lite power subject to the whims of outside forces, and even help reshape Chinese society and lay the basis for a pluralist civil society. The stakes could hardly be higher.

Convertibility of the currency, as with the notion of free trade, in the end requires China to abide by internationally agreed standards and accords. In the days before China barely signed on to any international agreements, it used to be said that when China did sign something, it was good at keeping its promises.[25] But since China has opened up to the outside world, there has developed far more doubt about whether China can be trusted. What concerns Western business leaders is whether China can be trusted to abide by agreements and what pressures can be brought to bear in case China breaks the rules.

The reasons for China's deteriorating record in abiding by agreements are as myriad as the features of its economic and social reform. The complexity of the problem is well evident when assessing why, for example, China has violated the intellectual property rights agreement with the United States in 1995.[26] Even before the accord was signed, it was clear that the central government would have great difficulty in ensuring compliance. Those parts of the Chinese economy that were violating intellectual property rights were in the free-wheeling entrepreneurial sector, often with good connections to the children of senior leaders or key parts of the establishment such as the armed forces. In a chaotically decentralised economy, Beijing found that it had little control and therefore its solemn pledges to the United States could not be implemented, even if there was the will to do so.

It is obvious that there is a great need for China to implement agreements already reached and there are growing doubts about China's ability to ensure compliance on its own territory. Chinese public security units are engaged in piracy and other crimes. Smuggling is so rife, often with official sanction, that the likes of Motorola find that more of their products are smuggled into China (and sold at a cheaper price) than are produced within China. Chinese authorities are unable to provide effective help in controlling the swelling drug trade, nor are they able to stop thugs closing the anti-intellectual piracy office established in China. The list could go on and on, but even a Chinese paper reported in 1995 that China had more trade and investment disputes with foreigners than any other country.[27]

Without a better record of implementation and control over what goes on in its territory, China's signature on a WTO entry accord is equally meaningless. Of course, part of the problem is political. A Beijing that admitted it was having trouble controlling its economy and society, and sought help and understanding from the outside world, might get a more sympathetic hearing than one that pretends to rule but cannot. Beijing is disinclined to be realistic because to do so would be to admit just how much it is constrained by its own reforms and the process of interdependence with the outside world. The result is a China that is harder for the outside world to handle. But it is difficult to see why the outside world should believe the fiction that Beijing tries to sell when it claims to be abiding by international accords. The outside world has an interest in seeing Beijing recognise its more Lite reality and come to terms with its diminished ability to act like an authoritarian state.

## SECURITY CHALLENGES

The international economic agenda will obviously be the most important battleground in the effort to ensure that China becomes enlitened. China can see the benefit of economic interaction and therefore will be more willing to make concessions in order to bring prosperity. A much more difficult battleground will be in the security realm where a China that is growing strong will see less reason to be constrained through interactions with the outside world.

A key concern for the world outside China will be to ensure China does not use force to settle territorial disputes. In 1994 China ejected fishermen from the Philippines from Mischief Reef and established a military facility on the disputed territory. In 1995–6 China closed air and sea-lanes and conducted major military exercises in its attempts to scare Taiwan into backing away from seeking a greater international status. While the specific rights and wrongs of Chinese claims to such territory remains in dispute, what is of concern to the international community is the right to have these issues settled without the resort to force. In the case of the South China Sea, China has agreed not to use force, but it used coercion when ejecting the fishermen. In the case of Taiwan, China even refuses to pledge not to use force.

These issues are crucial tests of the extent to which the world is prepared to constrain China and therefore defend the long-term strategy of enlitenment.[28] It will take time for Chinese society and politics to be changed by the liberalising forces: in the meantime, a firm line needs to be held against the use of force. The outside world need not defend Taiwanese independence or the claims of ASEAN states to the South China Sea, but it does seem more necessary to defend the right to settle such issues peacefully. If no defence is offered, then China will feel that it can use, or threaten the use of force, in order to manage its neighbours. It was in part concern about such a future that led Indonesia and Australia in December 1995 to sign a defence accord, and led Japan in 1996 to formalise its claims under the UN Law of the Sea and include territory disputed with China. It was similar concerns that led the United States to take a firm line against Chinese pressure on Taiwan in 1996 and to reconsider the wisdom of its previous policy of 'strategic ambiguity'. In short, there is a growing concern that China will use force to settle territorial disputes, and that China's neighbours need to resort to the balance of power as well as a long-term trust in economic interdependence in order to constrain Beijing.[29]

In theory there are also possibilities of tying China into arms control accords that might limit its propensity to use force. While China refuses to discuss any such accords in its maritime disputes, much has been made of its willingness to sign confidence-building measures with India and Russia. Yet what is instructive in both these cases is that China has done little to constrain its behaviour and nothing to constrain its realistic territorial claims. India has essentially accepted the 'line of control' as China has long demanded.[30] Russia has given up only its absurd claims that the frontier should run along the Chinese bank of the river, but all other major issues remain unresolved. Where tiny bits of territory have changed hands, it has always been Russia giving up land to China.

The pattern seems to be that where China is strong, it finds it easy to accept accords that confirm its superior position. Where China feels it will grow in relative strength, it sees little point in being constrained through arms control. This pattern is also evident when we consider current arms control negotiations such as the Comprehensive Test Ban Talks. After France and Russia agreed to a zero-level CTBT, China at first demanded exemptions for peaceful nuclear tests, and then capitulated when it was clearly the last power holding up an accord. As was the case in previous arms control accords, China eventually signs on once it is clearly the last power standing in the way.

The case for the virtues of the interdependence of security, which is often used in discussing arms control, has also motivated some attempts to get China to agree to schemes for military transparency. China does comply with the United Nations Conventional Arms Register and it published a 'White Paper' on arms control.[31] The latter revealed nothing that had not appeared in Xinhua press releases and adherence to the UNCAR was hard to avoid when other arms importers and exporters already provided embarrassing detail concerning China. Where transparency measures would really show that China understood the need to be more interdependent about security – for example, on the defence budget – China has been particularly unhelpful.[32]

Neither has China been helpful in international efforts to deal with piracy, illegal migration, or control of the drug trade. These are all areas of increasing concern because Chinese, and even Chinese officials, have become increasingly involved. The causes of these problems, as with the issue of violation of intellectual property rights accords, lie deep in the social, political and economic reforms in China.[33] Decentralisation of authority has made Chinese more able to operate in these illegal manners and more difficult for the authorities to get a grip. Once again, the unwillingness of the Beijing authorities to admit the extent to which they have lost control, is part of the reason why China is so uncooperative in dealing with the challenge. Just like an IPR accord is worthless under these conditions, so would arms control be with China, or even bilateral cooperation, for example in drug control. Only when China can implement such arms control, or seeks the outside world's help in dealing with problems that have internal origins, will China be truly said to have accepted the logic and constraints of interdependence. For the time being, China's resistance is a sign of its refusal to face the consequences of social change, and the need to recognise the consequences of its de facto surrender of important powers.

A related testing ground of China's approach to international security continues to be how it reacts to the role of the United Nations in international security. Like the United States, but unlike any other permanent member of the Security Council, China is very wary about putting its soldiers under UN command. It is a difficult decision for any great power to allow foreigners to put its troops into harm's way, but China refuses to do so. Although its non-combat units have been used in UN operations (for example in Cambodia), they have yet to be put into circumstances where foreigners would command Chinese troops at times when deadly force would be used. The United States does put its troops under these conditions when it is working with allies, but China has none. One trusts allies (and friends), but because China trusts no one with its security, it finds it very difficult to take serious steps which suggests it sees the value of interdependent security.

When issues of Chinese national security are at stake in the UN, China even abandons its relatively passive role of allowing the Security Council to intervene in other countries' affairs. Consider the case of the UN mission in Haiti in March 1996. China blocked, and then had amended, the efforts to alter the UN mandate not so much because it disagreed with the operation, but because the Haitian authorities dared to have ties with Taiwan.[34] The old pattern reasserts itself: China only takes an active interest if its direct interests are involved. Otherwise it is content to neither block nor support the wider will of the international community as expressed through the United Nations (or arms control).

MAKING ENLITENMENT WORK

China is on its way to enlitenment. It may still be ruled by a communist party, but it is a much weaker party in far less control of its country. The Chinese economy is less than half state-owned. Economic and social power has been decentralised throughout a far more complex society. Chinese citizens have far more contact with the outside world than they have ever had before. Contact with foreigners helps feed the processes of reform, both because it helps provide economic incentives and because it offers alternative models of governance.

So far so good. But while enlitenment works its spells, in the meantime there are also the inevitable difficulties and risks in sustaining reform. It is clear that human rights in China will not substantially improve until there is a far more plural civil society, and that will take generations.[35] In the meantime, as is often the case in times of rapid modernisation, elites are shattered and old leadership structures shudder. When those who made the previous so-called revolution pass from the scene, the shudder turns to judder and the system can become even more unstable. Weak leaders, as so often in the past, find that dead ideologies can be replaced with nationalism as a way of building unity. The result is often simultaneous social and economic reform, accompanied by a very conservative political system. This picture of China is well within the experience of other rapidly modernising but destabilised societies.

The actions of outsiders can have an impact on such societies. There are groups within China who want the developed world to help them get beyond nationalism. There are groups outside China who do not want confrontation with China and would prefer to just wait for the forces of enlitenment to take their course. Of course, there are also those within and outside China who would relish confrontation. Can these diverse views be accommodated in a policy towards China?

A sensible strategy towards China requires four components – all of which are necessary but none of which are sufficient on their own. China needs to be (1) given more space in the international system; (2) engaged with the international society, economy and patterns of security; (3) kept to a rules-based international system, and (4) constrained when it undertakes unwanted action. Until recently, much of the debate about policy towards a rising China has been foolishly based on the notion that one or two of these components would suffice as a policy. The puerile 'containment' versus 'engagement' debate was a symptom of this underdeveloped thinking about policy towards China.

Where there is common ground is in the view that it is good that China should be engaged with the outside world. While the motives behind such engagement undoubtedly differ, the policy output looks similar.[36] Some hope that engagement will hasten the enlitenment of China, while many Chinese expect that engagement will provide them with the tools to better resist the outside world. The correctness of one view or the other depends on how long enlitenment takes and how resistant China and its society is to liberalism.

It also depends on the policies adopted while we are waiting to see how long enlitenment takes. While China grows Lite, will the outside world resist China's unwanted actions? Unconstrained authoritarians can resist liberalism for far longer than those who are constrained and forced to submit to liberal forces. The challenge for the world outside China is both to persist with the agenda for enlitenment, and to continue constraining China until it works.

NOTES

1. Alastair Iain Johnston, 'Learning Versus Adaptation: Explaining Change in Chinese Arms Control Policy in the 1980s and 1990s', *The China Journal* No. 35, January 1996.

2. These issues are discussed in Barry Buzan and Gerald Segal, *Anticipating the Future* (London and N.Y.: Simon & Schuster, forthcoming 1997).
3. On pidgin scholarship see 'Intellectuals: The Self and the Other', *China News Analysis* No. 1556, 15 March 1996.
4. Francis Fukuyama, *Trust: The Social Virtues and the Creation of Prosperity* (N.Y.; The Free Press, 1995).
5. W.J.F. Jenner, *The Tyranny of History* (London: Allen Lane, 1992).
6. Raymond Cohen, *Theatre of Power* (London: Longman, 1987).
7. These trends are described in nearly every popular book about modern China, but an early and still entertaining analysis is Orville Schell, *Discos and Democracy* (N.Y.: Pantheon, 1988).
8. Jianying Zha, *China Pop* (N.Y.: The New Press, 1995).
9. Gerald Segal, 'Asians in Cyberia', *The Washington Quarterly* Vol. 18 No. 3, Summer 1995; Kim Gordon, 'Riding China's TV Dragon', *Prospect,* April 1996. pp.76–8.
10. On various aspects of these issues see *Financial Times* 18 July 1995; *New York Times* 20 August 1995; *China News Analysis* 1 June 1995; *The Economist* 14 October 1995; and more generally in 'China', *Strategic Survey* (Oxford: Oxford University Press for the IISS, 1996).
11. See various chapters in Gerald Segal and David Goodman (eds), *China Deconstructs* (London: Routledge, 1994).
12. Statistics based on *China Statistical Yearbook 1995* (Beijing, 1995). Other statistics from *The Economist*, 'Business in Asia Survey', 9 March 1996 and Xinhua, 3 March 1996 in BBC/FEW/6425/WG/1.
13. Goodman and Segal, *China Deconstructs.*
14. Gerald Segal, *China Changes Shape* (London: Adelphi Paper No. 287, Brassey's for the IISS, 1994).
15. Michael Yahuda, *The International Politics of Asia-Pacific* (London: Routledge, 1996).
16. Johnston, 'Learning Versus Adaptation'.
17. Mark Valencia, *China and the South China Sea Disputes* (Oxford: Adelphi Paper No.298, Oxford University Press for the IISS, 1995).
18. Banning Garrett and Bonnie Glaser, 'Chinese Perspectives on Nuclear Arms Control', *International Security* Vol. 20 No. 3, Winter 1995–6. See also Robert Mullins, 'Chinese Missile Proliferation', *The Pacific Review*, Vol. 8 No. 1, 1995.
19. *Financial Times* 7 November 1995 and *The Economist* 2 August 1995.
20. On 1 April 1996 China reduced its tariff level from 36 per cent to 23 per cent. World Bank research showed that numerous exemptions and rampant smuggling had reduced actual import revenue to 6 per cent. By bringing formal tariff levels to more realistic rates, the hope was that the actual import revenue figure would rise. See *Financial Times* 7 December 1995; *International Herald Tribune* 1 April 1996.
21. For example, Lu jianren, 'APEC's Objectives and China's Position'. An unpublished CASS paper.
22. *The Economist* 20 January 1996; the *International Herald Tribune* 17 January 1996; and Zhongguo Xinwen She 14 February 1996 in FE/2537/G/6. *The Straits Times* 29 March 1996.

23. *The Economist* 2 December 1995 and *The Far Eastern Economic Review* 21 December 1995.
24. *The Economist* 2 March 1996.
25. Harold Jacobson and Michel Oksenberg, *China's Participation in the IMF, the World Bank and GATT* (Ann Arbour: University of Michigan Press, 1990).
26. *Financial Times* 25 January 1996.
27. *Asian Wall Street Journal* 17 July 1995; *Far Eastern Economic Review* 13 July 1995, 8 February 1996; *Newsweek* 29 January 1996; *International Herald Tribune* 14 December 1995; United Press International 20 June 1995; *Financial Times* 21 March 1996, citing the Shangahi Business News.
28. Gerald Segal, 'East Asia and the "Constrainment" of China', *International Security* Vol. 20 No. 4, Spring 1996.
29. Douglas Stuart and William Tow, *A US Strategy for the Asia-Pacific* (Oxford: Adelphi Paper No. 299, Oxford University Press for the IISS, 1995) and more generally Paul Dibb, *Towards a New Balance of Power in Asia* (Oxford: Adelphi Paper No. 295, Oxford University Press for the IISS, 1995).
30. For a more positive spin see Rosemary Foot, 'Chinese-Indian Relations and the Process of Building Confidence', *The Pacific Review* Vol. 9 No. 1, 1996.
31. Malcolm Chalmers, *Confidence-Building in South-East Asia* (Bradford: Department of Peace Studies (distributed by Westview Press), 1996.
32 'China's Military Expenditures' in *The Military Balance 1995–96* (Oxford: Oxford University Press for the IISS, 1995).
33. Greg Austin, 'The Strategic Implications of China's Public Order Crisis', *Survival* Vol. 37 No. 2, Summer 1995.
34 *Xinhua* 1 March 1996 in FE/2551/G/1 and the *International Herald Tribune* 2 March 1996.
35. An American government study, not surprisingly, reports that there is little evidence that economic reform in China has made an appreciable difference to the poor state of human rights. See the *International Herald Tribune* 7 March 1996.
36. See a careful study of these issues in James Shinn (ed.), *Weaving the Net: Conditional Engagement with China* (N.Y.: Council on Foreign Relations, 1996).

# 10 The US–Japan Security Relationship in a New Era

Aurelia George Mulgan

## INTRODUCTION[1]

The US–Japan security relationship has been under sustained challenge since the end of the Cold War. First and foremost, its strategic relevance has been questioned by the decline in the Soviet threat. Other challenges have also emerged: from scholars who see Japan's protectorate status as perpetuating a state of political underdevelopment which effectively prevents Japan from engaging in more equitable risk-sharing and who argue that the United States naively provides Japan with a cheap defence while it enriches itself in American export markets;[2] from Japanese nationalists who view the terms and conditions of the US security guarantee as symbolising Japan's subservience to the United States; from populist politicians who express the justified grievances of Japanese residents wanting to rid their neighbourhoods of American bases; from Japan's economic ministries and business communities who seek greater independence from the United States in order to defy American trade pressures; from certain Asia-orientated sections of the Japanese establishment who see the US–Japan alliance as an impediment to their country's freedom of diplomatic action in Asia; and from observers of American politics who constantly predict a new wave of isolationism about to prompt a US military withdrawal from East Asia.

The response of the Japanese and US governments to this challenge has been an attempt to show that the bilateral alliance can be a resilient and flexible mechanism for adjusting to the changing security agenda in the Asia-Pacific region. In mid-April 1996, President Clinton and Prime Minister Hashimoto put the final gloss on what has been an extended process of detailed re-examination by American and Japanese defence officials of future directions in their security relationship.

The following analysis contends that Japan and the United States face three main problems in revamping and upgrading the US–Japan alliance. The first problem centres on how to restructure bilateral security arrangements to facilitate greater reciprocity in terms of the defence burdens assumed by each side. The possibility that conflict may occur in East Asia involving the United States raises the critical question of Japan's willingness to accept an expanded military and logistical support role in the alliance and therefore greater responsibility for regional defence. Retaining strong American support for the security guarantee to Japan is partly contingent on such an adjustment.

The second problem is how to manage the base issue in Japan. Diminishing public tolerance for the more intrusive aspects of the American military presence is seriously undermining the traditional basis of support amongst the Japanese people for the US–Japan Security Treaty. The result is a growing divergence between elite and mass attitudes towards the security relationship with the United States. For the first time since the early 1960s, the American military presence in Japan has become a domestic political issue. This is a new development which neither the US nor Japanese governments have had to accommodate before.

The third problem centres on the refocusing issue generated by the events that took place in the Taiwan Strait in early 1996. If a real strategic challenge from China were to emerge, Japan and the United States would face the problem of converting what was traditionally an anti-Soviet alliance into an anti-Chinese alliance. While China's display of military force in the seas around Taiwan underscored the continuing strategic relevance of the US–Japan Security Treaty, it also highlighted potential differences between Japanese and US policies towards China and consequently the difficulties Japan might confront in having to order its strategic priorities between the two powers with which it maintains 'special relationships'.

How the United States and Japan jointly face up to and resolve these issues will determine the capacity of the US–Japan alliance to adjust its internal dynamics to cope with a changing domestic and international environment. This chapter considers each of these problems from a Japanese policy perspective. It examines what kinds of military and logistical assistance Japan can render the United States in the event of a regional crisis or conflict in Northeast Asia, how reliable Japan is as a potential security partner of the United States against China, and what effects the weakening of the mass base of support for the US–Japan Security Treaty in Japan will have on the sustainability of the alliance.

## THE FUNCTIONS OF THE US–JAPAN ALLIANCE

Historically speaking, the US–Japan security alliance has always served two core objectives: the American defence of Japan which is guaranteed under Article 5 of the Mutual Security Treaty and the pursuit of American regional strategy in East Asia under Article 6, which permits the United States to maintain bases on Japanese soil. Both these objectives remain relevant and operative in the post-Cold War period. Japan retains quite significant levels of dependence on the United States for defence of Japanese territory against large-scale and nuclear attack and also for the defence of its interests further afield. On the other hand, Japan's generous host-nation support to the American military bases in Okinawa, Honshu and Kyushu enables the United States to pursue its regional defence strategy at a lower cost,[3] to deal more quickly and efficiently with military contingencies all the way from East Asia to the Indian Ocean and the Persian Gulf and to guard the sea lines of communication (SLOCs).[4] In addition, the US–Japan alliance furthers US economic and political interests in East Asia,[5] provides access to Japanese defence technologies[6] and facilitates joint weapons development with Japan.[7]

By anchoring the US military presence in Asia, the US–Japan alliance performs a number of regional security functions which are broadly acknowledged and supported by Japan as well as most other countries in the Asia Pacific. These functions include maintaining the regional balance of power, deterring regional conflict, constraining the potential expansionism of regional states and preventing the development of a destabilising power vacuum.[8] In the rhetoric of US declaratory policy, the US–Japan alliance is the cornerstone of stability and prosperity in the region.[9] Although it is a bilateral arrangement, it has a tremendous regional impact.

The US–Japan Security Treaty also prevents a regional arms race by containing Japan. The US security commitment to Japan underwrites Japan's self-defence posture by obviating the need for Japan to develop a fully independent military with a power projection and nuclear weapons capability. It makes the Japanese nuclear option irrelevant and thus helps to preserve the nuclear non-proliferation regime in East Asia. Without the US nuclear umbrella, Japan would confront two nuclear powers both full of uncertainty – China and Russia – as well as the possibility of a third country (North Korea) going nuclear. The pressure for Japan to acquire nuclear weapons in these circumstances would be overwhelming, and in Japan's wake, South Korea, Taiwan and a number of Southeast Asian states would follow.[10] A continuation of Japan's present military course is, therefore, almost entirely dependent on the credibility of the American commitment to Japan. The US East Asia Strategy Report (EASR) of February 1995 which committed the United States to maintaining 100 000 troops forward based in East Asia reaffirmed the US security guarantee by providing a firm assurance of continuing American willingness to maintain its force presence in East Asia.

The EASR's emphasis on the US–Japan alliance as the linchpin of East Asian security was echoed in the fundamental restatement of Japan's defence policy undertaken by the Japanese government in November 1995. The new

National Defence Programme Outline (NDPO) advocates stronger military ties with the United States and anticipates immediate joint action by combined US–Japanese military forces in the event of an invasion of Japan.[11] In part it is a culmination of the comprehensive security dialogue between the United States and Japan initiated in 1994 by former US Assistant Secretary of Defense, Joseph Nye. This process was designed to re-examine the continuing rationales for the security relationship, to define more clearly its operation in relation to a number of possible contingencies and to examine more specifically what roles Japan should play.

In defining the continuing relevance of the bilateral security arrangement in the post-Cold War period, attention has been drawn to the number of indirect benefits generated by the alliance in related security, political and economic spheres. First, from the Japanese perspective, the US–Japan security relationship is the basic prerequisite for Japan's acceptance in Asia because it 'reassures Asian states nervous about Japanese rearmament'.[12] Indeed, Japan's military build-up in the context of the US–Japan alliance has been made more acceptable to its Asian neighbours because it has alleviated residual suspicion of Japanese intentions and thereby helped Japan to 'implement its defense build-up programs'.[13] A Japan locked into an alliance with the United States, with American military forces based on its soil, is generally perceived as posing little expansionist threat to the region. According to former Vice-Foreign Minister Kuriyama: 'The security treaty renders regional and international credibility to Japan's fundamental stance that it will not become a major military power. The treaty thus facilitates the acceptance of a larger political and economic role for Japan by its neighbours.'[14] Sato argues along similar lines: 'Japan can maintain good relations with the Asian countries only as long as it maintains friendly and intimate relations with the Western countries. If the US–Japan alliance should fall apart, the Asian countries, including China, will certainly take much more suspicious attitudes towards Japan.'[15] Japan's alliance with the United States has, therefore, unquestionably assisted Japan's rising profile in Asian affairs from the late 1980s onwards, including its use of diplomacy to mediate in regional disputes, in promoting defence exchanges with Russia, China, South Korea and Southeast Asian states, in sending military forces to Cambodia in a peace-keeping support role, and in taking initiatives to assist the growth of regional security dialogue within multilateral frameworks.[16]

Second, the US–Japan Security Treaty sanctions the exercise of tremendous US leverage over Japan, enabling it to pressure the Japanese into taking on more responsibilities not only for the region but for world peace and prosperity. Indeed the Treaty acts like a basic law for the overall relationship; it is being reinterpreted as an agreement committing both countries to wide-ranging political, economic and security cooperation underpinned by a commitment to a common set of values.[17] This represents US–Japanese 'burden sharing' on a global scale.[18] It includes but is not restricted to the Asia-Pacific region and it extends across a broad range of security related and non-security related issues. It is evident in the rhetoric of 'global partnership' which was coined in the early 1990s to denote a wide-ranging cooperative and mutually supportive relationship extending across a range of 'global' issues. It envisaged the two countries pooling their economic, military, technological and diplomatic resources to manage and solve international problems in areas such as environmental preservation, drug trafficking, nuclear non-proliferation, the development of Third World and formerly socialist nations, the fostering of democracy, human rights and open markets, and the strengthening of UN peace-keeping operations. In July 1993 Japan and the United States established a 'Common Agenda' covering five different areas of global cooperation including education, the environment, narcotics and terrorism.[19]

The US–Japan global partnership has complemented a more productive diplomatic partnership in the pursuit of shared political and security goals in the Asia-Pacific region, with greater US–Japan consultation, cooperation and coordinated action in a number of areas. Examples include:

- the development of common strategies to deal with the North Korean nuclear issue. Japan and the United States together with South Korea acted as co-partners in the formulation and implementation of the Agreed Framework which attempted to provide a non-military diplomatic solution to the issue of North Korean nuclear weapons development;[20]
- mediation with North Korea by the United States on Japan's behalf in order that diplomatic normalisation talks might be resumed;
- joint participation by Japanese and American officials with their Russian counterparts in trilateral forums on North Pacific security;
- strong support by Japan for American nuclear non-proliferation goals in the region;
- the coordinated pursuit of mutually agreed goals, such as increased military transparency and confidence building amongst Asian states and the promotion of multilateral Asia-Pacific security mechanisms and dialogue, all of which are constructive gestures towards the creation of a stable and peaceful climate in the region.

At the urging of the US side, Japanese contributions to international security are also evident in parts of the world where no vital national security interests of its own are at stake. For example, Japan has agreed to make available large amounts of reconstruction aid to Bosnia in the wake of the peace settlement brokered by the United States. Similarly, at the beginning of April, Japan announced that it would be making a donation of US$21 million to the Palestinian Authority in Gaza, working on the principle that economic prosperity provides a foundation for peace.[21] An important American interest in upholding the security relationship with Japan is, therefore, that it enables the United States to make an ambit claim on Japan to underwrite financially an international security system led by the United States. The United States and Japan can draw on a powerful and productive complementarity of strengths in the pursuit of common political and security goals. Japan helps to prop up US global hegemony and in this respect is one of America's most valued 'supporter states'.

## PROBLEMS IN RESTRUCTURING AND REFOCUSING THE ALLIANCE

These more positive and productive aspects of the alliance relationship, although important in underlining the common interests of both parties in its maintenance and preservation, need to be balanced against possible stresses and strains arising from its restructuring and refocusing as a bilateral security arrangement. First and foremost is the issue of Japan's willingness to come to the aid of the United States by providing military and logistical support for US action in dealing with regional crises and possibly stemming regional conflicts.

In the changed strategic circumstances of the post-Cold War period, the issue of Japan's willingness to contribute to regional security beyond the defence of Japanese territory is critical to the future of the US–Japan alliance. As Sato explains:

> During the Cold War, given the US–Japan alliance, Japan was able to contribute to the West's security by focusing on the defence by conventional forces of the Japanese archipelago, which constituted a strategically important outpost in deterring the Soviet Union. Even if Japan refused to exercise the right to collective self-defence, and, in this sense, confined itself behind the walls of one-country pacifism, the US–Japan alliance was not seriously affected. Now, however, the US–Japan alliance is bound to be confronted with a grave crisis if Japan continues to cling to the security policies of the past.[22]

Sato's point is that Japan's geostrategic position during the Cold War enabled it to blur the distinction between individual and collective self-defence.[23] In exercising its right of individual self-defence in areas such as the Sea of Japan, the Sea of Okhotsk and the strategic straits, Japan could execute a joint strategy with the United States against the Soviet Union. The geostrategic dimensions of Japanese defence in the post-Cold War period, however, have changed. A joint US–Japan defence of Asia is much harder to justify in these terms.[24] Japan cannot maintain the illusion of individual self-defence in the wider Asia-Pacific region. This problem will become more acute as the regional focus of the US–Japan alliance broadens.

Operationalising the US–Japan security relationship in the Asia-Pacific region, however, will require a number of politically difficult and delicate steps for Japan. The Japanese government is concerned that if the United States asks Japan for assistance in a regional crisis, the government will have to approve it, and this will require a major political decision.[25] Japan is not yet politically and legally prepared to deal with such an eventuality and will, therefore, not be able to issue the sort of rapid and adequate response that would satisfy American expectations. Japanese security policy-making is effectively shackled by domestic considerations and sensitivities, including constitutional obstacles associated with Article 9 (the so-called 'Peace Clause' in the Constitution) as well as derivative legal impediments and mandatory political procedures, all of which put up strong barriers to an expansion of Japan's logistical and military support role in the US–Japan alliance. For these reasons Japan finds it difficult to cope adequately with rapidly changing external circumstances and to respond quickly and decisively in a crisis.

The question of Japan's ability to participate either directly or indirectly in military operations in concert with other nations beyond strictly territorial defence raises the issue of Japan's exercising the right of collective self-defence. Under the current interpretation of Article 9 of the Constitution, Japan is constrained from exercising this right. Japan cannot deploy the Self-Defence Forces (SDF) for any military purpose other than the defence of Japanese territory. The domestic debate is couched in terms of the contrast between the right of individual self-defence (*kobetsuteki jieiken*) which is granted under the Constitution, and the right of so-called 'collective self-defence' (*shudanteki jieiken*),[26] which is prohibited. According to the Japanese government, the current interpretation of Article 9 confines 'the use of armed strength ... to the minimum level necessary';[27] and 'because the exercise of the right of collective self-defense exceeds the minimum limit ... [it is] constitutionally not permissible'.[28] This interpretation also bans the overseas dispatch of the Japanese military 'to foreign territorial land, sea and airspace for the purpose of using force [*kaigai hahei*] because such a deployment of troops overseas generally goes beyond the minimum limit necessary for self-defense'.[29]

The practical effect of Article 9 of the Japanese Constitution is, therefore, to render 'ambiguous [Japan's] ... support role in regional contingencies'.[30] Two scenarios are of more pressing concern to security planners in both countries: military (including nuclear) developments on the Korean Peninsula and the possibility that China will attempt to resolve the question of Taiwanese sovereignty by force.

On the basis of present policies, what Japan can do to assist the United States in the event of a regional conflict is extremely limited. Apart from the territorial integrity of Japan being breached, there are very few triggers for a combined US–Japanese military operation to occur.[31] Even for Japan to exercise the right of self-defence, there must be 'an imminent and illegitimate act of aggression against Japan'.[32] Formally, at the request of either Japan or the United States, there may be consultations under Article 4 of the Mutual Security Treaty. Under this Article, Japan and the United States will consult at the request of either party whenever the security in the Far East is threatened. Second, under Article 6 of the Treaty, Japan provides bases for the US forces. If the United States wishes to bring major military equipment and forces into Japan and use its bases to mount a direct military operation from Japan, it must request the permission of the Japanese government under the Exchange of Notes based on Article 6 of the Treaty, something it has never done because of the implications for Japan's three non-nuclear principles.[33] If there were such a request, the Japanese government could grant or withhold its permission, but either way it would require a political decision. Political agreement under the present constellation of parties would not be easily forthcoming. One of the parties in Japan's current ruling coalition – the Social Democratic Party (SDP) – is on record as opposing the use of US bases for the Korean Peninsula. Opposition also surfaced to the United States' using its bases in Japan to enforce its military presence in the seas around Taiwan in early 1996.[34]

In addition to formidable constitutional and political obstacles, legal hurdles also serve to restrict Japan's options. No domestic law exists that would permit the SDF to extend direct military assistance to US forces or to undertake the kind of logistical support role requested by the United States in the Gulf War for example.[35] According to SDF Law, the only mission of the Japanese military forces is the defence of Japan and training. On these grounds, the SDF's potential is extremely limited with respect to supporting the United States in activities outside of the defence of Japan.[36]

The difficulties Japan faces in dealing with US requests were evident during the North Korean nuclear crisis of 1994. A Japanese media publication drew attention to the issue by pointing out that in the event of hostilities erupting on the Korean Peninsula,

all Japan could do without rewriting the law would be to swap intelligence with the allies, and treat wounded troops on Japanese soil. Anything else – supplies, transportation, communications or even the inspection of foreign ships in Japanese waters, would require Diet permission.[37]

In another report from Reuters, it was revealed that US forces asked the Japanese navy if it could send minesweepers and warplanes to Korean waters in the event that fighting started with North Korea. Specifically the US side wanted the Japanese navy to send a minesweeper flotilla and a squadron of P-3C anti-submarine patrol planes to protect a US navy task force to be deployed in Korean waters in case of war with North Korea. Japan's Defence Agency (JDA) replied that 'all it could do under the constitution was to provide the US navy with information from its regular anti-submarine patrols and give limited support to units stationed in Japan'.[38] The American request was denied because 'such an act would violate Japan's constitutional ban on collective security arrangements'.[39] Japan also refused an American request for help in blockading North Korea.[40]

The limits that apply to the deployment of Japanese military forces in the event of regional conflict in East Asia have been succinctly explained by Retired Lieutenant General Shikata of the SDF:

Direct participation, such as sending its Self-Defence Forces or any such personnel, in the organizing of multinational forces, even if legitimized by UN resolutions, cannot be a viable option for Japan to consider, as long as the current interpretation of the constitutional clause defining the rights to collective defence remains unaltered. Under the prevailing circumstances, Japan can only indirectly assist the multinational forces by providing support services to US units. In addition, given the constraints of the present constitutional interpretation, these support services remain limited to measures such as the exchange of information, assistance and accommodation for refugees coming to Japan, and a variety of support services for US forces like training support, logistic supply support, and medical care of casulties.[41]

Moreover, the vague wording of Japan's new NDPO does little to clarify the issue beyond underlining Japanese awareness that regional conflict may occur by referring to 'a situation in the areas surrounding Japan, which will have an important influence on national peace and security'.[42] The document offers assurance of an 'appropriate response' from Japan 'in accordance with the Constitution and relevant laws and regulations, by proper [sic] supporting the United Nations activities when needed, and by ensuring the smooth and effective implementation of the Japan–US Security Arrangements',[43] but what action Japan would actually take is not specified in concrete terms. Defence policy is an area long subject to deliberate obfuscation by the Japanese government primarily for domestic political reasons. The absence of specificity and clarity maximises latitude of interpretation and therefore greater flexibility of options. Terms such as 'appropriate measures' and 'smoothly and effectively implementing the Japan–US security system' have been left intentionally vague in order to permit a range of options for Japan depending on the situation. The terminology of the NDPO has certainly been viewed as a positive step by some American security experts who have interpreted it as 'the Japanese government ... trying to say it will do its best to accomplish its role'.[44] Others have argued that it 'could mark a substantial change in Japan's traditional position that its military forces cannot operate outside Japan or in "collective security" operations with the United States'.[45]

In addition, the new NDPO implies that the defence of Japan, while still the 'principal mission' of the SDF, is not their only mission, referring in vague terms to the Japanese forces playing 'an appropriate role in a timely manner in the Government's active efforts to establish a more stable security environment'.[46] This refers primarily to peace-keeping,[47] but it does leave the door open to other developments. In this respect, the new Outline contrasts with the 1976 version which described only the defence of Japan. The significance of such a development lies in the fact that the NDPO is like a constitution for the SDF. If something is included in the official statement of Japanese defence policy then the SDF must give priority to it.[48]

The new NDPO also puts great emphasis on operational issues in the section under 'Japan–US Security Arrangement', where reference is made to enhancing the credibility of this arrangement by making efforts '(1) to promote exchange of information and policy consultation ... [and] (2) to establish an effective posture for cooperation in operational areas including joint studies, exercises and training, as well as enhancement of mutual support in those areas'.[49] This is an attempt to lay the groundwork for more efficient joint operations between US and Japanese forces in the future. Thus far the extent of these operations beyond Japanese territory, sea and airspace has been restricted to minesweeping in the Persian Gulf in 1991 when the Japanese Maritime Self-Defence Forces coordinated with the US and other navies.

The objective of making the security relationship more operable is complemented by growing calls for Japanese contributions to enhancing the infrastructure servicing US forces to improve their readiness in the event of an emergency situation. The Defence Advisory Group's report to former Prime

Minister Murayama in August 1994 called for, amongst other things, 'improved logistics support, particularly reaching an acquisition and cross-servicing agreement; [and] increasing interoperability in defence systems by including more cooperative development in $C^3I$...and other areas'.[50] Former Prime Minister Hosokawa Morihiro in a speech to the Council on Foreign Relations in Washington DC in March 1996 also called for urgent decisions on

> what specific rear support Japan can provide the US forces. In this regard ... the most realistic course would be to conclude an emergency ACSA (Acquisition and Cross-Servicing Agreement), the kind of special agreement which Germany had with the United States during the cold war governing emergency host nation support.[51]

Hosokawa made this suggestion in the light of measures which could be taken 'without invoking the concept of collective security'.[52]

These recommendations anticipated the ACSA reached between Japan and the United States during President Clinton's visit to Japan in mid-April 1996. The agreement envisages much more substantial cooperation between the military forces on both sides, including permission for the SDF to supply 15 items such as food, fuel, spare parts and components, transportation, repair and maintenance and clothing to US troops. According to Chief Cabinet Secretary Kajiyama Seiroku, Japan will not apply its three principles on weapons exports in supplying weapons parts to the US military under the ACSA.[53] Initially, the agreement is expected to be applied only to joint exercises in peacetime, UN peace-keeping operations and humanitarian relief operations.[54] It does not apply to peacetime exercises conducted by the United States alone or the provision of help in regional conflict.[55]

The extent of this new commitment by Japan fully accords with existing limitations on its defence role. Provision of logistical support for joint military exercises by the United States and Japan can be justified in terms of Japanese self-defence because this provides the only trigger for SDF deployment. Supporting US forces acting alone, however, whether in the conduct of military exercises or in a conflict situation, has much more of the flavour of collective self-defence and therefore remains presently outside the limits of Japan's options. In other words, the commitments that Japan has given the United States in the ACSA of April 1996[56] do not breach the ban on participating in collective self-defence.

No sooner was the ink dry on the accord, however, than a proposal was unveiled for Japan and the United States to conduct a review to consider offering such support in an emergency, that is, in the event of conflict in the region.[57] In addition, Japanese Prime Minister Hashimoto Ryutaro reportedly gave permission for a study into ways of legally permitting American military forces to use Japanese civilian airports and ports in time of war.[58] These developments suggest that one of the important directions in which Japanese defence policy will continue to change is in the area of logistical support for US forces. The quality, quantity and circumstances in which this support is given may gradually be upgraded and extended to facilitate an expansion in Japan's roles and responsibilities, and this will form an important part of the alliance restructuring process.

Japan's Defence Agency also plans to revise the 1978 Guidelines for Japan–US Defence Cooperation in order to facilitate a wider range of joint military activities with the United States. This initiative was given subsequent endorsement in the 'Japan–US Joint Declaration on Security' of April 1996 in which Prime Minister Hashimoto and President Clinton agreed to initiate a review of the 1978 Guidelines for completion by November 1996. A joint US–Japan study group was set up 'with a view to establishing a framework for bilateral cooperation in regional emergencies'.[59] The significance of this development lies in the fact that the 1978 guidelines laid down procedures for US–Japan cooperation only in the case of defending Japan. The Joint Declaration, on the other hand, uses exactly the same terminology as the NDPO in referring to 'bilateral cooperation in dealing with situations that may emerge in the areas surrounding Japan and which will have an important influence on the peace and security of Japan'.[60] This section 'means that Japan will start studying how its military could cooperate with US forces in a future armed conflict in the region that threatens Japan'.[61] For Japan this was the most crucial section of the entire Joint Declaration because it broached the issue of collective self-defence.

While the potential scope of US–Japan defence cooperation has clearly been enlarged to encompass a regional focus, the limit of such a revision are that it will only involve studies on joint defence planning, not real planning. Although 'the JDA does not have to win Cabinet approval for the Guidelines and is therefore more free to consider potentially controversial policies',[62] it is highly unlikely Japan will make any formal commitment to operational plans binding both Japanese and American forces without first changing its policy on collective self-defence, and therefore the status of the new guidelines will be the same as the 1978 version – just studies and consultations.[63]

Nonetheless, while no Japanese commitments to regional defence have yet been made explicit, the idea that an expanded concern with regional security is part of the redefinition of the alliance is strongly evident on both sides of the Pacific. This development points to a changing emphasis in the security relationship from Article 5 (which envisages joint Japanese–US defence of Japan's territories) to Article 6 (which refers to conditions constituting a threat to peace and stability in the Far East).[64] One of the key features of the Japan–US Joint Declaration was the implied shift from a bilateral defence function to a regional security function for the US–Japan Security Treaty. Numerous references are made in the text to 'security in the Asia-Pacific region'.[65] Such a move will inevitably require a review of Japan's ban on collective self-defence.

Even prior to the April 1996 Clinton visit to Japan, leading politicians in the ruling Liberal Democratic Party (LDP) were contemplating serious policy discussions on the subject of collective self-defence and related issues. The Chairman of the LDP's Policy Affairs Research Council in early 1996 proposed that the government tackle Japan's emergency legislation system governing such matters as air traffic control, radio frequencies, the use of private land and traffic laws in order that Japan might be better prepared to deal with a military attack. The party's Security Investigation Committee (*Anzen Hosho Chosakai*) also began to work on guidelines to deal with threats to national security in the wake of Chinese actions in the Taiwan Strait in March 1996. The task of the committee was to 'make ... clear what measures [Japan] ... could take within the limits of the Constitution and relevant laws when [Japan faces] ... situations such as heightened military tension in the Taiwan Strait or on the Korean Peninsula'.[66] The Committee also undertook to review the government's policy on collective self-defence[67] against a background of calls from some LDP Diet members to extend cooperation between the Japanese Self-Defence Forces and US troops 'to include overseas military operations in time of war'.[68] Just prior to the Clinton visit the Chairman of the LDP's Policy Affairs Research Council, Yamasaki Taku, also announced that 'the issue of collective defense should be brought up ... we have to discuss in what way the SDF should cooperate when the US military is dispatched (from American bases in Japan)'.[69] He was also quoted as saying that: 'In problems which take place quite near to Japan, I believe some fields fall into the area of Japan–US security co-operation as well as Japan's individual self-defence.'[70] Another LDP spokesperson had earlier remarked that: 'The Japan–US security treaty has some elements of asymmetry. It is important for us to make it symmetric.'[71]

These initiatives represented something of a shift in policy direction for the LDP. In June 1994 when the Korean crisis was at its height, the party (then in opposition) used the collective self-defence issue to discredit the New Life Party under the leadership of former Prime Minister Hata (now Japan's main opposition New Frontier Party). The Hata Cabinet had suggested that 'Article 51 of the UN Charter, Article 5 of the San Francisco Peace Treaty, and the preamble to the Japan–US Security Treaty all implicitly gave Japan the right to enter collective defense arrangements.'[72] It is now possible that the collective self-defence issue might forge a new political realignment in Japan, if the LDP goes into coalition with the New Frontier Party to establish a stronger defence policy.[73] On the other hand, it is highly doubtful whether any change in existing government policy could be achieved under the present ruling coalition which includes the SDP and the moderate-pacifist New Party Harbinger.

In the absence of any official change in the policy banning collective self-defence, it would be up to the Japanese government to determine what sort of action by Japan constituted collective self-defence and what did not. It is possible that certain actions by the SDF which could conceivably assist the United States might be ruled in, but the room to manoeuvre would be very limited. Japan might approve American use of Japanese bases, something that has recently been discussed in the Diet in the context of what Japan could do if US forces engaged on the Korean Peninsula. A more substantial logistical support role than the current ACSA envisages, however, would remain contentious. The distinction between supplying the forces of another country engaged in combat and actually engaging in combat is not so clear-cut according to Japan's Cabinet Legislative Office (CLO) which argues that such an act could violate Article 9's ban on 'the threat or use of force as a means of settling international disputes'. The CLO has ultimate authority for the government's interpretation of the Japanese constitution and tends to interpret its provisions very strictly. In the CLO's view, Japan is not permitted to make a contribution that could be interpreted as a 'use of force' by Japan unless it has itself has been attacked. Determining what amounts to a use of force by Japan in turn encompasses a number of 'grey' areas. Medical treatment is possible because 'the threat or use of force' is very low. On this basis, Japan could offer to treat wounded American troops. Other areas such as transportation are more problematic. The case of Japan deploying a cargo transport aircraft to ferry supplies to a US base in Korea might be ruled out, for example, but using transport vehicles to ferry supplies to US forces within Japan would probably not be seen as a use of force. Similarly, if Japanese ships supplied US ships on the high seas it would become highly contentious, although in Japanese territorial waters, it might be possible.[74]

In terms of direct military engagement, Japan would face even greater difficulties. In some circumstances minesweeping might be permissible. It would generally be seen as the use of force in a combat situation in the seas around Japan, but following the termination of conflict (as in the Persian Gulf in 1991) or if there were imminent danger to Japanese shipping, it might be approved. Article 99 of the SDF Law states that the Japanese Maritime Self-

Defence Forces can dispose of mines and other dangerous materials in the sea. Such action has also been sanctioned by precedent and enunciations of government policy. In 1987 former Prime Minister Nakasone declared that action to clear mines did not constitute the exercise of force, and in 1991, former Prime Minister Kaifu also declared that the clearing of mines did 'not correspond to the overseas despatch of military forces as prohibited by the Constitution'.[75]

Other potential Japanese contributions include participation in an economic blockade if the overall mission does not involve the 'use of force',[76] the escort of merchant ships (but not combat ships) to protect them against acts of piracy, and patrolling by the Japanese navy and airforce which could be justified in a situation of high tension and imminent attack provided that such action were not designed to provoke. The intelligence gathered from such activities could be relayed to US forces although objections might still be raised on constitutional grounds.

In all cases, however, the Japanese government will be unquestionably slow and reluctant to engage its own military hardware and personnel in situations where there is no direct threat to Japanese security and no attack on Japan itself. The initial response will always be to cite the traditional constraint: 'Japan will take the maximum cooperative action allowed under its constitution.'[77] Any dramatic departure from existing policy will require both a change in constitutional interpretation and also Diet action to amend the SDF Law or to write a new law, both or either of which will submit the decision process to the vagaries of domestic politics at the time. Because of anticipated political difficulties, Japan will remain extremely reluctant to make any commitments in advance as to the nature of its undertakings in a crisis situation.

Japanese perceptions of possible threats to their own security will be a key determinant of the domestic environment of such policy change. The recent tensions between China and Taiwan, for example, were seen by the Japanese government as a cause of concern but not as a major threat to the nation's security.[78] In the event of real conflict in the region, however, attitudes might change quickly if the United States were operating direct combat sorties out of Japan, thereby converting it into an 'unsinkable aircraft carrier' and at the same time a legitimate target for attack by theatre ballistic missiles.

Another important factor will be the actual parties to the conflict. Not all regional crises are created equal in Japanese political terms. Key differences will inevitably emerge in Japan's response to a Korean situation compared to a military situation in the Taiwan Strait. The domestic constitutional and legal implications of either contingency will be the same, but, historically speaking, the Korean Peninsula has a much higher priority for the security of Japan. The Japanese would be much more inclined to consider an attack on South Korea by North Korea as a threat to Japan than a Chinese attack on Taiwan. In official policy terms, Japan backed away from a perception of a Chinese security threat arising from the Taiwan issue after normalisation of relations with China in 1972, but it never backed off Korea. Certainly in terms of the regional contingencies canvassed by the United States and Japan as part of their security dialogue in 1994–6, the most important focus of these discussions has been the Korean Peninsula. Japan and the United States worked well together on the North Korean nuclear issue at the diplomatic level and Japan's defence planners continue to watch very closely developments on the Korean Peninsula. In late 1995, concerns were raised about what appeared to be significant changes in the North Korean military posture and the North Korean violations of the armistice in the DMZ in early 1996 also caused concern.

The Korean situation is, therefore, fairly clear-cut. North Korea is patently the adversary from the Japanese as well as the American perspective. It is regarded as a rogue state without a formal relationship with Japan. The China–Taiwan issue, on the other hand, has a markedly different significance in these respects. Japan's policy on China recognises 'one China', and therefore Chinese claims to Taiwan. The temptation for Japan will always be to hide behind this official position, although in practice it has a complicated dual relationship with both China and Taiwan. Both countries are important trading partners of Japan with China's economic importance exceeding that of Taiwan at least in terms of its potential, in spite of extensive links between the Japanese and Taiwanese business communities as well as close ties amongst the older generation of politicians.[79]

In other areas such as human rights, democracy and economic liberalisation, Japan pays lip-service to shared values with the United States but these provide only a weak basis for a joint Japan–US policy on Chinese issues. Ostensibly Japan has incorporated democracy and human rights criteria into its declaratory policy on foreign aid, but on no occasion has Japan explicitly applied these criteria to its aid policy on China and, unlike the United States, Japan is not prepared to allow these values to determine its overall China strategy which is designed not to give offence. The only area where Japan displays an official 'get tough' attitude is on nuclear issues. In 1995 Japan cut its grant aid to China (which amounted to only a small proportion of its total allocation) in the wake of China's continued nuclear testing.

Generally speaking, Japan is like other Asian governments in believing that provoking China would not serve its interests.[80] Its China policy is dominated by economic pragmatism and a desire to engage China in networks of interdependence designed to increase Japanese influence over the Chinese government and mitigate potential Chinese hostility towards Japan. It has great difficulty talking about a 'China threat' because of the history of its own past aggression during the 1930s and 1940s.[81] Nor does it wish to be seen as closely allied with the United States in a containment of China policy. Until now Japan's main security concerns have focused on the prospect that internal destabilisation in China might affect Japanese trade and investment in that country and the possibility that Chinese refugees fleeing domestic conflict might flood into Japan.

The domestic political environment of Japanese policy towards North Korea and China also provides clear contrasts. Given North Korean actions in using Japan as a base for terrorist attacks against South Korea, the public mood towards North Korea is very negative. In the case of China, the situation is totally different. Japanese public opinion in the past has been highly favourable towards China.

Because the interpretation of the Japanese constitution is, in the last resort, a highly political matter, the fundamental mood of the Japanese people will strongly affect any statement of constitutional interpretation allowing or preventing Japan from making contributions to the US–Japan alliance, whether military or logistical, in the event of a regional crisis or conflict occurring. This makes such action much easier in the case of North Korea than it does in the case of China. For Japan the ideal crisis sequence is North Korea first and China second. In the North Korean case, Japan could much more actively pursue some kind of contribution because of the more serious implications for Japanese security and the more hostile domestic environment towards North Korea. Such engagement would have the effect of creating a precedent for action elsewhere – possibly in a contingency involving China. The worst scenario would be the reverse sequence: a China crisis first, followed by a North Korean crisis.

The choice for Japan on the China–Taiwan issue is, therefore, a complicated one. While Japan shares a one-China policy with the United States and opposes China's use of military force against Taiwan, Japan will hesitate about its options in the event of a crisis in the Taiwan Strait and will try at all costs to avoid taking sides. Its political response to Chinese military actions to intimidate Taiwan in the lead-up to the presidential election was cautious as well as ambivalent,[82] although calls emerged from some political quarters for the Japanese government to take a tougher stance.[83] Any military response such as the option of dispatching a Japanese naval presence to the area, however, was inconceivable. In terms of Japan's defence policy, its position was that although the Taiwan Strait came within Japan's 1000 nautical mile sea-lane defence zone,[84] the main sea-lanes lay to the east of Taiwan, not to the west. The latter were simply too close to China for the Japanese to contemplate a military presence in that sea zone.[85] Furthermore, for Japan to act in defence of its sea-lanes, the Chinese would first have to attack Japanese ships.

Given the complex realities of Japan's relationship with China, US military involvement in a China–Taiwan dispute will provoke a policy and diplomatic crisis for Japan well short of a decision to engage in military terms. A nightmare scenario for Japan would be an extension of Chinese military demonstration in the Taiwan Strait into a fully-fledged military blockade which would raise the stakes for all parties and create prospects for a much more direct and lengthy US military engagement. In these circumstances, Japan would be much more likely to have to field requests from the US side for assistance.

Japanese action in support of the United States over the Spratly Islands issue is even less likely than in the case of contingencies arising further north because of the distance of the Spratly Islands from Japanese shores. Even though Japanese and US official policies towards this issue appear similar on the surface, in reality they are very different. Both retain a neutral position with respect to sovereignty claims over the islands, both have strong interests in freedom of navigation, both want the issue solved peacefully by negotiation in accordance with international law and neither want conflict in that region. In Japan's case, its SLOCs are directly affected, particularly the shipment of oil from the Middle East. Only if a situation in the South China Sea evolved into a large-scale conflict affecting shipping would Japan consider the option of engaging in supportive political and military activities in close coordination with the United States. What form this might take, however, is highly uncertain.

Japanese reluctance to endanger its important relationship with China and divergent US–Japanese priorities and tactics in handling issues involving China may undermine the value of Japan as a strategic partner from the American perspective. A regional contingency might generate a severe test of the US–Japan alliance because of the difficulties the Japanese government would face in meeting American demands. The Japanese response would in the initial stages be predictably passive and minimalist, but according to Okazaki Hisahiko, in the end 'Japan would have no choice but to allow the United States to use bases on Japanese soil to support Taiwan and might feel compelled to participate in operations if passivity endangered the US–Japan security alignment.'[86] In other words, Japan would do the minimum necessary to preserve its more important relationship with the United States.

## PROBLEMS IN PUBLIC SUPPORT FOR THE ALLIANCE

The role of public opinion in constraining Japan's options is another factor that cannot be overlooked if the issue of operationalising the US–Japan alliance arises. In the event that the United States deploys its forces in armed conflict in East Asia, this will raise all sorts of difficult political issues for the Japanese people, particularly if there are no direct security threats to Japan. Although one of the strong elements of continuity between the Cold War and post-Cold War alliance has been the conviction of diplomatic and military elites on both sides of the Pacific that the US–Japan security relationship remains in the best interests of both countries, the equally powerful anti-militarist[87] and anti-nuclear sentiments of the Japanese people show no signs of diminishing. Indeed, these ideals have become deeply embedded in Japan's political culture. On all defence issues, but particularly those involving the dispatch of the armed forces, the pacifist sentiments of the Japanese people will significantly narrow the options available for the government. The public shares a strong residual suspicion that a Japanese military that operates internationally cannot be trusted. A majority opposes any involvement by the Japanese military in international conflicts and the use of force to resolve international disputes. A 1994 public opinion survey conducted by the Prime Minister's office showed that only 4.7 per cent of those polled thought the SDF should emphasise international contributions in the future, whilst 37 per cent thought the SDF should emphasise disaster relief and 39.3 per cent national security.[88]

A regional crisis will, therefore, throw into sharper relief the increasing divergence between elite perceptions of Japan's larger national security interest and popular inclinations which are much more predisposed towards questioning the need for the security alliance with the United States in the wake of the Cold War's end and resistant to an expansion of Japan's regional military role. Because of public opinion, Japan may choose not to support America in a crisis and be unwilling or unable to provide timely and adequate military or logistical support in the midst of conflict. Compounding public hesitation on traditional pacifist grounds are the powerful populist sentiments being generated by the base issue in Okinawa. At the moment the political divisions fall very much between centre and periphery. The central government led by the Foreign Ministry (FM), the JDA and mainstream conservative politicians in the LDP consider the US–Japan Security Treaty as non-negotiable and are not prepared to contemplate a substantial closure of US bases in Japan. Their position is diametrically opposed to that of large numbers of Okinawan residents with justified grievances against the dislocation of their personal lives caused by the American military bases on the island.[89] Much of the resentment of Okinawans is directed towards the central government[90] rather than the US government. The bases are regarded as symbolising the central government's infliction of second-class status on the Okinawan people who have to bear a disproportionate share of the burden of the US military presence in Japan.

Confusing the issue is the fact that neither side is completely unanimous in its position. Many landowners in Okinawa oppose the closure of the US bases because of the income their leases provide.[91] On the other side of the debate, some degree of reassessment about the bases is going on in mainstream political circles. In a March 1996 speech in Washington DC, former Japanese Prime Minister Hosokawa Morihiro complained that

> in the last fifty years Japan, so far as we know, has not seriously discussed the level of forces deployed on Japanese territory or even the need of them with the United States of America, its security partner. If there has been any such discussion the people have not been told .... Why are 47 000 US troops necessary in Japan? What specific usefulness is served by the Yokota and Kadena air bases? ... More than ever before, convincing explanations must be provided if the present security system is to be maintained.[92]

Hosokawa's view is shared by the majority of the Japanese people who feel that they are not being given full and convincing explanations as to why the US needs to maintain 100 000 troops in East Asia, including the 47 000 military personnel in Japan.[93]

Clearly there is a credibility gap perceived by the Japanese public in relation to the US–Japan alliance which both the American and Japanese governments need to fill. Vogel lays the blame squarely with the Japanese side. He argues that the absence of public debate in Japan on the merits of the alliance has allowed its public image to fall into a state of disrepair.[94] For any such debate to be successful, however, the discussion will need to engage the US and Japanese governments in a more detailed justification for the presence of specific bases and their operational rationale in terms of US regional strategy as well as the attendant security benefits to Japan. As Japanese media commentators only too readily admit, the Japanese people seem incapable of appreciating the larger strategic interests at stake.[95]

The recent events in the seas around Taiwan provide mixed signals as to what a likely Japanese public response might be in a future crisis. Japanese officials have been reported as saying that they welcomed such a development as a way of educating the Japanese public to become more conscious of the security issues in East Asia which might impact on Japan. The escalation of tensions so close to Japanese territory was seen as 'just the thing to awaken the Japanese people to new realities in national security needs'.[96]

The domestic political utility of such an issue related both to its liberating effect on domestic security debates and the fact that it potentially generated greater public recognition of the need for the American military presence in Japan for its own protection. In general terms, the increased tensions in the region served to reinforce the case for the US military presence in East Asia, with the bases in Japan providing the launchpad for a regional defence.

CONCLUSION

The Joint Declaration on Security issued by President Clinton and Prime Minister Hashimoto in April 1996 reaffirmed the mutual interests of the United States and Japan in maintaining strong bilateral security ties. It also incorporated changing Japanese perceptions of the appropriate division of security responsibilities between the two sides. The US–Japan security partnership now envisages a greater support role for Japan in relation to US forces.

In the volatile strategic environment of Northeast Asia, there will be continuing pressure on Japan to define its security strategy more clearly and to be more explicit about any enlarged role in the US–Japan alliance. The US–Japan security relationship has undoubtedly entered a period of transformation with the emphasis shifting to broader regional defence. It only remains for Japan's domestic policies to catch up with the new rhetoric and emphasis.

In particular, Japan will have to decide the extent to which it can offer logistical support to the United States and whether or not it will be prepared to contemplate a role that breaches the boundaries of collective self-defence.[97] Japan's utility as an alliance partner of the United States in the event of a regional crisis is contingent on liberalising policy response in both these areas. Resolving these sensitive policy questions will depend on the complex interplay of domestic political institutions, including constitutional and legal norms, popular attitudes and external pressures which together make up the principal determinants of Japan's defence and security policies.[98] In the past, Article 9 has served as a pre-emptive policy commitment against American pressure for extended military obligations,[99] but in future the manoeuvring room permitted by the Peace Clause may not satisfy the demands of alliance maintenance, particularly if the security relationship is put under pressure by developments in the region. A regional crisis in which the United States calls on Japan for support may expose the underlying fragility of the relationship associated with public reservations about expanding Japan's security commitments and Japanese ambivalence about the shift in the strategic focus of the alliance towards countries such as China.

The pace and extent of future developments in Japan's regional defence role will primarily be responsive to strategic developments in the region. In a benign security environment, the pace of change will be slow and incremental. On the other hand, rising tensions leading to a state of conflict in which the United States becomes involved is likely to catalyse the Japanese political process to deliver more expansionist changes in policy. In the absence of a precipitating crisis, a fundamental reorientation in Japan's regional security role is unlikely to occur. This suggests that conflict in Northeast Asia might play the same domestic political role in relation to the collective self-defence issue as the Gulf crisis did for Japan's venture into international peace-keeping – as a catalysing force for the assumption of an expanded security role. If this eventuated, American pressure and supportive domestic political forces might again combine to defeat the forces of the status quo.[100] Opportunistic elements within Japan led by the conservative-nationalist who leads the New Frontier Party, Ozawa Ichiro, remain eager to expand Japan's contribution to international security as part of a comprehensive agenda designed to restore Japan to so-called 'normal statehood'. A collective self-defence role for Japan is seen as a vital step in this process.

Not all regional crises, however, are necessarily of equal value in altering the domestic political configurations of Japanese defence policy. A Korean conflict is much more likely to facilitate change than one involving China, unless there is a direct security threat to Japan. Whether China will step into the former Soviet Union's shoes as the common adversary binding Japan and the United States together in a shared security enterprise remains an open question. In the event that China displays an increased readiness to use military force or the threat of military force to achieve its national objectives, Japan will become more sensitised to security risks posed by China in the region. In the wake of the military tensions in the Taiwan Strait in early 1996, the SDF may unconsciously shift their main threat perceptions from an historical emphasis on the Soviet Union to a growing focus on China as the main rationale for maintaining the impetus of Japan's military modernisation and defence budget acquisition. Although Japanese defence planners are not worried about the conventional capabilities of the Chinese navy and airforce in the short term, they are concerned about China's medium-range ballistic missiles, both nuclear and conventional, which could pose a threat to Japan.

In this regard, it is significant that the enhancement of the US–Japan security relationship at the operational level envisaged by the new NDPO is not directed at any particular state. In fact the purpose of this enhancement is left intentionally hidden in order to accommodate possible changes in strategic focus. Furthermore, while the United States has given assurances that the reaffirmation of the US–Japan alliance is not directed at any one country,[101] and while neither Japan nor the United States want their alliance to be seen as directed against China, the essential point of the expanded regional focus of the alliance is to encompass China as well as the Korean Peninsula.

More broadly, elements in the FM and the JDA are concerned about China's future impact on the power balance in East Asia. But the picture at both the political/bureaucratic and public levels is complicated. China has both supporters and critics amongst Japan's elites and its general public and as a result Japan has no clear position. The situation could change dramatically, however, if China made negative moves involving nuclear weapons. A recent poll in Japan reveals that China's persistence in nuclear testing is already having a negative impact on public opinion towards China. The proportion of respondents who felt close to China fell below 50 per cent for the first time since the survey began in 1978.[102] A nuclear issue could very quickly turn the Japanese public against China and provide a more productive environment for Japanese defence policy change. The fears of other countries in the region about the Japanese military build-up and any decision to engage in collective self-defence may also diminish because of their perceptions of Japan's value as a military counterweight to China. Southeast Asian nations generally welcome the added deterrent power Japan could provide against China, provided that the SDF operate in concert with US forces. Nishihara calls these countries the 'hidden supporters for the strengthening of the US–Japan alliance ... [who] have kept silent because of fear of the threat from the Chinese giant. They welcome the alliance as a counter to China.'[103]

With respect to the base issue, there is little possibility that popular anti-base sentiment will undermine the US–Japan security alliance to the point of dissolution. Undoubtedly it will force accommodation on the part of both the Japanese central government and the US military to the complaints and grievances of the Okinawan people,[104] but this is essentially a political management problem. The outcome depends on the quality of joint US–Japan finessing of the base issue and whether the adjustments agreed to will appease popular anger[105] or whether a strong anti-US military movement is brewing in Japan. As long as the protests are localised amongst those most directly affected and do not spread to the general populace, the problem can be politically contained. In these circumstances, Japan's larger security interests will prevail on the issue of maintaining the US–Japan security relationship itself.

The key factors shaping public attitudes are, of course, perceptions of security threats to Japan and the absence of any widely supported alternative to the US security guarantee. Public opinion surveys in the wake of the April 1996 Japan–US Joint Declaration on Security showed that a majority of the Japanese people supported the alliance,[106] although they did not welcome with unquestioned enthusiasm closer military ties with the United States.[107] Most would still reject the prospect of Japan becoming involved in conflict that went beyond Japan's own defence.[108] Moreover, many share the view that providing the land for US bases is something Japan does as a favour to the United States; that despite the implicit asymmetry in the US security guarantee, the alliance primarily serves US interests, and that US actions in the name of regional security may not necessarily be in Japan's own defence interests.

## NOTES

1. The author is grateful to the Japanese government officials who kindly consented to be interviewed for this study. Not all remarks and observations have been directly attributed because of their sensitive nature. The author bears responsibility for any errors of fact or interpretation.
2. Chalmers Johnson and E.B. Keehn, 'The Pentagon's Ossified Strategy', *Foreign Affairs*, July/August 1995.
3. This is because it is cheaper to station American troops on bases in Japan than it would be on bases in the United States, given the Japanese contribution to the operations and maintenance of US bases on Japanese soil.
4. Robert Manning, 'Futureshock or Renewed Partnership? The US–Japan Alliance Facing the Millennium', *Washington Quarterly*, Autumn 1995, p.96.
5. United States Department of Defense, *East Asia Strategy Report*, February 1995 and Joseph S. Nye, Jr, 'The Case for Deep Engagement', *Foreign Affairs*, July/August 1995.
6. Young-sun Song, 'Prospect for US–Japan Security Cooperation', *Asian Survey*, Vol. XXXV, No. 12, December 1995, pp.1089–90.
7. The new Japan–US Joint Declaration on Security signed by Prime Minister Hashimoto and President Clinton in April 1996 includes a commitment to 'enhance mutual exchange in the areas of technology and equipment, including bilateral cooperative research and development of equipment such as the support fighter (F-2)'. Japan and the United States also agreed to 'cooperate in the ongoing study on ballistic missile defense'. Text of *Japan–US Joint Declaration on Security – Alliance for the 21st Century*, 17 April 1996, p.5.

8. Norman Levin, 'Prospects for US–Japanese Security Cooperation', in Danny Unger and Paul Blackburn (eds), *Japan's Emerging Global Role*, Boulder and London, Lynne Rienner, 1993, p. 82.
9. Worldnet Interview on 'US Policy in East Asia and the Pacific' with Ambassador Winston Lord, Assistant Secretary of State for East Asian and Pacific Affairs, Canberra, 29 March 1996.
10. This is the view of one of Japan's foremost strategic analysts, Sato Seizaburo, interviewed by the author in Tokyo, July 1995.
11. In the 1976 Defence Program Outline, which the 1995 Outline replaced, Japan's role is first to try and repel a limited invasion, only calling on American forces in the event of a large-scale or nuclear attack.
12. Levin, 'Prospects for US–Japanese Security Cooperation', p.82.
13. Song, 'Prospects for US–Japan Security Cooperation', p.1091.
14. *Far Eastern Economic Review*, 10 October 1994. This is very similar to remarks made elsewhere, namely: 'The US–Japan security arrangements add credibility, particularly in the eyes of Asian countries, to Japan's policy of not becoming a big military power.' Yukio Satoh, 'The Japanese Role' in T.B. Millar and James Walter (eds), *Asian-Pacific Security after the Cold War*, Allen & Unwin, 1993, p. 74.
15. 'The Perils of Pork-Barrel Politics: The Birth of the Murayama Government', *Asia-Pacific Review*, Vol. 2, No. 1, Spring 1995, p.29.
16. See Yoshihide Soeya, 'The Evolution of Japanese Thinking and Policies on Cooperative Security in the 1980s and 1990s', paper presented to the Conference on Economic and Security Cooperation in the Asia-Pacific: Agendas for the 1990s, ANU, July 1993.
17. Levin notes for example that 'the treaty articulates a set of values that underpin the alliance [such as] ... the principles of democracy, individual liberty, and the rule of law'. 'Prospects for US–Japanese Security Cooperation', p.72.
18. On the Japan–US global partnership, see Aurelia George, 'Japan as America's Global Partner: Problems and Prospects', *Journal of Northeast Asian Studies*, Vol. XI, No. 4, Winter 1992.
19. President Clinton's official visit to Japan in April 1996 highlighted two projects: eradicating polio in the world by the year 2000 and establishing a natural disaster watch system for the Asia Pacific.
20. Japan, for example, is one of the three major financiers for the light water reactor project for North Korea. Song, 'Prospects for US–Japan Security Cooperation', p.1094.
21. Interview with Foreign Ministry official, ABC Parliamentary and News Network, 1 April 1996.
22. Sato, 'The Perils of Pork-Barrel Politics', p.28.
23. See also Hashimoto Motohide, 'Security in Asia: Roles and Tasks for Japan and the United States', *IIPS Policy Paper* 149E, March 1996, p.11.
24. *Ibid.*
25. Interview, Defence Agency official, Canberra, February 1996.
26. Collective self-defence is defined in the Japanese Defence White Paper as: 'the right to use force to stop armed attack on a foreign country with which [a state] ... has close relations (read the United States), even when the state itself is not under direct attack'. *Defense of Japan*, 1994, p.63. Under international law Japan has this right which is recognised in the Preamble to the US–Japan Security

Treaty. But because of the Constitution, Japan is prevented from exercising this right.

27.  *Defense of Japan*, 1994, p.63.
28.  *Ibid.*
29.  *Ibid.* According to the official government interpretation of the Constitution in 1980, 'if the mission of a "U.N. force" includes "the use of force," the SDF is not constitutionally allowed to participate in it'. Akihito Tanaka, 'Japan's Security Policy in the 1990s', in Yoichi Funabashi (ed.), *Japan's International Agenda*, New York and London, New York University Press, 1994, p.48.
30.  Manning, 'Futureshock or Renewed Partnership', p.88.
31.  Interview, US military personnel, Canberra, March 1996.
32.  *Defense of Japan*, 1994, p.63.
33.  Major forces include nuclear weapons, which would contravene the ban on the 'introduction' of nuclear weapons into Japan.
34.  *Weekend Australian* 16–17 March 1996.
35.  According to Ozawa Ichiro, during the Gulf War, the United States requested that Japan 'deploy transport craft to carry military supplies. The Japanese government refused without giving the issue any serious thought, citing constitutional restraints. America then requested supply ships. Japan again said "No". Next came military tankers. Again, "No". ... The same happened regarding cooperation in airlift efforts.' Ichiro Ozawa, *Blueprint for a New Japan: The Rethinking of a Nation*, Tokyo, Kodansha International, 1994, p.37.
36.  Interview, Defence Agency official, Canberra, February 1996.
37.  Ayako Doi, 'The Korea Crisis and Japan: Politics as Usual', *The Japan Digest*, 8 June 1994, p.5, quoted in Patrick Cronin, 'The Future of the Japan–US Alliance', *Asia-Pacific Review*, Vol. 2, No. 1, Spring 1995, p.41.
38.  Reuter Textline, *Reuter News Service – Far East*, 26 November 1995.
39.  *Ibid.*
40.  *The Economist*, 2 December 1995.
41.  Toshiyuki Shikata, 'Japan's Security Strategy: Meeting the Needs of a New Era', *IIPS Policy Paper* 145E, November 1995, p.13. Retired Japanese Rear Admiral Sumihiko Kawamura, on the other hand, 'calls for Japan to provide an oiler to deploy with and support the USS Independence (which is home-ported in Japan). He makes several other proposals, including the use of Japanese minesweepers to fill the void in US Seventh Fleet capabilities throughout the Western Pacific.' Ralph A. Cossa, 'Northeast Asia Security Challenges: Looking Toward the 21st Century', *Korea and World Affairs*, Spring 1994, p.55.
42.  Government of Japan, *National Defense Program Outline in and after FY 1996* (tentative unofficial translation), p.6.
43.  *National Defense Program Outline*, p.6.
44.  *Nikkei Weekly*, 8 January 1996.
45.  Peter Ennis and Takashi Sato, 'Reading Between the Lines of Japan's New National Defense Program Outline', *Tokyo Business Today*, February 1996, p.21.
46.  *National Defense Program Outline*, p.4.
47.  On page 1 of the *National Defense Program Outline*, the phrase 'contributing to building a more stable security environment' is mentioned directly in

relation to SDF 'participation in international peace cooperation activities'. *National Defense Program Outline*, p.1.
48. Interview, Defence Agency official, Canberra, March 1996.
49. *National Defense Program Outline*, p.5.
50. As reported in Manning, 'Futureshock or Renewed Partnership', p.94.
51. Hosokawa Morihiro, 'Restructuring the Japan–US Alliance', quoted on Internet, H-ASIA, 18 March 1996.
52. Hosokawa, 'Restructuring the Japan–US Alliance'.
53. Reuter Textline, *BBC Monitoring Service – Far East*, 16 April 1996.
54. *Nikkei Weekly*, 25 March 1996.
55. *The Australian*, 15 April 1996.
56. The formal title is 'Agreement Between the Government of Japan and the Government of the United States of America Concerning Reciprocal Provision of Logistic Support, Supplies and Services Between the Self-Defense Forces of Japan and the Armed Forces of the United States of America'.
57. This review had already been mooted by the Chairman of the LDP's Policy Research Council, Yamasaki Taku, in late March 1996.
58. *The Australian*, 15 April 1996.
59. Reuter Textline, *BBC Monitoring Service – Far East*, 16 April 1996.
60. Text of the *Japan–US Joint Declaration on Security – Alliance for the 21st Century*, 17 April 1996, p.4.
61. Reuter Textline, *Reuter News Service – Far East*, 17 April 1996.
62. Ennis and Sato, 'Reading Between the Lines', p.21.
63. As was stated in the 1978 Guidelines for Japan–US Defence Cooperation: 'These draft guidelines shall not be construed as affecting the rights and obligations of Japan and the United States under the Japan–US Security Treaty and its related arrangements. It is understood that the extension of facilitative assistance and support by Japan to the United States, which is described in the draft guidelines, is subject to the relevant laws and regulations of Japan.' *Defense of Japan*, 1994, p.254.
64. Toshiyuki Shikata, 'The Security Environment', Paper presented to the Berlin Trilateral Conference on 'Challenges of the 21st Century', 11–13 June 1995, and reported in *IIPS News*, Vol. 6, No. 3, Summer 1995, p.2.
65. For example, the Joint Declaration states that the Japan–US security relationship 'remains the cornerstone for achieving common security objectives for maintaining a stable and prosperous environment for the Asia-Pacific region as we enter the 21st century'. Text of the *Japan–US Joint Declaration on Security – Alliance for the 21st Century*, 17 April 1996, pp.2–3. Hashimoto later back-pedalled on this point, emphasising that Japan's security cooperation with the United States extended to areas near Japan, but not to all the Asia-Pacific region. *Nikkei Weekly*, 29 April 1996. This is despite the fact that Chief Cabinet Secretary Seiroku Kajiyama said after the Clinton visit: 'My understanding is that the area that the security treaty would cover may be extended to Oceania and member states of the Association of Southeast Asian Nations.' In 1960, the Japanese government defined the Far East as an area covering Japan, South Korea, Taiwan and the Philippines, as well as the surrounding oceans. *Nikkei Weekly*, 22 April 1994.

66. Yamasaki Taku, Chairman of the LDP's Policy Affairs Research Council describing the task he had set the Security Investigation Committee. Quoted in *Nikkei Weekly*, 18 March 1996.
67. *Nikkei Weekly*, 25 March 1996.
68. *Ibid.*
69. *Nikkei Weekly*, 15 April 1996.
70. *The Australian*, 10 April 1996.
71. *Nikkei Weekly*, 25 March 1996.
72. Johnson and Keehn, 'The Pentagon's Ossified Strategy', p.110.
73. This prospect is known as *'ho-ho rengo'* (conservative-conservative union), which envisages a sweeping realignment of conservative politicians across party boundaries. It is a concept being pushed by a group of hawkish conservatives, including former Prime Minister Nakasone, with Ozawa (leader of the New Frontier Party) as the key partner outside the LDP, with the objective of uniting the LDP and New Frontier Party at the expense of the LDP's other coalition partners, the SDP and New Party Harbinger. *Nikkei Weekly*, 13 May 1996.
74. Interview, Defence Agency official, Canberra, March 1996.
75. Glenn D. Hook, *Militarization and Demilitarization in Contemporary Japan*, London and New York, Routledge, 1996, p. 80.
76. This argument is put by Tanaka, 'Japan's Security Policy', p.48.
77. Shikata, 'Japan's Security Strategy', p.11.
78. *Nikkei Weekly*, 18 March 1996.
79. On the other hand, pro-Beijing politicians in Japan who have traditionally been concentrated in the socialist party are losing ground. *Nikkei Weekly*, 29 April 1996.
80. *Nikkei Weekly*, 18 March 1996.
81. Ezra Vogel, quoted in the *Weekend Australian*, 28–29 October 1995.
82. The Japanese government expressed 'great concern' at the actions of China, and also lodged an official protest through diplomatic channels.
83. Nationalist LDP politicians, for example, habitually accuse the government of kowtowing to China, and one member of the New Party Harbinger which participates in Japan's ruling coalition pressed the Japanese Prime Minister to adopt a much harder line towards China. Within the LDP there was also criticism of the government's low-key response and calls for a freeze of Japanese aid to China. *The Australian*, 14 March 1996.
84. One of China's missile target zones off Taiwan is less than 65 km from the Japanese island of Yonaguni on which about 1700 Japanese live, and is, therefore, approximately midway between Japan and Taiwan.
85. Interview, Japan Defence Agency official, Canberra, March 1996.
86. Reuter Textline, *Reuter News Service – Far East*, 25 April 1996.
87. In a public opinion poll conducted in 1991 for example, only 10 per cent of Japanese answered that they had 'much trust' in the SDF, although the vast majority supported the existence of the armed forces for the defence of Japan. *The Japan Times*, 28 March 1995.
88. Makiko Ushijima, *Japan's Defense Policy-Making Process*, Occasional Paper 95-10, Program on US–Japan Relations, Harvard University, 1995, p.7.

89. These resentments are not confined to the Okinawan people. For example, those living and working close to Yokota air base, which is 40 km west of central Tokyo, share many of the same sentiments.

90. The Director General of the Okinawa Peace Movement Centre stated: 'Our anger is not against the US, but against the Japanese government that has been making us a sacrifice for the US–Japan Treaty.' He added that 'Tokyo should think of a way by which the entire country, not Okinawa alone, can bear the burden.' Quoted in *Far Eastern Economic Review*, 23 November 1995.

91. *Nikkei Weekly*, 20 May 1996. Under 10 per cent of landowners renting land to the Japanese government for the US bases want their leases terminated. Of the 32000 landowners with plots used by the US military, only 2937 refused to renew their lease. *Associated Press*, 9 February 1996.

92. Hosokawa, 'Restructuring the Japan–US Alliance'. Hosokawa goes on to recommend that 'it may be possible to reduce the US facilities and base areas during peacetime with a prior arrangement allowing for pre-stockpiling of materials and stationing of personnel in case of emergency. More specifically, it should be realistically possible to relocate the main base of the marine corps stationed on Okinawa to Hawaii or Guam.'

93. *Nikkei Weekly*, 20 May 1996.

94. Vogel, quoted in the *Weekend Australian*, 28–29 October 1995.

95. Japanese media representatives on the Worldnet Interview on 'US Policy in East Asia and the Pacific', with Ambassador Winston Lord.

96. *Nikkei Weekly*, 18 March 1996. A Foreign Ministry official was quoted as saying: 'If [Beijing's military demonstration] has any effect on Japan ... it would be a good one.'

97. In the wake of President Clinton's April visit to Tokyo, the Chief Secretary of the Cabinet, Kajiyama Seiroku, stated that even though he was an advocate of greater military support to the US, 'we will not change our interpretation of "collective defence"'. *Weekend Australian*, 20–21 May 1996.

98. Hook, *Militarization and Demilitarization*, p.1.

99. Peter Cowhey, 'Domestic Institutions and the Credibility of International Commitments: Japan and the United States', *International Organization*, Vol. 47, No. 2, Spring 1993, p.319.

100. Aurelia George Mulgan, 'International Peacekeeping and Japan's Response to the Challenge of Collective Security', Seminar, Department of International Relations, RSPAS, ANU, March 1996.

101. This assurance was given by Winston Lord in his Briefing on Clinton trip to Japan and Korea. The White House, Office of the Press Secretary, 'Press Briefing on the President's Upcoming Trip to Asia', *US Wireless File*, 11 April 1996.

102. *Nikkei Weekly*, 19 February 1996.

103. A comment made by Nishihara Tadashi, quoted in *The Australian*, 19 April 1996.

104. On the eve of President Clinton's April visit to Japan, the United States agreed to shed seven military facilities, including Futenma air base, training grounds and communications centres, and cut back four more. One US defence spokesperson put the cost to the Japanese taxpayer at about US$1 billion. In total, the land returned in Okinawa will amount 4800 hectares out of the total 24500 hectares set aside for American bases and facilities, although actual

numbers of US military personnel in Japan will not be reduced. *The Australian*, 12 and 15 April 1996; *Nikkei Weekly* 15 April 1996; Reuter Textline, *Reuter News Service – Far East*, 15 April 1996.

105. During President Clinton's visit to Japan, Governor Ota said he was 'grateful' for the concessions offered by the American side, but stated that he wanted all Americans out by 2015, and that 'Okinawans are still strongly dissatisfied with the conditions attached to the removal of the bases.' Reuter Textline, *Reuter News Service – Far East,* 18 April 1996.

106. According to a survey done by the *Nihon Keizai Shinbun* after the Clinton–Hashimoto summit, 60 per cent of respondents agreed that Japan should maintain the US–Japan security relationship, while one-third were in favour of a Japanese withdrawal from the alliance. In a October 1995 survey, opinions were split evenly at about 40 per cent each. *Nikkei Weekly*, 29 April 1996.

107. In the April *Nihon Keizai Shinbun* poll, of those supporting the US–Japan alliance, 27.1 per cent wanted closer cooperation, while 70.3 per cent expressed satisfaction with existing levels of cooperation. Only 11.6 per cent were in favour of amending the Constitution to enable Japan to take part in collective self-defence. Close to 80 per cent of the respondents backed the government's current interpretation that any exercise of this right was unconstitutional. *Nikkei Weekly*, 29 April 1996.

108. *Nikkei Weekly*, 20 May 1996.

# 11 The Strategic Dynamics of Post-Cold War Southeast Asia

J. Soedjati Djiwandono

While the ultimate effects of the post-Cold War changes in Southeast Asia's security environment remain uncertain, these changes have encouraged a rethinking of strategic concerns and interests, and in turn strategic policies, among Southeast Asian states.

The most dramatic change with the most fundamental implications for Southeast Asia, for the Asia-Pacific region of which Southeast Asia forms an integral part, and for the world at large was certainly the demise of the Cold War. For the Asia-Pacific region, however, the end of the Cold War has removed just one dimension of its security problem. It is true, and welcome, that the countries of the region will no longer face the danger of getting embroiled in an East–West confrontation or the threat of great-power interference in the context of East–West competition. From that perspective, the end of the Cold War has created a more peaceful international climate in the Asia-Pacific region, including Southeast Asia. Either directly or indirectly, the new climate has been favourable to the development efforts of the countries of the region. It has provided greater opportunity for the promotion of economic and trade relations among states without the political constraints upheld by Cold War bipolarisation.

Peace and stability, however, do not automatically follow, for the problem of security in the Asia-Pacific region has always been complex and multi-dimensional – more so than, for instance, Europe, the birthplace as well as the deathbed of the Cold War. Indeed, the Sino-Soviet dispute, which represented a conflict between communist countries rather than between the communist and non-communist camp and which occurred during the height of the Cold War, was no less significant than the Cold War for the security of the Asia-Pacific region, and particularly Southeast Asia, as it ushered in a period of constant realignment among communist nations in Asia.

Aside from the the Cold War, the region has always contained the seeds of potential conflict, both domestic and interstate. The Cold War often exacerbated existing conflicts of both types because of the support given by one of the two Cold War blocs for its respective protagonist in support of the superpower's own perceived interests. The superpowers, therefore, were not above creating regional or domestic conflict in Southeast Asia if they believed this would give them an advantage in the East–West struggle. Yet

170

the superpowers were not necessarily the only or even the primary source of regional conflict. Some regional conflicts, such as those in Cambodia and Myanmar, are basically domestic conflicts, although the former had from the beginning involved external powers; thus they persist after the end of the Cold War. The region also abounds with interstate conflicts whose origins are basically independent of the Cold War. In Southeast Asia alone, that between Malaysia and the Philippines over Sabah is the oldest and the most serious of all existing intra-ASEAN territorial disputes.[1] There are overlapping claims over a small island (Batu Puteh) between Malaysia and Singapore, the dispute between Malaysia and Indonesia over the two small islands of Sigitan and Lipadan, and conflicting claims over the Spratlys in the South China Sea, which involve not only four of the member states of ASEAN, but also China and Taiwan. Beyond Southeast Asia, the Russians and Japanese continue to dispute ownership of the Kurile islands; the China–Taiwan question remains unresolved; and tensions remain high on the divided Korean peninsula, a lingering legacy of the Cold War.

Moreover, it may be assumed that despite the end of the Cold War, international politics will continue to be marked by competition among nation-states, especially the great powers, one of the Cold War's classic characteristics. With the end of the Cold War, the competition is no longer between East and West, and it is likely to be less characterised by military confrontation. It may be more likely to involve contests over economic and trade benefits such as access to natural resources and markets of export goods and services, as well as over political, cultural, and other forms of influence.

## REGIONAL IMPLICATIONS

This means the Asia-Pacific region, particularly Southeast Asia, may continue to face a possible threat of external interference, if less military in nature than before. This is likely to be true whether or not there is to be a 'power vacuum' in the Asia-Pacific region. Some observers have predicted the emergence of such a vacuum because of the dissolution of the Soviet Union and the withdrawal, at least in part, of the US military presence since, and indeed even prior to, the end of the Cold War. Some believe this may encourage other great powers, particularly China and India, to fill the vacuum.[2]

As far as the question of external interference concerns the member states of ASEAN, it may be recalled that the Association was established primarily on the basis of their common concern with the threat of external interference. This can be seen in various documents, including the founding Bangkok

Declaration of 1967, the Kuala Lumpur Declaration of 1971 on ZOPFAN (Zone of Peace, Freedom and Neutrality), the Declaration of ASEAN Concord, and the Treaty of Amity and Cooperation in Southeast Asia, the last two having been signed at the first ASEAN Summit held in Bali, Indonesia, in February 1976.

Thus, the nature of international relations being as it is, the regional cooperation of ASEAN will remain significant and relevant in the post-Cold War era. External interference, however, is made possible or facilitated by existing conflict situations, either of domestic or interstate nature, in the Southeast Asian region itself. In other words, domestic and interstate or regional conflicts tend to induce external interference. Such interference may intentionally be invited by the countries involved in the conflicts in search of external support or initiated by external powers for their own ends in the context of their own competition.

Again, the principle underlying the regional cooperation of ASEAN, that the member states bear primary responsibility for the peace and security of the region and its freedom from external interference, remains relevant. And while it is the responsibility of each member state to prevent and overcome domestic conflicts in its efforts to promote 'national resilience', it is the collective responsibility of all the member states through regional cooperation to prevent, contain, and settle differences and disputes among them by peaceful means for the promotion of ASEAN 'regional resilience'.

The end of the Cold War has eliminated the prospect of a world war. But while gone are the days of wars by proxy, the world has continued to be beset by local and regional conflicts. Some of these have been going on since well before the end of the Cold War, and some others have broken out thereafter. Hence the significance of sub-regional and regional approaches and cooperation, or simply regionalism. The countries of various regions of the world should now bear the primary responsibility for the peace, security and stability of their respective regions. The ASEAN member states realised this responsibility from the very inception of the Association. The founding Bangkok Declaration of ASEAN states that 'the countries of South-East Asia share a primary responsibility for strengthening the economic and social stability of the region and ensuring their stability and security from external interference in any form or manifestation'.

During the Cold War, many nations of the so-called Third World were factors in the strategic calculations of the great powers engaged in East–West competition. For that reason, the importance of such regions as Southeast Asia, which in fact has remained ill-defined geographically, was for a long time derived from their strategic significance to the great powers. In the post-Cold War era, however, the great powers would most probably no longer have as great an interest in either instigating or exploiting local and regional conflicts. Unfortunately, it is also unlikely that they have great interest in involving themselves in attempts to solve such conlicts. Hence the greater responsibility of regional powers for peace, security, and stability in their respective regions. And in that sense, the regions will increasingly have their own inherent importance, quite apart from the interests of external major powers. Increasingly, they will become subjects in their own right, rather than objects, in international politics.

Furthermore, while not necessarily a decisive factor in determining the identity of a region, geographical proximity is likely to facilitate interaction in a multilateral framework limited to a region or sub-region more than in a wider context. It will ensure greater intensity in the relations and cooperation among states. This in itself will help determine the identity of a region. And in regional cooperation, it would be generally much easier to find areas of common interest and common problems among states than in a wider sweep. Mutually beneficial interstate relationships may thus be easier to attain.

Regional cooperation would also serve as a cushion or an umbrella that would ensure the maintenance of bilateral relations and cooperation, often dampening existing differences or even conflicts in the bilateral relationship of any two nations involved in regional cooperation. This is true especially after each of them has developed an increasing stake in regional cooperation. ASEAN is a good example: it continues to flourish despite the fact that disputes are to be found in practically every bilateral relationship among its member states. One lesson to be learned from this experience is that nations can still promote and maintain mutually beneficial relations and cooperation in spite of the existence of differences or even disputes. Without ASEAN such disputes might have developed into armed conflicts.

At all events, ASEAN has succeeded in sweeping such problems under the carpet, at least pending their final settlement by peaceful means. ASEAN governments are committed to the notion that disputes should not be the focus of relations among nations, nor should they hinder the promotion of the favourable relations and close cooperation that might eventually resolve the dispute.

## SECURITY COOPERATION

A sub-regional approach is the most realistic, feasible, and therefore the most appropriate means of promoting cooperation in a wider framework such as the Asia-Pacific region in any field, particularly in that of security. Cooperation in the security field is not something new to the countries of Southeast Asia, on either a bilateral or multilateral basis. We may recall the Soviet–Vietnamese Treaty of Mutual Defence and Security of 1978, and bilateral security and defence arrangements the United States maintained with Thailand and the Philippines during the Cold War. And although ineffective, multilateral security and defence cooperation in Southeast Asia took the form of SEATO, while the FPDA (Five-Power Defence Arrangements), which is an agreement to consult Great Britain, Australia and New Zealand if the security of either Malaysia or Singapore is threatened, is still in force. As far as the ASEAN member states are concerned, however, cooperation in the security field has continued to be conducted outside the framework of ASEAN regional cooperation, be it on a bilateral or multilateral (if mostly limited to trilateral) basis. What clearly distinguishes the present security cooperation between ASEAN member states from any previous security arrangements is the absence of the involvement of any external great power.

The central question is whether in the post-Cold War era security cooperation is still of relevance and significance to the countries of Southeast Asia. And if so, we may ask what purposes it should serve, whether it is to be promoted on a bilateral or multilateral basis, and how it would be related to external great powers. Although not yet involving all the countries of the region, if that is the aspiration, ASEAN may serve as a good model, precisely because its establishment as a vehicle for regional cooperation was motivated primarily by security considerations, and aimed, if in general terms, at the promotion of individual and collective peace and security for its member states.

While security cooperation among the ASEAN member states has been maintained outside the ASEAN framework, not all member states have been involved in such bilateral or trilateral security cooperation. The limited scope of security cooperation among the member states of ASEAN, even at the bilateral level as officially endorsed for the first time by the Declaration of ASEAN Concord of 1976, and the absence thus far of such cooperation at the multilateral level within the framework of ASEAN regional cooperation, may be due to various reasons: First, as mentioned earlier, unresolved territorial disputes remain between certain member states of ASEAN.

Second, probably as a remnant of the Cold War, multilateral security cooperation has continued to give the image of a military pact with the involvement and backing of an external great power. Past experience shows that the presence or involvement of a great power in such multilateral security cooperation may invite external interference whenever a domestic or interstate conflict occurs that involves one of the parties to the security arrangement, or a neighbouring state.[3]

Third, member states of a multilateral security cooperation framework are usually bound together by a common perception of an external threat, as in the case of NATO, SEATO, and the Warsaw Pact during the Cold War. As far as the countries of Southeast Asia, particularly the ASEAN member states, are concerned, such a common perception of external threat has never developed, and probably never will. The diversity among ASEAN member states in geopolitical circumstances, size of territory and population, and historical backgrounds will continue to yield different and perhaps unchanging perceptions of external security threats.

Fourth, the nature of security problems between any two member states of ASEAN in their bilateral relations is unique in each case. Between Malaysia and Indonesia, for instance, there is a common problem of illegal border crossing, just as between Indonesia and the Philippines. And Malaysia and Thailand share security problems along their common borders, as have Malaysia and Indonesia in Kalimantan in the past.

Thus, fifth, common problems and common approaches to such problems are likely to be easier to find on a bilateral basis between two states than in a multilateral framework.

TOWARD MULTILATERALISM?

Since the withdrawal of the American military bases from the Philippines, pressure has mounted for the promotion of multilateral defence and security cooperation within the framework of ASEAN. This seems to indicate a recognition, an awareness, or a premonition that the end of the Cold War has not automatically created peace and stability in the Asia-Pacific region, including Southeast Asia. On the contrary, the demise of the Cold War seems to have created more complex problems of defence and security, at least as far as the Asia-Pacific region is concerned. And in any event, the end of the Cold War has created considerable uncertainty in the region, as elsewhere, over what kind of power structure is likely to emerge in lieu of the Cold War.

The main problem for the countries of Southeast Asia, particularly for the member states of ASEAN, is not whether security cooperation is still necessary. The problem is whether the form of security cooperation that has been undertaken so far among the ASEAN member states should be continued on a bilateral basis, so that eventually there will develop what former Foreign Minister Tan Sri Gazhali Syaffie of Malaysia has aptly called a 'web of interlocking bilateral relationships', or whether such cooperation should be promoted to the multilateral level, within the framework of ASEAN. If so, how should it relate to the great powers? And should such security cooperation, bilateral or multilateral, be expanded so as to involve the other Southeast Asian countries that have remained outside ASEAN regional cooperation until now?

It is uncertain whether the non-ASEAN Southeast Asian states will be drawn into security cooperation before the end of the twentieth century. The domestic political situation in Myanmar will apparently remain unsettled for several more years. The conflict in Cambodia, in spite of the general elections sponsored and supervised by the United Nations which have resulted in the formation of a coalition government minus the Khmer Rouge, has not been completely resolved, as the country continues to be torn by civil strife. It therefore seems most realistic to expect security cooperation in Southeast Asia to be limited to the ASEAN member states for the foreseeable future. The need for the present is the strengthening of bilateral security cooperation, for even among ASEAN member states, the bilateral web is not yet complete.

That is by no means to suggest that the possibility of promoting security cooperation on a multilateral basis is to be ruled out altogether. But present circumstances would not favour such an undertaking even for the member states of ASEAN, let alone for a wider framework that would cover the entire Asia-Pacific region. This is likely to be a long-term process, and we should move slowly and with caution. Certain factors may nevertheless be considered and certain steps taken to pave the way for future security cooperation on a multilateral basis.

It has been suggested that a common perceived external threat is necessary to bind the parties together in a successful multilateral security organisation. Such a common enemy, however, may not be necessary. Alternatively, ASEAN multilateral security cooperation may serve as a confidence-building measure (CBM). Such cooperation will have no need for a formal structure of its own, but it may form an integral part of ASEAN regional cooperation as a whole. Of prime importance will be its common programme of activities. These may cover coordination in the procurement or manufacturing of weapons and other military equipment that may lead to some form of balance among the member states, which in turn will increase transparency and enhance confidence building; coordination in training, education, and exchange of military cadets and their teachers; joint military exercises; exchange of information and coordination in the formulation of strategic concepts and planning; joint search and rescue operations (SAR); and exchange of military intelligence. The benefits extend beyond confidence building. Cooperation in such fields will also result in greater efficiency in human and financial resources for the development of skills and the advancement of weapons and military technology.

Of greater importance, however, is that such a multilateral security cooperation will not be a military pact in the traditional or conventional sense of the word, and will not be directed against any particular nation. Nor will it involve or require the backing of any external great power. Apart from confidence building, such cooperation will help prevent and contain possible differences or conflicts among member states. And in that sense it will help prevent any possible threat of external interference, a preoccupation that, as noted earlier, motivated the establishment of ASEAN in the first place.

TOWARD A WIDER FRAMEWORK

Multilateral security cooperation is a long-standing issue in the Asia-Pacific region. In 1969, for instance, Soviet leader Leonid Brezhnev proposed the establishment of an Asian collective security system. And in 1988, Mikhail Gorbachev in his famous speech at Vladivostok suggested the establishment of a security cooperation framework after the model of the Helsinki Accord or the Conference on Security and Cooperation in Europe (CSCE). After the end of the Cold War, a similar idea was proposed by Australian Foreign Minister Gareth Evans and later by his Canadian counterpart Joe Clark under the name of Conference on Security and Cooperation in Asia. Australian Prime Minister Paul Keating wanted APEC used as a basis for a security forum.[4]

None of those ideas on the establishment of some form of security cooperation on a multilateral basis that have been put forward until now for the Asia-Pacific region with a definite structure or organisation have come to see the light of day. Each was unrealistic. The Brezhnev proposal was a non-starter, for nobody could fail to see that the real motive behind it was to encircle China, at that time enemy number one of the Soviet Union. The idea of emulating the CSCE model, whatever its name, did not receive a positive response from most of the countries in the Asia-Pacific region basically for the same reason: it ignored the fundamental differences between Europe and the region.

One essential element of the CSCE that those proposals seem to have overlooked is the fact that the CSCE served above all to affirm the status quo – namely, the postwar borders in Europe. This is irrelevant and inapplicable to the Asia-Pacific region. The idea of emulating or applying the CSCE model to the Asia-Pacific region is often criticised as simplistic or 'Eurocentric', and rightly so. This objection is not based on mere prejudice, but on the recognition that such an approach is fundamentally irrelevant and inapplicable to the conditions and circumstances prevailing in the region. References above to the various unresolved conflicts afflicting the region, especially territorial claims and counterclaims, actual as well as potential conflicts, some of which have survived both the Cold War and the Sino-Soviet dispute to this day, should suffice to explain why a widely accepted status quo is out of the question in the region, most probably for a long time to come. Therefore, multilateral security cooperation would make sense for the Asia-Pacific region as a whole only after the various conflicts are settled by peaceful means.

Most countries of the Asia-Pacific region, however, have proved amenable to the idea of dialogues, especially of an informal nature, among all the countries of the region on security issues affecting their vital national interests. The reluctance demonstrated by some countries in the region is not an aversion to dialogue per se, but apprehension about moving too fast towards a definite structure or organisation for multilateral security cooperation while no region-wide consensus on the meaning of 'security' has yet been reached.

Indeed, only at the Fourth ASEAN Summit held in Singapore in January 1992 did the ASEAN member states agree that the Association would use established fora such as the ASEAN Post-Ministerial Conference (PMC) to promote and intensify external dialogue over political and security matters. The ASEAN PMC, however, is certainly not the only forum for such dialogues. Other existing informal fora such as APEC may serve a similar purpose, in addition to economic matters that may be the focus of their concern. Informal exchange of information, ideas, viewpoints, concerns, perceptions and perspectives on security matters among the countries of the Asia-Pacific region will definitely help prevent or at least reduce misperceptions, misunderstanding and suspicion, and at the same time help to build mutual confidence.


## THE NEED FOR CONFIDENCE BUILDING

Confidence building is what the countries of the Asia-Pacific region need most at this stage. In the meantime, areas of common interest should continue to be sought, identified and expanded, on which multilateral cooperation in many fields may be founded and promoted for common benefit. This can eventually create an atmosphere conducive to the peaceful settlement of existing disputes. Only then would the countries of the region be ready to embark on more structured security cooperation on a multilateral basis.

The security of a region may be defined in terms of the relations between its constituent states. And although the prospect of a world war, particularly in the form of war between alliances, is now unlikely, war is not inconceivable between major powers, between a regional power and a major power, or between regional powers themselves. In the latter case, the situation would become even more tense if some other regional power should take sides. This realisation provides even greater incentive for efforts to establish a regional or sub-regional approach that will ensure greater interaction and cooperation among states in areas of common interest and common problems. Again the importance of confidence-building measures comes to the fore.

As mentioned before, traditional forms of security cooperation, particularly Cold War-style military approaches backed by a superpower and aimed at a well-defined enemy, are no longer relevant. In today's Asia-Pacific region, confidence-building measures are the most appropriate vehicle in an era of unresolved disputes, ill-defined security concerns and perceptions, and mutual suspicion. The concept of CBMs understood in Europe within the context of the OSCE has a strictly military content, such as 'the prior notification of major military manoeuvres on a basis to be specified by the Conference, and the exchange of observers by invitation at military manoeuvres under mutually acceptable conditions'.[5] For the Asia-Pacific region, however, security must be understood comprehensively, so as to include numerous other non-military fields. Furthermore, there are great differences among countries and between sub-regions in respect of security problems and concerns. In this region, CBMs are generally understood broadly as including 'both formal and informal measures, whether unilateral, bilateral, or multilateral, that address, prevent, or resolve uncertainties among states, including both military and political elements'.[6]

Such measures are aimed at contributing to a reduction of uncertainty, misperception, and suspicion and thus helping to reduce the possibility of armed conflict. The intent is to alleviate tension and reduce the possibility of armed conflict. A CBM is not to be conceived as an institution, but rather as a stepping stone or a building block; it represents a means to an end rather than an end in itself. By forming part of the security groundwork, it may serve as a useful precondition for effective institution building in the future.[7]

CBMs help manage problems and avoid confrontations between states, but they do not include mechanisms for conflict resolution or other attempts to settle ongoing crises, for which preventive diplomacy is needed. Thus the concept of CBMs is used here to demonstrate that a regional security consensus can be developed through a relatively informal approach, built upon a base of personal political contacts and relationships, and taking into account the security situation that prevails in each region or sub-region. The approach should be a graduated one, and its broad objectives should include the following: reducing tensions and suspicion; reducing the risk of war by accident or miscalculation; fostering communication and cooperation in a way that helps to de-emphasise the use of military force; bringing about a better understanding of one another's security problems and defence priorities; and developing a greater sense of strategic confidence in the region.

The ASEAN Regional Forum (ARF), which first convened in July 1994 and included the six foreign ministers of ASEAN, seven of its dialogue partners (Australia, Canada, EC, Japan, South Korea, New Zealand, and the USA), two consultation partners (China and Russia), and three observers (Laos, Vietnam, and PNG), may itself be regarded as a form of CBM. Now that Vietnam is a member of ASEAN, India has become a dialogue partner, and the European Union is also represented, the ARF can be considered a bridge spanning the Asia-Pacific region understood in the broadest sense. These developments perhaps foreshadow the emergence of a new world order in which Europe has lost its centuries-old dominance over international relations and the Asia-Pacific region has become the new focus, not only for its economic dynamism but also for its strategic, political, and security importance.

## NOTES

1. See J. Soedjati Djiwandono, 'Intra-ASEAN Territorial Disputes: The Sabah Claim', paper presented at the *Seminar on ASEAN into the 21st Century: Dealing with Unresolved Issues*, organised by ASEAN-ISIS in Manila, 14–15 January 1994.
2. See the discussion in Jeshurun, 'Southeast Asia', 60–1.
3. See George McTurnan and Audrey Kahin, *Subversion as Foreign Policy* (Ithaca: Cornell University Press, 1995).
4. Kusuma Snitwongse, 'Post-Ministerial Conference of ASEAN', Disarmament, Topical Papers 16, Disarmament and National Security in an Interdependent World (New York: United Nations, 1993): 117.
5. Victor-Yves Ghebali, 'Confidence-building measures within the CSCE process: Paragraph-by-paragraph analysis of the Helsinki and Stockholm regimes', *Research Paper* No. 3 (New York: Unidir, 1989), 3.
6. Ralph A. Cossa, *Confidence and Security Building Measures: Are They Appropriate for Asia?*, Summary and Analysis of the Council for Security Cooperation in the Asia Pacific's Confidence and Security Building Measures Working Group Seminar (Honolulu, Hawaii: Pacific Forum CSIS, January 1995), 6.
7. *Ibid.*, 7.

# Index

Printed in Great Britain
by Amazon